TEACHER LEADERSHIP

for the 21st Century

Fourth Edition | Thomas S. Poetter

Teacher Leadership for the 21st Century

Thomas S. Poetter
Miami University, Oxford, Ohio
Fourth Edition

Printed in the United States of America
10 9 8 7 6 5 4 3 2 1
ISBN: 978-1-61740-568-6

Van-Griner Publishing
Cincinnati, Ohio
www.van-griner.com

CEO: Mike Griner
President: Dreis Van Landuyt
Project Manager: Brenda Schwieterman
Customer Care Lead: Julie Reichert

Poetter 568-6 Su18
206637
Copyright © 2019

About the Author

THOMAS S. POETTER is Professor of Curriculum Studies and Chair in the Department of Educational Leadership at Miami University, Oxford, Ohio. Tom has been teaching and writing about teacher leadership since he came to Miami in 1997 after three years at Trinity University in San Antonio, Texas, where he began his career in higher education in 1994 as a teacher educator after several years as a high school English teacher and athletic coach. His first book, *Voices of Inquiry in Teacher Education* (Routledge, 1997), chronicled his work with beginning teacher inquirers. From the beginning, he has been writing and publishing in the education field, authoring, co-authoring, and/or editing more than 20 books and monographs as well as more than 50 journal articles and book chapters. Tom also works to engage with citizens and teachers to reverse the school reform movement of the past decade that has damaged students, teachers, and public education (*www.tspoetter.weebly.com*). This book is dedicated to my doctoral advisor and mentor at Indiana University, Norman V. Overly, who inspired my inquiries into the fields of curriculum studies and education and who made me a better person.

Contents

Foreword by Morna McDermott . . . . *ix*

Preface . . . . *xiii*

Prologue. *1*

Chapter 1   Situating the Self as a Teacher Leader **9**

Freeze Frame: Tom Teaches Ibsen's *The Wild Duck*. 9

Making a Decision to Teach 14

Chapter 2   Pursuing Reflection as
Grounds for Teacher Leadership **25**

Suzanne Reflects on Practice 26

Acknowledging Your "Apprenticeship of Observation" 29

Chapter 3   Reflection for Teacher Leaders:
Autobiography and the Teaching Platform **35**

Creating a Teaching Platform .41

Write a Teaching Platform 43

Chapter 4   The Teacher Leader as Reflective Agent. . . **63**

A Case of a Reflective Agent 63

Some Initial Thoughts on Teacher Education and
Building a Learning Community as a Teacher Leader. 66

Extending Your Autobiography and Platform: Toward
Personal, Practical Theories of Action in Teaching 68

Considerations of "Theory" for Teacher Leaders. 70

Chapter 5   Creating a Classroom
and School Learning Community. **75**

The Possibilities for Classrooms and Schools as Communities .76

The School as Community/The School as Organization 78

Four Areas of Focus for Creating a Classroom
and School Learning Community 80

Standards for Authentic Pedagogy: Instruction 92

Standards for Authentic Pedagogy: Assessment 92

Grant and Sleeter's Five Approaches
to Multicultural Education .100

Chapter 6   Inquiry for Teacher Leaders **113**

What Is Action Research? 135

How Do I Do Action Research? 136

What Can I Get Out of Action Research
as a Beginning Teacher Leader? 141

Chapter 7   School Reform and Teacher Leadership . .**145**

Defining School Reform 145

A Historical Perspective 146

The Current Reform Agenda 149

Mindscapes for School Reform 150

Considering School Reform .152

Considering Varying Conceptions of School Reform 153

Three Prominent Conceptions of School Reform 155

Preparing to Lead: What You May Be
Asked to Do as a School Reformer 161

Chapter 8   Teachers' Unions and Leadership **165**

Union Organization, Structure, and Issues 166

Unions and the Reform Debate:
In Whose Interests Do They Work? 173

"Right to Work" 174

Unions, Teacher Leadership,
and (Curriculum) Deliberation 175

Chapter 9   Curriculum Perspectives **179**

The Curriculum Defined? 184

Personal Curriculum Q-Sort 187

Some Foundational Concepts for
Thinking About Curriculum 199

Chapter 10 Curriculum Deliberation and Teacher Leadership 207

Deliberating on Curriculum: A Scenario 211

Student Curriculum Projects. 217

Chapter 11 The Zoo Trip: Objecting to Objectives* . .237

The Zoo Trip 239

Learning to Let It Be. 244

Chapter 12 Stemming the Tide: Calvin's High-Water Mark and Teacher Resistance* 247

Standardized Schools 248

From Words to Actions 248

Teaching with Autonomy 249

What a Difference Five Years Makes 249

Common Practice 251

Not Giving Up the Fight 252

Glimmers of Resistance 252

Final Thoughts 254

Chapter 13 Critical Issues for Teacher Leaders 255

Your Rights and Responsibilities as a Teacher 256

School Finance and the Classroom 266

The Common Core Standards .272

Human Difference and the Curriculum. 276

Chapter 14 Continuing to Learn: Professional Development for You and Your School 279

Creating a Teaching Portfolio .280

Surveying Your Assumptions About Professional Development. 283

Professional Development Models. 286

A Final Case Study. 292

References. 297

Foreword

Anyone who has studied the history of educational leadership and change in the United States will note that many ideas touted as "innovations in education" are really not new at all. While oftentimes academics and practitioners package and market catchy coined phrases for the latest "thing" that supposedly "all schools need to adopt," we might consider that many of these same ideas were being pushed in the name of educational change decades ago. Tom Poetter offers no "10 easy steps to success." (I am grateful he does not!)

Such approaches are disingenuous. What *Teacher Leadership for the 21st Century* <u>does</u> do is reignite contemporary teachers' passion for ideas such as democratic classrooms for a democratic society. Poetter provides guiding ideals, critical questions to ponder, and suggestions for how to find and maintain this passion. While these ideas were being promoted over a century ago, we sadly have yet to see them come to fruition. Educator/activists such as Marion Thompson Wright (1941) believed that "education in America, which must be education for a democracy, must be democratic in theory and practice" (p. 202, as cited in Crocco et al. [1999], p. 70). And yet today a passion for creative, meaningful, and democratic schooling is still conceived by many as unrealistic. These ideas and practices are also in great jeopardy now more than ever of being extinguished from the dialogue and practice of public schooling altogether. Educators *right now* are facing a tipping point, and Poetter's book has arrived at the moment when it is needed most if teachers are to reclaim their profession.

Poetter never shies away from tackling the politics, morality, or economics of "reform." Instead he clearly outlines how each historical moment has led us to this tipping point, and more important, guides his readers on how to use this information in order to effect democratic rather than corporate changes. Until recently I would have agreed with Taubman (2007) who sadly suggests that "we missed the chance." He states:

One can only wonder why educators would willingly collude in what many view as an educational nightmare. 'There must have been a moment,' Guildenstern says, 'at the beginning when we could have said—no. But somehow we missed it.' (p. 153)

Poetter's book gives me hope that maybe Taubman was wrong. Maybe, in 2007 when he wrote this passage, the moment just hadn't happened *yet.* Now, *right now,* is the moment for democratic educational change.

There are both problems and promise in this particular historical moment. One thing of promise has been the advent of social media such as Facebook and Twitter, which have created free-moving lateral avenues for communication beyond the control of the dominant mainstream discourse promoted by proponents of corporate models of education. Second, and more problematic, is the post 9/11 culture of fear, and that an ensuing curriculum of fear has emerged. Surveillance, control, and accountability in the name of national safety have become the "norm," and while we are accustomed to having our freedoms stifled at airports, we have inadvertently also allowed our educational rights and freedoms to be stripped from us as well. And educators have been silenced from challenging new accountability measurements out of fear. Test scores are made public, pay is being attached to student "performance," and schools that do not make AYP (annual yearly progress) are being shut down. I call this historical educational moment one of "fear and loathing" (Thompson, 1972). This leads me to the third criteria that makes this moment unique. Loathing.

Recently, I heard a student in Howard County, Maryland (one of the "top performing" counties in the country), say he would "rather be homeless than complete another worksheet." *That's* true loathing for education. Additionally, mainstream media's support of the corporate agenda, including the film *Waiting for Superman* (2010), has placed public school teachers under attack. Teachers—whether in support of collective bargaining or simply standing up and speaking out in the form of public protests against core curriculum or high-stakes testing—are being confronted by hateful images of pig masks and having expletives hurled at them for their efforts. This virulent mistrust of public educators is unparalleled with any other time in American educational history.

So I will say this plainly and as clearly as I can: Educators are at war with policy "reform." They are fighting to defend the professionalism of their vocation. They are in a war wrought at the hands of a dominant ideology called capitalist or corporate "reform" that generates a fear-based culture in which panic leads to the surrender of critical thought and democratic rights; ironically, the movement is cloaked in an ideology of morality and freedom.

Teacher leaders must be at the forefront of this battle. As leaders they need to speak for what they know works in education—resisting the funding cuts for everything from The National Writing Project to arts education. Teacher leaders need to support the work of teacher education programs that are at risk of being eliminated in favor of "alternative certification programs" which claim to "train" teachers to perform successfully in this profession in a matter of weeks. If students are merely products, curriculum little more than a scripted one-size-fits-all database for mass consumption, and teachers no more than "delivery specialists" for textbook and testing companies, then I suppose that would be true.

Therefore, anyone leading the way for educational change can gain much insight from Poetter's suggestion that we reframe the dialogue, not in terms of reform, but in terms of what John Goodlad calls "educational renewal." In this way Poetter remains critical yet hopeful. To be hopeful, from Poetter's perspective, is not simply a feel good attitude, but a vital and necessary tool for all educators if we are to avoid losing the public in education. Hope is the instrument of democratic action, not merely a slogan for a Hallmark card. But to be hopeful, one must have a vision. Poetter's vision, most simply stated, is this. He writes:

> We should rebuild school cultures with connections to children's lives, their worlds, so that the best, most appropriate influences will affect them, support them, and enhance their chances for success in school and in life.

Poetter weaves together a framework that enables his readers to see history in light of the present, grassroots, and community-based action in light of the "larger national picture," and educational leaders in light of the people they seek to lead. He creates a meaningful and accessible vision of the educational spectrum from a range of angles, and brings them together into a call for action. If teacher leaders are to confront the powerful media, lobbyists, business entrepreneurs, propaganda, politicians, and policy makers, all of whom claim to know more about "what's best" in classrooms than teachers themselves, then they are required to be well-equipped with the tools to dismantle the push toward privatization and standardization.

Several years ago Poetter wrote a wonderful "fictional" piece entitled *The Education of Sam Sanders* (2006) which prophesized what is now coming to pass with current and future legislation. *Sam Sanders*, though written as a futuristic piece, is coming to pass as a frightening glimpse into our present and future condition. In this book, *Teacher Leadership for the 21st Century*, Poetter crafts together another vision: One that can divert us from the nightmare.

This historical moment in educational shape-shifting, with a generation of teacher leaders who are facing educational crises that are coming to a head, needs his vision. Weaving together narrative experiences from "the trenches" with a critically informed analysis of history, curriculum, theory, policy, and practice, this book provides educational leaders with the tools to keep creative and democratic decision making where it belongs: in the hands of educators, students, families, and communities. We need public education with, by, and for the public.

Morna McDermott
Towson University

References

Crocco, M. S., Munro, P. & Weiler, K. (1999). *Pedagogies of resistance: Women educator activists, 1880–1960*. New York, NY: Teachers College Press.

Guggeheim, D. (Writer/Director), & Kimball, B. (Writer). (2010). *Waiting for Superman* [Motion picture/Documentary]. United States: Paramount Pictures.

Poetter, T. (2006). *The education of Sam Sanders*. Hamilton Books.

Taubman, P. (2007). The tie that binds: Learning and teaching in the New Educational Order. *Journal of Curriculum and Pedagogy, 4*(2), 150–160.

Thompson, H. S. (1972). *Fear and loathing in Las Vegas: A savage journey to the heart of the American Dream*. New York, NY: Vintage Press.

Preface

Before the turn of the century, my friend, colleague, and mentor Bernard J. Badiali invited me to work with him on a new book called *Teacher Leader*. He confirmed a book deal with a publisher, Eye on Education, and we set out to produce a book for a course on teacher leadership that we were developing at Miami University. Over the course of several years, we produced a book that we were very proud of and that we used in the course on Teacher Leadership for undergraduates in our professional teaching programs. For that first book, which was in use for more than ten years, several beginning teachers supplied outstanding reflections and insight pieces that were included and most of which still appear in this revised text.

Those beginning teachers were Molly Cheek, Pat Travieso, Teria Fields, Kelli Fox, Bethany Lawson, David Parry, Deannah Bair, John Healy, Kara Kane, Lindsay Bolandar, Ashley Myers, Kari Koerner, Suzanne Clements, Anne Milbratz, Michele Welser, Trista Diangelo, Emily Hall, Kristina Moffo, Jenn Reid, Lauren Steidl, Bridget Oaks, and Abby Gard. Not every piece made the new version of the book, but all of their contributions were timeless, and the ones included here still hit home in this edition of the book. Thank you to everyone mentioned above and to all of our previous students for contributing to this volume.

I would also like to name and thank the student authors whose pieces appeared in the second and third editions: Katherine Young, Angela Yingling, Kelsey Browne, Allie Walsh, Jackie Ziegler, Jake Strauss, Troy Phillippe, Todd Tracy, Sean Mormino, Kayla Angermeier, Gordon Donahue, Jessica LeFevre, Kelsey Martinez, Bethany Brown, Quentin Russell, Allyson Klovekorn, Erin Worrell, Cody Dye, Victoria B. Ellis, Brian Veil, Sarah Zaffiro, Kelsey Oros, Jacob Morris, Melina Hazzard, Rob Cron, and Ashley Martin.

The following students contributed pieces to the revised fourth edition: Allie Skorcz, Ashley Kemper, Cassidy Conerby, Annie Frazee, Nicole Geygan, Lianna McDonald, Rachel Murray, Pearl Whistler, Grace Olsson, Sammi Kushen, Leslie Jason, Maddie Charles, and Morgan Silinsky. I name every student above whose writing has appeared in any of the editions of this book; they all made tremendous contributions to the class when they took it, and following the class through the consumption of their written work included herein by future preservice teachers.

And, I want to extend my great appreciation to my colleague Kevin Talbert, who authored Chapter 8 on Teacher Unions, which was added in the second edition and then revised with new material by Dustin Hornbeck for the fourth edition. It's an excellent piece of work, and I appreciate the time and energy they put into creating this new version. Also, I want to thank my colleagues Nelda Cambron-McCabe and Dennis Carlson at Miami University for their feedback and commentary on certain passages of this text. Their checks for accuracy and appropriateness of language on complicated and sensitive topics greatly improved the text. Debra Freedman and Morna McDermott reviewed the original book and made excellent suggestions for revision. Morna, my longtime friend and colleague, wrote the inspiring Foreword, and Debra wrote the back cover text. I would also like to thank Brenda Schwieterman, Jenny Luebke, and Janelle Lange for their efforts in updating the text for the fourth edition. Dreis Van Landuyt, Van-Griner publisher and my friend, gave this project new life, and he has been the most supportive publisher I've ever worked with on a book project. Thank you, Dreis.

After a long run with the book, and after Eye on Education gave the rights to the book back to us, Bernard signed over his rights to me and allowed me to revise it as a solo author. I want to thank him for that, and reiterate how much we miss him at Miami. But his career at Penn State has continued to blossom, and I continue to count him as friend and mentor in the work at hand. I want to mention that there are two significant places remaining in this book where he had a profound impact on the text. First is the survey of curriculum orientations for students in Chapter 9 and second is the overview of professional development models in Chapter 14. He provided the scholarship and insights behind those prominent sections, and I thank him for his graciousness in allowing me to include the material here.

So, this book is a revision of a previous text, and this is the fourth edition of that earlier revision. There is new material and a slightly different organizational pattern. The process has been enlightening, I've learned a lot, and I hope the book sings for students taking a course on teacher leadership course and who want to have a strong, productive career in teaching by practicing teacher leadership.

I intended for the book to address a gap that has existed for me in the field, that is, for a book to use as an anchor text in a course on teacher leadership with preservice or beginning teachers that is readable and engaging, that focuses on the narrative of real experiences of teacher leaders in schools, and that pulls together many sound ideas by means of an interactive, multilayered text. At root, I'm advancing several important, primary ideas. For instance, we need beginning teachers who set the bar for themselves extremely high. Competence in the classroom is critical, but as important as an initial threshold of competence are the following qualities/approaches: caring for children, schools, and communities; focusing on learning and inquiry; working well with others; creating productive environments where everyone can learn, question, and practice democratic living; and improving every day upon the previous day so that students benefit. In essence, I view teacher leaders as such from the very beginning of their careers, from the first moment they think that teaching is for them through their last day on the job. Teacher leadership happens when teachers take their professional development seriously, when they try their best every day in the classroom and with peers, when they see themselves and their work as making a difference, and when they engage others with honesty and integrity as they persevere through the exciting work in the field every day of teaching. Teacher leadership is action, a function, not just a role to play. We need teachers who see how important it is to be successful in the classroom with students as the primary concern, but who also see themselves as having a wider perspective all at the same time, who consider deeper ideas, question the status quo, pursue justice, and reflect/act as stewards of public schooling for the wider community and society.

To these ends, the book has three movements. The first part of the book pushes the reader to consider deep, educational issues regarding teaching and to reflect on his or her decision to teach on a very personal level. I ask the reader to consider the implications of developing theory, style, and practice in teaching that is based on reflective action. The second part of the book focuses on the wider questions surrounding teaching and learning today through the lens of curriculum leadership. The curriculum (not standards, which are preset by outsiders and are concerned mainly with ends, not means) offers a way for teachers to act with some autonomy and with professionalism together. It is one of the last areas in the field where this is the case, and teachers need to develop skills, orientations, and predispositions to excel as curriculum leaders. And last, the book closes with critical issues that all teachers have to face today, including the connection between personal professional development and the improvement of school and society.

Throughout the book I use different forms of writing to engage the reader, from vignettes about teaching and learning written from a first person perspective, to cases of experiences that students have had in the field as beginning educators. These stories weave the main points of the book together, and sometimes the main points emerge from the stories. Teaching and learning are narrative experiences. A book with a narrative feel stands a chance of incorporating multiple discourses and engaging the reader more effectively than a straight textbook, which I could have written much more easily!

A brief note about defining teacher leadership: I implicitly try to define it by showing the reader what it looks like. I never define teacher leadership unequivocally, like a typical textbook might. If pressed, I'd say Gerald comes as close as anyone I've ever met to embodying teacher leadership (see Chapter 4). The fact of the matter is that you will be defining teacher leadership as you practice it in the field. This is part of the vital energy surrounding the notion of teacher leadership: it exists, and beginning teachers can create it. You will, too. Read on …

Prologue

Writing a book about teaching and leadership might seem a pretty daring act when you consider that both topics have been written about in thousands of pages of text during the last 50 years and more. Both topics are familiar because we have all experienced teaching and leadership in some form or another; most of us have very definite ideas about what these concepts mean but interpretations vary widely. After working in schools and universities for the past 25 years, I decided to present perspectives on teaching and leadership in this text. In fact, the concepts and practices of teaching and leadership blend together so strongly that I call this book *Teacher Leadership for the 21st Century*.

This book is about ideas, propositions, concepts, and viewpoints of what it means to be a teacher leader and to exercise teacher leadership. I hope to make clear in the book's chapters what it means to be a teacher leader. Of course, I want to persuade you to my point-of-view, but I invite and encourage you to take issue with my positions (taking issue with ideas is part of teacher leadership). In the pages that follow, you will find that I emphasize some very complex ideas. For instance, teacher leaders are morally grounded and committed to public education. Teacher leaders are reflective and efficacious. Teacher leaders are skilled pedagogues committed to democratic education. Teacher leaders strive to improve the status quo. Teacher leaders take responsibility for their own as well as student learning. Teacher leaders create and take part in communities of learning inside and outside of their classrooms.

The book springs from experiences assisting undergraduates and first year teachers in their quests to enter the worlds of schooling, teaching, and leading. Students of teaching have taught me a great deal about how they think about teaching and leadership. I endeavor here to pass along what they have taught me about the journey to teacher leadership. I hope that this text enhances your understanding about what it means to commit yourself to a life of helping others learn.

From the beginning of this project, I identified multiple grounds or perspectives from which to legitimately begin to undertake writing a book on teacher leadership. I thought that I should speak from experience of teaching and leadership in schools, during which I have found new ideas, experiences, things that actually work and some that don't, and deeper questions about teaching and leadership in schools.

The dilemma for all teacher educators is that we need to prepare students to work in the schools as they exist today without simply contributing to the status quo. Certainly there are many excellent schools in America right now, but there are also schools that currently are not serving children well. Teacher educators try to prepare preservice teachers for all schools using the notion that every school, regardless of its current quality, could and should improve. There are two conflicting axioms that have almost become trite in our language today: "If it ain't broke, don't fix it," and "There is no standing still—either you get better every day, or you are getting worse." In the discourse on school improvement, I tend to ascribe to the second axiom. The challenge for teacher education is to prepare a generation of teachers who will dramatically improve the settings in which they work. This may sound simple to you, but it is not. Improving schools will require uncommon effort, clear understandings on the parts of those involved concerning what the multiple purposes of school are, skillful actions, and above all, commitment to all children, regardless of their backgrounds or circumstances.

Over the years educational pundits and professional associates have claimed that I am writing a book with expectations that are too high and that are unrealistic for the audience. They say that beginning teachers like you cannot be leaders. They claim that new teachers have all they can do to fit into the existing system, to get by, to survive. Some suggest that the idea of leadership should not be introduced until a teacher has had a few years of experience. I say in response, "Baloney!" The students I teach know more and can do more than anyone gives them credit for. I argue, instead, that the best time to marry the concepts of teaching and leading is when aspiring teachers are entering the profession. Recasting the role of teachers as leaders early is the only way to avoid maintaining the status quo. It is the most promising way to renew the role of teaching and consequently renew schools as we know them. Contrary to conventional wisdom, I believe that encouraging teachers to see their work as leadership enhances their commitments and has the potential for holding them more firmly in the profession. I believe that involved and committed teacher leaders are more likely to stay in teaching and thrive.

When I was first learning to drive I made a critical error in judgment. Picture this common, everyday scene. I pulled up to a stop sign at a busy intersection. There was one car in front of me seeking to enter a highway with the fast-moving traffic. The car in front was turning right and I also intended to turn right. Both the driver in front and I were looking to our left for a break in the flow of cars so we could get onto the highway. After several long moments a space appeared. I was driving a standard shift so I revved the engine to get ready for a speedy start. The opening came, I gunned the engine, popped the clutch and off I went—smack into the car in front of me. Obviously, the driver in the car ahead wasn't as quick to pull out. Fortunately, she was driving one of those big expensive cars with real bumpers, so the damage to her car was minimal. On the other hand, my Volkswagen was a wreck.

—Vignette told by colleague Bernard Badiali

Bernard's story illustrates the classic mistake educators and other reformers make by trying to renew schools by any other means than through promoting teacher leadership. Administrators want to create policies that improve schools. College professors want to promote theories about school change based on their research. Legislators and corporate pundits want to press the idea of accountability to insure school reform. But all of these groups and individuals are at the equivalent point of being one car back at the stop sign. The only way to get onto the highway of educational renewal is through the teacher. (The metaphor breaks down a bit when you imagine teachers driving expensive cars!) After all is said and done, the most critical component in school improvement is the classroom teacher. We all may want to get on the highway of educational renewal, but we go nowhere without exceptional teachers. Few people disagree with that fact, yet so many groups look past teachers who are right in front of them for some other magic elixir that will renew schools.

At some point in our lives, virtually everyone teaches. Parents teach, sisters teach, brothers teach, coaches teach, clergy members teach, and college professors teach. Some are very good at teaching. Some of these teachers are painfully awful. To complicate matters, learners have conflicting views about who is good and who is awful. Nonetheless, because we all have taught and have been taught, we have very definite ideas about what good teaching is. There is a difference, however, between teaching as an instinctive social act and professional teaching. To illustrate, most of us could build a garden shed. But a professional architect and master cabinetmaker could certainly build a better one than we could because she has specialized knowledge and skills.

Becoming a professional teacher requires an intricate level of understanding, artistry, and a lifetime of study. It is true that anyone can teach, but great teaching is so complex that it makes shed building, architecture, cabinetmaking, and rocket science all look relatively simple.

In every classroom there are incredible challenges to be met. Every student is a puzzle partly because each student is so unique and partly because learning preferences vary so widely. Motivation is a puzzle because different children respond to different actions. Learning itself is a puzzle because humans do it in such a variety of ways. Understanding curriculum content to be taught is a challenge, not so much because concepts are difficult, but because knowledge has exploded and there is so much to know. Important decisions must be made before, during, and after teaching to help students build connections between what they know and need to know. Knowing content is not a sufficient condition for becoming an excellent teacher. The challenge is knowing content well enough to present it in different ways for the learners, and knowing the learners well enough to create experiences from which they will develop and engage the content. On top of the challenges to good teaching, there are the problems presented by the current structure of school environments. Many veteran teachers say that the easiest part of the job is actually teaching. The difficult part is dealing with the demands of the state and school bureaucracies—the paperwork, the reports, and the sometimes difficult relationships with administrators, other faculty members, parents, and community members.

I relate some of the difficulties of learning to teach not to discourage you from pursuing your goal to become a great teacher, but to point out that the job, done well, is challenging and far more demanding than it appears on the surface. I also acknowledge that teaching does not have to be difficult. Some teachers make the job easy. They teach from the book, assign homework, go through the motions, do what they are told, and collect their checks at the end of the week. I am not interested in perpetuating that approach to teaching. Instead, I'm interested in preparing thoughtful, caring, skilled individuals, individuals to whom we can entrust the next generation of learners. This text was created to help you become one of those teachers, one who understands from the outset that he or she is a teacher leader.

Leadership is another one of those terms that has a thousand definitions and the definition in use usually depends on who's talking. In the navy, leadership means "running a tight ship," being well organized, directing

subordinates, and so on. In politics, leadership means mobilizing constituents and getting elected. How do you define leadership? What ideas, or
actions, or perspectives come to mind when you think of leadership?

Sirotnik (1997) coined one of the best definitions of leadership, saying
that leadership is "the exercise of significant and responsible influence." This
definition is powerful in its elegance. Consider the key words: exercise implies that leadership is a dynamic, deliberate decision-oriented activity. It is
an action or set of actions. Significant suggests that leadership is not without
content of importance. Responsible means that leadership in education has
moral implications, especially for teachers. "Embedded in this word is the
moral core that derives from the tacit agreement entered into by educators by
virtue of an occupation directed at significantly and profoundly influencing
the lives of children and youth" (p. 237). Influence in this case means leading
others to a reasoned point of view.

In this book leadership is considered to be a function, not a role.
Everyone in school can lead and should be enabled to do so. Schools that do
not encourage teacher leadership as a function will never be good places for
students or for teachers.

The text that follows has several structural layers of organization and
styles of presentation. First, vignettes in each chapter capture the energy and
essential ideas of the entire chapter. Students and teachers should interact
with each other and the text through these vignettes, challenging each other's
assumptions, speculating about possible resolutions to dilemmas, and spur-
ring the creation of related personal stories of experience among readers. The
narrative form holds a certain power for opening windows of thought and
interaction. Narratives in the forms of stories or first person accounts have a
certain affinity for communicating notions and images of teacher leadership
that are important for readers to experience. Your interpretations of the
narratives will vary, of course. I think they will enrich your experience of the
ideas in this book.

Second, I direct the reader to relevant research and pertinent readings
while discussing in an expository fashion the chapter's primary topics. In some
places I paraphrase or more extensively document a theoretical perspective or
describe a unique school practice that is a central concern of a chapter. But I
also give numerous references to materials for further study including books,
articles, and websites to visit, believing that students of teaching will want to
read outside the assigned readings in order to grow and excel in their work.

Third, I illuminate nearly every chapter's core ideas by providing examples from students' and colleagues' perspectives and writings on the topics at hand. This adds multiple voices and perspectives to the discussion and situates the challenges, joys, and problems of teaching and leadership in the lives and experiences of teachers in real schools and in real professional teacher preparation programs.

Last, throughout much of the book I ask questions for further consideration and discussion called "Reflections." They do not appear in any systematic way throughout the book except "often." I mean for you to interact with these reflective prompts as you read. Some may lead to more extensive thinking and writing on your part. I strongly suggest that instructors include a journal component in the course if this book is used as a class text; perhaps these "Reflections" can serve as a baseline of prompts to which students can more formally respond.

I hope that reading this book will make a positive contribution to your development as a teacher. I have intentionally written it in a style that is conversational and in a structure that is modestly unconventional. My approach is more indirect than conventional texts. It is created with the idea that you will read these stories, vignettes, cases, and problems from real school settings and try to understand the messages embedded in them. In this way I hope to foster the habit of critical reflection so necessary to your success as a teacher leader. I also honestly aim to press on you a particular point of view about the functions of teaching and leading as well as the organization of schooling. Obviously, I invite you to take issue with the assumptions and viewpoints put forth on the pages to come.

Consider this a fair warning that this text is not a "how-to" book on teacher leadership. While many of the things taken up here are practical, and have the potential to shift and enhance professional practice in schools, I don't claim to have the best recipe to cook up "teacher leadership" or a "teacher leader." I do take strong positions on matters here, and suggest things that teacher leaders ought to do, from educational, moral, and ethical standpoints, but this is not a manual. Contexts and situations dictate decision-making opportunities for teacher leaders that shift, change, expand, detract, grow, and move in experience. Making decisions about what to do in context is teacher leadership; perhaps this book will help you understand how to go about positioning yourself to make good decisions, on a daily basis, for yourself, students, colleagues, school, and community.

What I mainly hope for is that those who read this book will discuss and challenge deeply their assumptions about teaching in schools and commit themselves to actions that can be defined in context as teacher leadership. This reflects the position that teacher education is not a training regimen filled only with methods of "how-to," but a practically philosophical undertaking that seeks clarity to questions about the "whats" and "whys" of teaching and leadership. The "how-to" trick bag will last a few of your first days in teaching; a disposition to inquire, question, and study the "whats" and "whys" of teaching will last a lifetime and lead to exemplary practice.

From this point on I invite you along on a journey of self-discovery and to ponder the mystery of great teaching. I want you to construct a thoughtful approach to pedagogy and to develop your own teaching style. I also want you to begin placing yourself in the world of schools, not simply as a cog in the wheel, but as an intellectual person with knowledge and insights into how to make schools better places. Most important, I want to make clear that the life of a teacher leader demands your full attention and all the mental and physical resources you can bring to bear to the task. Your students deserve no less.

1
SITUATING THE SELF AS A TEACHER LEADER

Freeze Frame: Tom Teaches Ibsen's The Wild Duck

During my student teaching experience, the senior English class charged to my care during week three was slated to begin reading the great Norwegian playwright Henrik Ibsen's *The Wild Duck*. My cooperating teacher told me I would take over this class and start with this play. I had been observing for a week or so, and she gave me another week to get a better feel for the classroom and students and to plan for the unit on Ibsen before "taking over."

I had not read any Ibsen before this, so I dug into the play as well as some background about his life. I remember how difficult it was just to read the play. Ibsen is subtle, dark in his humor, and difficult to read. But I was enjoying reading and learning about Ibsen's life and even found some old slides in the school library on Ibsen that had been used by another teacher in the school. I took the slides and started planning for an opening lecture on "The Life and Times of Henrik Ibsen."

The night before the first class of the unit, I wrote out every word of a lecture by hand, and marked the text of the lecture at the times when I would change the picture in the slide projector. I was so nervous, edgy, un-sure. "This is it," I thought. "Time to teach, to see if I have what it takes to actually do it." I put immense pressure on myself. I thought, "After all of this preparation, especially after leaving another career behind already, what if I don't like teaching or can't do it? What if the students hate me or do things I can't respond to adequately? What if they are smarter and see right through my obvious ignorance?" I also thought briefly that scripting a lecture would come across as boring, but at this point I didn't know how I could just stand up there and talk about Ibsen without a script, let alone extemporaneously engage the students in a literary discussion.

My cooperating teacher—a classic, master teacher of literature for over 25 years at the high school level—always taught beautifully. As far as I could tell, she simply came in to school daily and started talking and engaging students in the text. The students always seemed interested, challenged, and engaged. I didn't know how to do this, but I did know that I had learned something about Ibsen from my studies that could be transmitted to the students.

So I walked in Monday morning, literally sweating on that cold winter day, and so nervous I could barely speak a coherent sentence. After fumbling nervously with the slide projector and the screen, I started in on Ibsen. I read from my script, several pages of it actually, until I started feeling more comfortable. At one point, I left the script and just began talking and walking about the room. "I'm teaching," I thought, "This is it. I've got it." At that precise moment, I started to speak a sentence, one that mirrored one written in the notes of my lecture, and I froze in mid-sentence. I couldn't recall a particular word in the sentence and I just stared into space, frozen, paralyzed by this lost word. I had rehearsed the lines, but now I had nothing except a blank slate.

I remember wanting to speak but not being able to. It was like falling perilously, out of control, in a dream. There's nothing you can do but wake up. But I couldn't snap out of it. Now this pregnant pause was probably only a number of seconds, maybe ten or so. But try staring, silently, willfully, for that long without flinching, in mid-sentence, in front of a group of students. It lasted long enough for the students to be at the edge of their seats and for my cooperating teacher finally to whisper from the back of the room, "Tom? Tom? Say something, anything ... Tom?"

"Oh?" I said, turning to her, "I lost my place. I can't remember a word."

"It's okay," she said, "Just say anything. You're doing fine."

"Okay," I said wanting to run and cry at the same time, "I just can't remember the word."

I turned like a robot, with mechanical preciseness, which is all I had left, first toward the teacher and then toward the students and then toward the door. Then I spoke these words as I walked toward the door: "Well, so much for Ibsen. How about *The Wild Duck?*" I asked, grabbing the handle and opening the door up wide. I remember the students' faces distinctly as I turned back to face them, worried and relieved at the same time, and their voices helping me as I eked out a few questions about Act I. I scrapped the notes and the slide show and decided to teach. The students saved me that day, never laughing or making fun about my freeze up, just going on about their business of learning. My cooperating teacher never brought it up later in any way, a potentially deadly glitch to hold over one's head or to base a label of incompetence upon, "Candidate for teaching can't remember words mid-sentence—freezes up." I could see it all in plain script, written on my final evaluation, but it never appeared. Over the years, after getting stuck on a word or losing my place during a class session, I fondly recall the moment I first taught and how glad I am that I didn't keep on walking through that open door, but turned back.

REFLECTION

What was Tom's dilemma as a beginning teacher? What do you think he meant when he said, "I scrapped the notes and the slide show and decided to teach?"

A Response to "Tom Teaches"

"I scrapped the notes and the slide show and decided to teach." This quote really stood out to me. Oftentimes you find teachers who are unwilling to change no matter what happens. They are set in their style of teaching and do not find a problem, for instance, with monotonous lecturing. It sounds as if Tom was trying such an approach during student teaching. His daily schedule someday could have looked like this: teacher enters classroom, teacher lectures, students take notes, teacher answers questions, class dismissed. That day Tom threw out the script in his own "how-to" manual and decided to engage the students in learning. What that means is he used the students' knowledge of Ibsen to guide him through his *teaching, rather than just lecturing. Teaching is a process of showing and involving students, rather than just telling. Tom used even his beginner's understanding of the class to teach more effectively.*

—Molly Cheek, preservice teacher

During our course on teacher leadership, in addition to reflections like Molly Cheek's above, students also write case reports, which are short treatments of significant incidents in classrooms. We use these reports to situate beginning teachers' fledgling understanding of teaching and students. Below, Jacob Morris writes about a field experience that led him to teaching.

Case Report: Teaching Is for Me

—Jacob Morris, preservice teacher

I have not had a "traditional" four-year college experience. I have transferred universities twice now, which has left me a little behind in my teacher education program. This situation, however, has given me two extra field experiences, both from which I feel that I gained a lot. This case report is about my second field experience because I feel like I had more opportunities to learn about teaching in this setting. Of course, I was nervous and unsettled but very excited to have this opportunity.

The first day of my field experience I walked in and met with the teacher, and right away, I felt very excited about how the experience was going to go. The teacher made me feel at ease and welcomed me into her classroom with encouraging words and enthusiasm. The semester went far better than I imagined it would have. There was a lot of observation involved but there was also ample student interaction and I was always included in what was going on in the class.

About my fourth or fifth week into the field experience, I was starting to get more familiar and comfortable with the students and the flow of the classroom. It was 12th grade U.S. Government, and I met with the first and second period classes three times a week for one semester. During the fifth week, my cooperating teacher started to give me more things to do, and she had let me pretty much be in charge of coming up with and teaching a lesson plan, which had to cover certain material in the textbook, and I had to come up with specific learning objectives and outcomes. The material being covered was about political parties and things that different parties were associated with, as well as just general knowledge about the function of political parties in government.

I was so excited about having this chance to lead the class in discussion and to see what it's like to stand in front of students and actually teach. I was even more excited when I turned in my copy of the lesson plan and the objectives to my cooperating teacher to look over, and she was kind enough to have the confidence in me to even let me create my own quiz to give to the students at the end of the week. I still remember the uneasy looks on the students' faces when I first stood up and started talking about political parties. But the more I got into the material, the more the students seemed to be interested in it.

All of these students were seniors deciding what the next steps in their lives would be, and they were very mature and understanding, seeing as how many of them were about to go off to college. The students were the main things that helped me get though this experience. They were understanding with me and interested enough to give me the privilege of teaching them. Halfway through the week we had even broken down into small groups and were talking about political parties. It was one of the most magical experiences in my entire life, and I wouldn't trade it for anything in the world because the discussions I had with those students and the great ideas that they had are priceless. Being able to teach something to these students pretty much on my own gave me a feeling that I can't get anywhere else except for in the classroom. I walked away from this experience with so many great new outlooks on life and teaching, and knowing that these students actually learned gave me great joy.

It was the first time in my entire educational career that I had really gotten a chance to take the reins and lead the class. But it was more than just coming up with a lesson plan and doing it because it was "just another thing I had to do to get through class." Instead, it was the first time I had really thought about and became passionate about knowing that teaching is what I really want to devote my life to. It was an important part of my experience because without it I don't know if I would still even be pursuing teaching today. It was a moment that I had that gave me the confidence and will power to see that teaching is something that means more to me than just a paycheck or an occupation, or something I'll just try until I find what interests me. Not to say that there weren't challenges and bumps along the road, because there were, but the overall experience was worth every second I spent in that classroom. This short field experience with these students and that teacher in a particular school that I had in my junior year of college is what spoke to me and what made me see that teaching is what's important, what I'm most passionate about.

Making a Decision to Teach

Deciding to teach is one of the most crucial decisions of your life. It should not be made casually, because it will not just affect you, but countless others you will be charged to teach, as well as the community and the common good. So how you situate yourself in the following discussion will have a great deal to do with how you view teaching as a profession and teaching as leadership. One of the things you should know is that for me the status quo isn't all that great. I am interested instead in helping your generation develop into teachers who carry a set of foundational commitments that make you teacher leaders from the very beginning.

> ## REFLECTION
>
> Some people "work to live" while others "live to work." What does choosing one position or the other mean for teachers? Is teaching a "calling" or a "vocation"?

In the preceding narrative, I faced several problems and decisions at the beginning of my career as a teacher leader. For me, all of the uncertainties about teaching got wrapped up in one event. I wondered if I were cut out for teaching, if I would be any good at it. To protect myself, I over-prepared and taught in a mechanical way. But locking up on a word, and the necessity in the moment that the mistake produced, allowed me the opportunity to make a decision to use my extensive preparation and knowledge about the subject to engage learners. As a result, I was able to draw them into the material by discussing their reactions to it, coming to some sense and meaning of it together in the classroom. I started down the path of reflecting on what good teaching is and can be. I took a step toward becoming a teacher leader. Similar questions for you as you become teacher leaders will be: How will

I plan for teaching? How will I interact and communicate with students? What degree of involvement will students have in the curriculum and in the generation of knowledge in my classroom, school, and community?

As a university professor working with beginning teachers, I worry that some of you will retreat from teaching at the first sign of trouble, like I almost did. This is a real temptation given the great sacrifice and commitment that constitutes teaching. Many teachers never recover from the first set of bad experiences in classrooms. Without appropriate support from other teachers, administrators, or family, they sometimes struggle through a couple of years and quit out of frustration, or they work themselves so hard toward excellence in the classroom that they quickly burn out and move on to another less strenuous career. Neither approach is healthy or helpful for the teacher, the students, or schools.

Parker Palmer (1998) insightfully writes about heartbreak in teaching. He points out that every "bad day" takes a little more out of the teacher. As bad days accumulate, commitment flags until eventually the job becomes too hard or too hurtful. Some teachers leave the profession. Some teachers harden to it. But teacher leaders learn from their mistakes and the mistakes of others. They carefully consider what needs to be done differently in the future. With reflection and support, good teachers survive and thrive in schools. They renew themselves through professional development opportunities and by developing a personal view of themselves as teachers and of their students in schools as able, worthy, and succeeding.

I also had to figure out quickly how to continue on in that moment given the seeming catastrophe of it. In actuality, lessons that go bust usually are not nearly as bad as they seem, and one aspect of professional development for teachers is learning to give yourself time to reconstitute approaches to teaching, even during and following negative experiences. Now, this position does not mean that you can responsibly experiment on students while you struggle to find a level of professional competence, but it does mean that there is a realistic understanding that teachers will be learning to teach as they begin teaching. Even the most accomplished veteran teachers learn something new every day. That's what makes teaching challenging and satisfying for them. The teacher leader's learning never ends.

No beginning teacher comes to the classroom able to teach like a master teacher, with years of experience and answers to many of the classroom's most difficult questions. Even the most capable beginners do not stack up to the best veterans. This does not mean that beginners cannot be effective and productive. In many cases they rival veterans in terms of effectiveness in the classroom. What it means is that beginning teachers have to give themselves permission to take intelligent risks. This is a crucial aspect of teacher leadership; of course, teacher leadership exists and flourishes when a supportive faculty and administration understand well the struggles for beginning teachers and provide adequate support for them.

REFLECTION

What concerns do you have regarding your initial teaching experiences in schools?

Student Journal Excerpt

There are many things that I wonder about as I get ready to go into the field next week for my first field placement with a cooperating teacher and real students in real classrooms. I wonder what I will be expected to do while I'm there? Will I have to teach the whole time (scary thought) or will I be stuck in the back of the room watching the teacher lecture all day long (also scary)? I'm hoping for something in the middle. This will be the first time that I will be in a classroom situation where I might be "in charge." It's a little nerve wracking.

—Kari Koerner, preservice teacher

Many similar concerns no doubt dot your mental landscape at this point. You may begin with questions such as "What if the students don't like me? How will I handle the first act of student defiance? Will other teachers help me? Can I count on the administration for support? How will I deal with parents?" These concerns are legitimate, important. But you will soon be facing even wider, more personal, and even public concerns such as "Is teaching the right profession for me? What is the purpose of a good public education for every citizen?" I would like you to consider these wider concerns now, as well as the issues surrounding the remarkable commitment that teaching entails. Embedded in these concerns are hopes for the future of teaching and schools, particularly in the hope that children will have a capable and competent teacher who cares for them and for learning, every day of every year, consistently and without fail. Fulfilling this dream starts with you and your commitment with regard to these early decisions.

In my opinion, teaching is second only to parenting in difficulty. Teaching is unimaginably complex to those who take the job seriously. It requires a deep knowledge of subject, a deep understanding of students, and an inventive facility for combining that knowledge and understanding into performances that result in learning and into opportunities for students to engage the topic at a deep level that tap into their own concerns and interests. Great teaching is a truly awesome thing. I have the utmost respect for those who teach well. I view teaching with a great deal of respect and admiration. Under difficult circumstances, teachers do more to serve and preserve society than any other profession. They not only help us to learn, but they inspire us to do so as well.

I understand that other professions require personal and professional commitment, but teaching will require that you invest much, often for intangible gain. The financial rewards will not be great in teaching. I have always supported reasonable pushes for higher salaries for teachers and for their well-earned rights to bargain. Teachers constitute one of the most underpaid professional groups in our society. But if you are seeking a life of monetary wealth, then teaching may not be the career you want.

If you think of teaching as something for you to do while you decide what to do with your professional life, as in, "I don't know, maybe I'll teach a few years and see what happens," then we do not want or need you in teaching. There is plenty of room for teachers who come to teaching after years in other professions, for those who feel a call to contribute to the lives of the young after other successful undertakings, and also for those who are unsure about whether or not they will ultimately have what it takes to teach at the beginning of a professional career. But if you are wandering, maybe thinking that teaching is a good placeholder on the way to something or somewhere else, there really isn't room for you in teaching. Consider what is at stake if you enter teaching without a full commitment. A half-hearted effort won't do you or your students much good. Spending much time trying to find your own way, while perhaps even exploring other career opportunities, leaves little time to really focus on the needs of your students and their learning and your own professional development.

It's important to note that students sometimes ask me about entering the Teach for America corps. I always answer that going through a legitimate teacher education program prepares teachers in the best way possible for a career in teaching. The idea that you can just walk into a classroom and be effective is naive, and it can be very damaging not only to the new teacher but also to the actual students in the classroom who deserve to have a real, certified teacher in the room. For me, choosing to teach, preparing for it, and pursuing long-term professional development opportunities is a social justice issue. Students and schools with the greatest needs deserve the best teachers. You should be well-prepared, dynamic, responsive, and in for the long haul. This is what students, schools, and society need for their long-term viability and for the pursuit of excellence. "Just passing through" gets you and schools nowhere fast.

Teacher leadership requires a commitment to and love for working with students in schools. These things can be developed in the process of learning to teach. I hope that as you make your way through this book that your decision becomes clearer or that the book and your classmates, friends, and instructor help you to confirm the view you brought with you.

Parker Palmer (1998) places the roles of identity and integrity as central features of good teaching, and focuses on the activity of connecting students and teaching with heartfelt passion:

> Good teaching cannot be reduced to technique; good teaching comes from the identity and integrity of the teacher. ... In every class I teach, my ability to connect with my students, and to connect them with the subject, depends less on the methods I use than on the degree to which I know and trust my selfhood—and am willing to make it available and vulnerable in the service of learning. ... The connections made by good teachers are held not in their methods but in their hearts—meaning heart in its ancient sense, as the place where intellect and emotion and spirit and will converge in the human self. (pp. 10–11)

Throughout this book I will encourage you to consider the possibility that while good teaching does have something to do with technique and method, since you will be required on your first day on the job to "teach" and no doubt to teach well, teaching is so much more. Teaching is about the choices you make and the reasons for those choices. Teaching is about what you believe in and how those beliefs mesh (or not) with those in your community of learners. Teaching is about having a sense of the purposes of teaching and learning. Teaching is about being committed to a life of learning and exploring and creating and risk-taking. Teaching is about having passion, caring for children, and connecting your life with something greater than yourself, like other people's and communities' lives and dreams. Teaching is a lot about having "heart."

Many students of teaching and leadership think that teaching is only about the transmission of relevant information in discrete bits from one generation to the next in isolated, controlled classrooms. This could not be further from the truth, no matter the punitive attributes that society attaches to the classroom. Teaching has always entailed a panoply of activities, including but ranging far beyond mere instruction: from planning lessons and studying academic/intellectual materials, to inventing meaningful learning activities, to assessing student work, to disciplining students and creating a positive classroom climate for learning, to accompanying students on field trips, to working on committees, to coaching athletics and directing the fine arts, to collecting lunch money, and on and on. All of these things constitute teaching. Some days require more discipline than instruction, more clerical work than coaching, and more instruction than paper work. In the end, however, all of it is teaching, and all of it is leadership. Teacher Leadership.

I know people who have left teaching early because, according to them, it changed too much during these last 40 years, right along with culture, society, and children. Some have claimed in disgust at the bitter end, "I'm not a baby-sitter," or "I didn't train to be a teacher to tell kids to 'be quiet' all day long." But I contend that the conditions in schools depend upon teachers' abilities to conceptualize their work for teaching academic material, creating appropriate settings for learning, and relating to children as social human beings who bring lives and problems to school. These perspectives and positions are essential and really cannot be separated and never could be.

Perhaps children are less compliant and parents less involved in their children's lives today than in yesteryear (I'm not all together convinced of these things, by the way), but those are not problems for teacher leaders to solve in their own classrooms. After all, there are things teachers can control and things they can't control. One thing they can't control is what students bring or do not bring to the table, which includes in many cases the level of involvement in or value for education their parents or guardians have. In fact, a focus on these perceived problems as lacks or as insurmountable obstacles to learning shuts down energy that should be spent working with children. What teacher leaders can control is how they face the issues. "We have students to teach, regardless of what they do or do not bring from home, so the question is: 'Given what I am charged to do and what my students bring to the table, how can we progress and learn together responsibly, with vigor and purpose?'" Teacher leaders have a profound sense of learners and their lives and how to maximize their learning in the classroom given whatever factors are at hand, and no matter what learners do or do not bring to the table in terms of cultural capital.

In this postmodern information age, in which students bring a range of experiences to school that their parents never had, teachers have a remarkable challenge and responsibility to channel the talent and ability of students into productive learning. All students are motivated to learn, but not always in the ways we may want them to be motivated for learning or even understand completely. As a result no doubt, for most teachers reaching students will take more than assigning pages to read from a textbook and creating worksheets. Again, Parker Palmer (1998) eloquently writes about commitment to students:

> Whatever tidbits of truth these student stereotypes contain (the ones naming them as having no direction or motivation), they grossly distort reality, and they widen the disconnection between students and their teachers. Not only do these caricatures make our lives look noble in comparison to the barbaric young, but they also place the sources of our students' problems far upstream from the place where our lives converge with theirs. Criticizing the client is the conventional defense in any embattled profession, and these stereotypes conveniently relieve us of any responsibility for our students' problems—or their resolution. (p. 41)

We must not blame students or their families for their perceived lack of interest in or motivation for learning and caring, but instead look at ourselves and our schools for answers about how to respond. We should rebuild school cultures with connections to children's lives, their worlds, so that the best, most appropriate influences will affect them, support them, and enhance their chances for success in school and in life.

I also believe that there is nothing more important than for the teacher leader to be passionate about learning whatever it is that he or she claims as a specialty area, whether working with children in early childhood, middle childhood, or adolescence, or math, language arts, music, art, physical education, and/or special education, etc. A teacher's intellectual excitement helps create a positive learning environment as well as the engagement of students in meaningful and relevant learning activities. What never ceases to surprise are teachers who continue to lecture, pass out worksheets, give "objective" tests, and complain that discipline and student learning/interest have eroded. Of course they have, because the learning environment in their classrooms is impoverished. Who would want to be there, especially when students learn exponentially more outside the classroom through other experiences and media? If you want to find teachers with few discipline problems and rich learning environments, watch those teacher leaders who create interesting curricula that engage students and their lives. These teachers exist in every school.

Finally, I want beginning teachers to resist being socialized into foot soldier status. Foot soldiers, quite literally, are well-trained soldiers who will ultimately lay their lives down at the request of their superiors, whether the order to fight is reasonable or not. It is their duty to go to battle, and not to question. And teachers are often treated as such, especially beginning teachers. They are often given assignments with the most difficult students and coerced into taking on a multitude of outside activities. Happy to land a job in a good district or just to be teaching at all, they do what they are told and they don't question, merely waiting to hand off unwanted assignments to the next wave of newcomers. They hear the march of standards-based curriculum and step tight, vowing not to get too "fancy" or "innovative" for fear of getting off track. And with heightened self-interest at hand in terms of the tying of merit to test scores, many beginning teachers will be all too happy to simply stick to the script, dumbing down the profession and teaching and learning in schools even further.

Maybe following orders is all there is to becoming a teacher, but I don't think so. Short of being so radical and obstreperous that they jeopardize their jobs, I envision vocal, knowledgeable, critical, and effective beginning teachers ready to contribute to students' learning and to develop professionally, even if these things require them to speak up and take risks from the beginning. In a bygone era, beginning teachers could bide their time before becoming engaged in activities of teacher leadership in the school; but now schools, administrators, colleagues, and students expect beginning teachers to get involved right away in the complete life of the school community. Part of your teacher education should attempt to ready you for the multitude of facets that constitute teaching and leadership in schools.

I envision a generation of teachers who view themselves as public intellectuals who engage ideas and life in every activity they take up in schools, from teaching students to discussing curriculum with colleagues (Giroux, 1994). I hope for a generation of teachers who have committed themselves to discourse in schools about how to address problems constructively and have not fallen (and vow not to fall) into the destructive discourse that reinforces close-minded prejudices and despair regarding students and their families or the school community. After all, among some teachers, this type of negative talk is common. Teacher leadership entails not participating in it and perhaps countering that discourse.

I hope for a generation of teachers who turn the discussion in the teachers' lounge from diatribes of blame against students and families to questions about their own responsibilities for student learning and their own professional development necessary to meet student needs. They will ask, "What is our responsibility for teaching the students we have regardless of what they bring or do not bring to their desks each day?" At times I sense a strain of anti-intellectualism and defeat among teachers and the public today that runs counter to the purposes of schooling. Organized, purposeful efforts to routinize, technicize, and mechanize teaching always "de-skill" teachers and contribute to this problem. For instance, teachers are "de-skilled" when we create curriculum or learning programs that have well-educated teachers reading a script prepared by others (these teachers don't even have room to prepare *their own* doomed script for teaching, like I did). What frightens the most is when efforts to limit teachers come from inside the teaching profession. Our task in teacher education isn't to produce automatons who can recite facts and figures and pass teacher tests or student achievement tests, no matter the political landscape; instead I charge you to help people learn to think productively in an intellectual and technological age that will tax all of our talents and resources, and to help create the next wave of well-educated citizens who can function in a social and political democracy. Much is at stake if we do not reach these ends in our work.

I believe that most students and teachers today are smarter and more able than they have ever been; they may know different things than students from generations ago knew, but they know more and have experienced more than other, older human beings. This goes for you as well, in relationship to the teacher educators you work with. Students are also more aware of the impact of the wider culture on their lives and in many cases have committed themselves to acting on behalf of the personal social welfare of their peers and strangers. How do we tap and guide this enormous potential and talent? This is a question for a teacher leader.

In this chapter I presented several beginning ideas concerning teacher leadership and discussed the commitment necessary to become a teacher leader. I intend to build on this beginning by asking you to look more deeply at yourself and your personal commitments to teaching in the next chapter.

REFLECTION

What motivating factors have led you to teaching? What assumptions, beliefs, values, and/or ideas do you hold about teaching so far?

2
PURSUING REFLECTION AS GROUNDS FOR TEACHER LEADERSHIP

Teacher reflection is at the core of what makes an outstanding teacher leader, one who constantly and critically examines the assumptions he or she has and the actions he or she takes based on those assumptions as well as the impact of those actions on others, especially learners. Teachers have to make thousands of decisions each day. Careful reflection strengthens those decisions.

Schon (1990) and Zeichner (1989) each developed frameworks to describe reflection. Each perspective helps to situate this discussion of reflection and provides a theoretical basis for the chapter. Schon writes persuasively about how reflective practitioners practice "reflection-on-action" and "reflection-in-action." Reflection-on-action refers to "thinking back to what we have done." Reflection-in-action describes the point at which "our thinking serves to reshape what we are doing while we are doing it" (Newton, 1994, pp. 20–21). Teachers engage in this reflective cycle as they teach and plan. They serve students and their own professional development well when they are conscious of the meta-cognitive processes that shape their teaching practices and understand that outstanding teaching practice involves a high level of "reflection-in-action."

Zeichner (1989) discusses "technical reflection," "practical reflection," and "critical reflection" for teachers.

- Technical Reflection: "the best way to get somewhere, when somewhere is already determined." (Adjust the plan at the moment the need presents itself.) (Zeichner, 1989, p. 15)
- Practical Reflection: "teachers deliberate both about the means and about the purposes." (Justify the adjustment.) (Zeichner, 1989, p. 15)
- Critical Reflection: "teachers raise issues that have to do with ethical and moral dimensions of teaching that aren't necessarily explicit within other forms of reflection. It goes beyond asking, 'What are kids learning and should they be learning that?' Instead, critical reflection raises questions related to moral dimensions of teaching, such as what kinds of things are particular groups of children learning?" (Wonder about the implications of their adjustment.) (Zeichner, 1989, p. 16) (All cited in Newton, 1994, p. 2)

Suzanne Reflects on Practice

Suzanne, a reflective teacher, practices all three of Zeichner's types of reflection when she teaches. One day, as her fourth grade students worked on several math problems at their desks, she realized that when she gave clarifying remarks or worked samples at the board, students in groups three and four contained students who couldn't see her. She quickly decided to ask them to turn their seats around to face the front during the activity (*technical reflection*, she changes the means of what she is doing to facilitate the meeting of her ends). Things went much more smoothly in the lesson after that. She answered fewer repeat questions than she had all week. But she still noticed that students struggled with applying their math skills to the problem solving questions at the end of their math workbook's chapters.

That night while planning she began thinking about the nature of the problems the students were working on and how she had been teaching math. The state achievement tests focus so much on skills that students spent most of their time practicing those skills in class, which left little time for thinking about math or brainstorming solutions to real-world problems with students, let alone for connecting math to other subjects. She wondered if her reliance on skill-based teaching and drills had actually stunted the students' mathematical thinking, making them even more fearful of math and seeing it as distanced from their everyday lives (*practical reflection*, she questions the legitimacy of her means of constructing a teaching response to the curriculum as well as the legitimacy of the curriculum itself).

The next day in the fourth grade team meeting, she asks her colleagues if the students in their classes are doing well on the problem-solving exercises at the end of the math workbook's chapters. When the other teachers say they didn't use them much, focused mainly on skills, and saw little point in discussing it, she pressed the issue further. "What are we doing as math teachers if our students cannot use their math skills to solve simple problems that require them to think in mathematical ways? Is the point of our math teaching just to get them to do well on the skills part of the state test, or do we have a greater responsibility to teach them more than skills, maybe how to think mathematically in the world? I guess I'm wondering if our focus on skills has actually made it harder for them to do well on these tests. Maybe our approach is actually backfiring on us right under our noses?" (*critical reflection*, she wonders about the deeper implications of their teaching decisions on students and questions the fundamental concepts/theories that lie at the heart of their teaching and curriculum).

REFLECTION

Describe a classroom event or experience working with children in an educational scene in which you engaged in some form of reflection. How did the process have an impact on your teaching, if at all?

I acknowledge that idiosyncratic, local knowledge of situations and scenes will be brought to bear during reflective moments and that you will be reflecting upon technical and practical matters (such as how to proceed with a transition from one lesson to the next given the current flow of the class) and/or upon more critical matters (such as questioning the political and power structures that do not permit you to schedule the length of your lab periods) (see Brookfield, 1995). While you are teaching, you are reflecting, just as you might think about and reflect on teaching beforehand and afterward.

As you take weeks to figure out an assessment strategy for an upcoming unit, make split-second decisions about discipline matters in a classroom scene, consider the mistakes you made in drawing up test questions at exam time, and/or represent the sixth grade teachers at a curriculum meeting for selecting the district's new social studies textbooks, you are reflecting before, during, and after the action of teaching, and your reflection has an impact on your teaching. To be aware and reflective means you are leading an examined life, paying attention, and looking more deeply at the issues that are political, economic, cultural, and power-oriented and that have an impact (or not) on your teaching. You aren't, as a result, living the life Plato found wanting: "An unexamined life is not worth living."

It's true that some teachers are not reflective and that you know them already and will meet them in schools. Their apparent lack of reflection reveals a set of assumptions regarding students and teaching. To many of them, teaching is a simple matter. They believe that when teaching is done right, it is done authoritatively, clearly, conveying information that can be given back in a similar form by students. The students' responsibility is to learn the information and show that they know it. When things do not go well, the blame game begins. "These kids aren't motivated"; "I never get any support from the principal or faculty"; "How can I be expected to help students if no one else in their lives will support them?"

Reflective teachers, on the other hand, know there are many ways to teach well. They believe that they are effective, making a difference, changing for the better, and making strong adjustments in order to have an impact on student learning. Reflective teachers always believe they are capable of reaching students; they look for new ways to approach them; and they struggle to improve their practice, especially when things do not go well. They never fall into cycles of cynicism or blame. Too much is at stake to allow this to happen. Instead they build on successes, even if they would seem miniscule to an outsider.

The story in Chapter 1 about freezing up in front of my first class is personal and autobiographical and constitutes a form of reflection. Thoughtful veteran teachers take time to write and reflect about the ideas, events, and decisions (like those embedded in my story) that make up their own personal story of becoming a teacher and living the career of teaching every day over a number of years. They get these opportunities in graduate coursework and as teachers in schools that offer and/or mandate extensive professional and personal development opportunities for faculty and staff. Writing these stories and discussing them offer wonderful opportunities for reflection.

Stories of veteran teachers are well chronicled in several good books on teachers' lives such as Connelly & Clandinin's *Teachers as Curriculum Planners*, 1988; McCutcheon's *Curriculum Development*, 1995; Meier's *The Power of Their Ideas*, 1995; Mitchie's *Holler If You Hear Me*, 1999; and Christenbury's *Retracing the Journey*, 2007. The stories of beginning teachers appear in print as well and are worth a closer look such as McKamey et al.'s *Becoming a Teacher*, 1995; Gitlin & Bullough's *Becoming a Student of Teaching*, 1995; and Codell's *Educating Esme*, 1999. Other classics about becoming a teacher are Jesse Stuart's *The Thread That Runs So True* (1950), Stuart Palonsky's *900 Shows a Year* (1985), and Jane Jacobs' *A Schoolteacher in Old Alaska* (1997). A very recent and elegant piece about returning to teaching is Keizer's "Getting Schooled: The Re-education of an American Teacher" (2011). My own memoir about returning to the high school classroom just came out in 2012 entitled *Teaching Again*. These autobiographical and biographical texts, taken as a whole, make a case for the importance of examining the personal assumptions and experiences that bring people to reflect deeply on teaching and sustain them in the work.

Acknowledging Your "Apprenticeship of Observation"

Daniel Lortie developed a concept in his book *Schoolteacher* (1972) that he called the "apprenticeship of observation." He claims that every teacher comes to teaching with a set of experiences and ideas related to previous school experiences that define the teacher's position as a teacher and that shape the teacher's behaviors. We gain these apprenticeship experiences as students in schools, watching and learning from our own teachers and developing concepts about what constitutes good and effective teaching (as well as bad and ineffective teaching) over a long "apprenticeship" of observing such things. This apprenticeship of observation is served from our own classroom seats as we experience thousands of hours of teaching, over 13 to 17 years of schooling (or more depending on preschool and postsecondary preparation), with many, many teachers. We also learn about teaching from our experiences in the wider contexts of schooling—in the hallways, on buses, and on playing fields. Unfortunately, some unflattering cultural images of teaching get shaped through films and television. Nevertheless, these images shape our conceptions of teaching as well.

Every day, our "apprenticeship of observation" grows and moves us toward a base of beliefs, ideas, images, and concepts of teaching; not surprisingly, we tend to reproduce these conceptions or models in our own teaching. These conceptions or models of practice may be good or bad; what is usually the case is that they are adopted without being critically examined. What I want to argue is that growth as a teacher leader comes from constantly examining and questioning practice and reflecting on the assumptions and perceptions that lead you to make the decisions about teaching that you make.

If we all experience apprenticeships of observation, and if we are influenced a great deal by our experiences as students, then our apprenticeships of observation constitute very powerful experiences. One could argue that we come to teaching with a great deal of knowledge about teaching through early experiences with our own teachers. Some argue, in fact, that teacher education programs have little impact on moving students past their initial perceptions about teaching that they have gained through their observations as students. The tendency is for students of teaching to adopt practices witnessed during their apprenticeships of observation. This happens for several reasons.

We often adopt practices because we only see them from a student's perspective, not from the other side of the desk. Therefore, we do things as beginning teachers because we personally liked the teacher who did them for us, or because the approaches used by certain teachers were effective with us. We do not usually do these things because we have determined that the people or practices we liked or that worked for us will lead to learning by our own students. For instance, you might have loved Mr. Jenkins in high school because of his personality and his ability to inspire you to enjoy history. So you watch him closely as a student and later as a teacher you adopt many of his practices, including his method of quizzing, using true-false questions that barely scratch the most surface level knowledge of history and that often confuse the most able students. Or, you may have excelled as a student in high school math classes centered on computational skills, when most of your district and state assessments these days focus on problem-solving skills. But you continue to focus your pedagogy and curriculum on skills and drills, forsaking the challenge of higher order thinking in mathematics for the comforts found in your own previous successes in school, simply mimicking others and thinking that your minimalist approaches lead to higher test scores.

This all becomes extremely problematic, especially when new teachers employ long-standing practices because they "worked for me" or they "worked for my best teachers." One fundamental mistake in this reasoning is thinking that your own students will be like you were. Perhaps your students come from such different backgrounds and experiences than you have that your assumptions and perceptions about teaching them, in actual fact, damage them and you in practice. It is infinitely easier to teach less effectively, using approaches that "work" (as in "work" to keep the students orderly and quiet in the short run) and not pursuing those that might lead to deeper learning for students.

The question becomes: "What can we accept into our own teaching that comes from our observations as students?" Not all of our observations of teaching as students are bad or antithetical to learning. They may be extremely effective when we employ actions based on those observations and perceptions. But our answer to the question must be something like, "I can accept nothing to be true about teaching well without careful reflection on the soundness of the pedagogy under consideration for use with my own students." We must commit ourselves to a thoughtful examination of our conceptions of teaching and learning and our practices in classrooms. If we do not, chances are we will merely find and keep practices that we ourselves experienced and liked. Chances are that many of those practices we remember as "fun" or "effective" for us really were not "fun" or "effective" for other learners then, and, in turn, will not be helpful for your own students today.

I realize that this discussion of reflection and your apprenticeship of observation may be unsettling to you. I expect that you may be struggling with a question such as, "So how do I determine or find the concepts and principles of good teaching?" One problem is that this is not a book on specific teaching methods, so I spend little space telling you specifically what good teaching according to a certain method looks like. Actually, I spend no time on it! It is up to you to figure out what good teaching is and what methods to use to get there. But good teaching doesn't just take shape out of experience. There are sources that complement the apprenticeships of observation that we have all experienced, and all that we have learned from personal experiences and personal beliefs regarding teaching and learning.

For instance, field knowledge you gain from working in schools with teachers and students and studying teaching through books, ideas, theories of instruction, and other sources will inform you as well. There has to be a balance of drawing upon a personal sense of things (common sense, practical wisdom) *and* the wisdom of others, written, or spoken, or enacted. Students of teaching must be aware that educational literature does exist to help them make decisions about teaching. For example, I can't imagine trying to implement "cooperative learning" strategies in the classroom without first reading Robert Slavin's book *Cooperative Learning: Theory, Research and Practice* (1994).

When I address this matter more completely in the chapter on teacher inquiry for the teacher leader, I will show you ways to go about systematically examining questions, ideas, problems, and issues in teaching that will present themselves in practice and in experience. Teacher leaders reflect, make reasoned decisions, trust their experience and instincts, and constantly adjust. They also study. What I am assuming here is that reflective teachers will ask several questions as they attempt to determine just what good teaching is for them and for their students:

- Is the teaching approach I employ good for all students? How? Why or why not?
- Is the teaching approach based on my hunches? Which ones?
- How have I used others' work (theories and assumptions) to support my own decisions for teaching, i.e., the hunches I originally considered essential?
- Do I get the results I want? How do I make adjustments as students progress (or not)?

Following are two short cases designed to engage you in a discussion of the implications of an apprenticeship of observation and reflective teaching:

REFLECTION

Describe a teacher you had in school who was inspiring or who was really awful. Explain and/or illustrate what you mean.

Case 1

Sarah became a second grade teacher because her second grade teacher, Mrs. Hanlon, greatly influenced her. Reading was so much fun in second grade, and Sarah loved her reading group. When Sarah began teaching, she decided to assign students to reading groups by perceived ability level just like Mrs. Hanlon had done. She made this decision even though she learned in her teacher education program that there are several profound and negative impacts of grouping readers by ability. As Sarah's class progressed through the year, she noticed that groups four and five were struggling with their reading. They demanded more and more of her time, pulling her away from other students she really enjoyed working with. They became disruptive, too, and she had to discipline them. She could tell that several of the students were losing their confidence, especially those assigned to group five, supposedly the lowest level readers in the class.

Case 2

Robert really enjoyed sixth grade social studies as a student. He especially remembers a simulation in which the social studies teacher challenged him to view his role in the world as an "active" citizen and even gave him opportunities to act as an agent of positive social change in the world through experiences such as working in a homeless shelter. When he got the opportunity to teach social studies to his own sixth grade class, he used the Wednesday afternoon period set aside for community service and other outside academic activities to construct opportunities for his students to serve citizens with fewer advantages. In fact, his class became the most active and successful in the school community, helping lead a campaign to persuade city leaders to refurbish an unsafe nursing home for low-income residents. In a newspaper article about the class' efforts, Robert mentioned that "my sixth grade teacher's commitment to me and certain causes inspired me to guide the class forward on this project." But Robert knows that his commitment to connecting students to means for helping others to exercise their human and democratic rights, for building stronger social communities, and for serving others—all critical ends that he values in his teaching platform—comes at some cost. The other sixth grade class used the Wednesday afternoon time when Robert's students were in the community to prepare for the "history bowl," learning names and dates in history and winning the district competition and finishing with higher scores on the state social studies exam than his classes did. Despite this, Robert continued to plan with his students for next year's community project.

Suggested Questions for Discussion of Cases

- What are the criteria we should use to determine whether or not a teaching practice is sound?
- Both Sarah and Robert used activities during teaching that they enjoyed as students themselves. Why do you think Robert, apparently, was more "successful" than Sarah in this regard? What is the difference in their stories?

These brief cases reveal the conflict created by apprenticeships of observation and reflective teaching. Given that you have experienced such an apprenticeship, how do you as a beginning teacher capitalize on the aspects of your apprenticeship that might help make you a productive, ethical, and effective teacher? And conversely, how do you come to recognize and eliminate those aspects of your experience that are negative and that might make you less able to educate all children well? I suggest that it is crucial for beginning teachers to reflect on their assumptions about teaching, learning, and curriculum; these assumptions lie embedded in your apprenticeships of observation.

3
REFLECTION FOR TEACHER LEADERS: AUTOBIOGRAPHY AND THE TEACHING PLATFORM

In order to address the issues surrounding your apprenticeship of observation and how your commitments and actions as a teacher are and will be shaped, as a beginning teacher you can write an autobiographical sketch that helps to mine the ideas and possibilities for moving forward as a teacher. Be careful to write a story mainly about yourself, not just about others and their influences on you, though key relationships and events are critical to anyone's development as a person and as a professional.

WRITE AN AUTOBIOGRAPHICAL SKETCH

Describe your life and family history, focusing on significant events and their impact on who you are as a person today.

I would be remiss if I asked you to focus exclusively on how previous experiences in school have an impact on your conceptions of self as teacher. It is likely that we learn at least as much as a result of life experiences outside of school as we do inside schools. Surely the time we spend outside of school and our experiences there have profound implications for who we are and who we become as people, as teachers. Examining our autobiographies, the stories, experiences, and relationships that shape us as people as well as our apprenticeships of observation is crucial for becoming aware of and challenging the assumptions we bring from the world as citizens and as teachers.

Following are excerpts from a preservice teacher's autobiographical sketch. In it, Pat examines experiences with family, home, and community as especially constructive for situating himself as a teacher leader. Following Pat's sketch, I quickly transition to a discussion of the teaching platform. The idea is that the creation of an autobiography and the teaching platform constitute a continuum of reflective practice. The autobiography traces the development of self as a result of life experiences and relationships. The teaching platform, explained in more detail later, builds on the autobiography and reveals the beliefs and commitments that constitute your emerging conceptions of the best teaching practices for you and your students.

Pat's Autobiographical Sketch

Part One—The Transition

"It's time to move on,
it's time to get going.
What lies ahead,
I have no way of knowing."

—Tom Petty

I remember the night vividly. "Patrick, we need to talk," my father said in a humble tone. His voice was nearly silent, making me feel as if I had entered into a vacuum. My mouth was dry and my hands wet with sweat. I had just returned home from my first semester of college in California, my father had picked me up from the airport, and on the drive home he said, "I'm sorry, but it is better to tell you now than to wait. I need your help here at home and you won't be going back to school in California."

Just like that, my life as I knew it was no longer. It was like a quick one-two jab to the nose. No, it was worse, like an explosive upper cut to my jaw that left my whole body paralyzed, and trembling all at once.

I believe that every person experiences one situation that will forever alter his or her life. It can be a subtle event, or it can be an obvious one; the magnitude doesn't matter, as long as each individual realizes that at these types of moments she needs to grasp them for what they are in terms of their true, deeper meaning.

In my case, I realized that I had been a naive child up until this point in my life. I had taken for granted the thick shell that had been shielding me from the troubles and problems that engulf this world. I had taken for granted my life and my socioeconomic status. However, just as fast as I had left the warmth of California and was slapped in the face by the cold Chicago wind, my life changed drastically.

The next morning was a blur that lasted for nine months. Wake up at 4:30 a.m., drive to work, work until 7 or 8 p.m., drive home, eat, and go to bed. Start over the next day. Same routine, day after day. Gradually the family business began to gain strength again. At glacier-like speed, we were moving out of a financial hole that we entered sometime while I was out playing around at school in California.

What I found during these days was a new respect for my family and myself. When the economic problems came, I became a part of a nucleus that helped pull things together. We became a family unit, and because of this situation, I was forced to become a leader.

As I began to see how the world works, I discovered how difficult it is to lead, and at the same time how rewarding it can be. I was teaching men twice my age how to do the work they needed to do to turn the company around. I was doing taxes for the company and running meetings with distributors.

I call this time in my life the period of transition because eventually, with luck and hard work, the company stabilized, and it was time for me to return to school. As I left home again, I realized that I had new goals and aspirations. I returned to a new college with a new focus in my life. At first, I couldn't explain it, but I knew that I wanted to teach. I believe it was this transitional experience at home combined with my previous educational experiences in school, which I had come to appreciate much later, that drove me toward teaching. I had taken authority in my life and had become a leader.

Part Two—The Enlightening

When I came to this new university, I began to question myself, "Why do you want to become a teacher?" I thought, at first, that it would be more appropriate to focus on business and possible careers in that field. But I forced myself to critically evaluate what my future might hold and in so doing had several flashbacks from my childhood.

In elementary and middle school, the last thing that I wanted to be was a teacher. I was the lost child: the one who sat in the back of the room faceless, unnamed. Quiet, obedient, I constantly prayed that the teacher wouldn't call on me. It remained so through my first two years of high school. My high school classes were large, and it was easy for me to continue hiding out in the back of the room. As the years passed, I became more distant, more withdrawn from school. I guess I found some comfort in not letting teachers know who I was.

My junior year, however, changed things drastically. Two teachers, a classroom filled with 50 other students, and an awakening on my part were the ingredients that would help me see the possibilities for becoming a teacher myself. The class was called American Studies, a class combining English and history, and the teachers were Ms. Bergin and Ms. Bertain.

Inside their classroom, everything was relevant. They had a way of making the past relevant and tying it to our current lives. Bergin and Bertain had a remarkable way of leading us while also treating us as equals.

Whether through architectural boat tours of the city, or tours of Frank Lloyd Wright houses, or visits to museums and graveyards that held famous paintings and people, Bergin and Bertain allowed us to feel, taste, touch, see, and hear every topic. They allowed us to experience the subject at hand. Some of us went to a play for the first time, and I don't think we could have learned or remembered as much or would have been so eager to learn if we had just read a few pages from a textbook.

They also encouraged us to trust, confide in, and respect each other. Because the class met for two hours everyday, a unique relationship developed among the students and teachers. We actually developed into a community where people felt free to laugh, cry, and share their feelings. After this experience my junior year, the class continued to meet on an informal basis, even organizing a "reunion" picnic my senior year. This experience forever changed my previous conceptions of what a school experience could and should be.

—Pat Travieso, preservice teacher

For a further look at the power of autobiography in learning to teach, see Rousmaniere's (2000) "From Memory to Curriculum," and Poetter's (1994) "Making a Difference: Miss Conner and Bunker Hill School."

Lianna's Autobiographical Sketch

Lianna McDonald's autobiographical sketch also analyzes life experiences that led her to teaching, a journey that ranges now far beyond the confines of the premature warnings of others, even those of close friends and relatives. Are you, too, made of such stern stuff?

Defying Popular Opinion

"You can't wear green! You're not Irish!" These were the first words that greeted me on St. Patrick's Day as I boarded the school bus. One boy was upset with me because I was wearing green, but did not appear to be of Irish decent. This really upset me and affected the rest of my school day. I went home to my parents, upset, and told them what he shouted at me that morning. My parents looked at me and told me "You can be anything you want to be." Ever since that morning in fifth grade, I understand that the only person I have to justify my choices and actions to is myself. I am the only one whose opinion truly matters. My parents' words that day have resonated with me throughout all of the ups and downs of my life. I truly believe that those words struck a fire beneath me to never give up or give in. Thanks to my parents I was able to learn the lesson of perseverance at a young age.

Perseverance, passion, and hard work are the three main driving forces that have kept and continue to keep me on my path to become a teacher. Throughout the years I have heard countless reasons to dissuade me from a career path I believe I was made for. Whether it was close friends, roommates, family or even strangers, they all had one clear message: Don't go into teaching.

The first time I really recognized this negativity was in high school my junior year. My friends and I were dreaming of future careers and what our lives would look like after high school. I mentioned that I wanted to become a teacher, and they all gave me looks of pity, disbelief, and confusion.

> *"Why would you want to go into that career?"*
> *"You know teachers make like no money."*
> *"Good for you???"*

These were the initial reactions of some of my closest friends. I told them it wasn't about the money and that I intended on dedicating my life to making a difference for future generations. I wanted to inspire and encourage my students to dream endless possibilities and have a chance at making those dreams come true. My friends looked at me like I had grown a second head. They could not understand the passion and drive I had for teaching. These were the same friends that intended on going to college to become doctors, lawyers, dentists, engineers, and successful business men and women. To them, teaching was nothing compared to their careers. I chose to continue pursuing my dream and decided to brush off what my friends had said, but that was just the beginning of the judgment to come.

Every November my family goes to Columbus for a big Thanksgiving celebration with all of my extended family on my dad's side. There are typically two types of questions relatives like to ask about: relationships and school. Many of these relatives are retired teachers, so I thought they would have uplifting or inspiring stories or pieces of advice for me. Unfortunately, they had exactly the opposite: a long list of reasons not to go into the field of education. Their reasons ranged from horror stories of students they had trouble with to complaints that teacher retirement is taking a downturn. One of my relatives even looked me straight in the eyes and said something along the lines of "get out while you still can." This behavior started during Thanksgiving of my junior year in high school and has continued every Thanksgiving since.

If family attacking my future career wasn't close enough to home, my roommate and her parents sure were. I have lived with her for two years now and have been good friends since freshman year. I find myself very close to her, except when she criticizes and ridicules my major. She was pre-med throughout freshman and part of sophomore year and thought that my coursework and major didn't hold a candle to hers. If I tried to talk about struggles or difficulties I was having in my education major, I would get nothing more than an eye roll and a sarcastic response about how my major was "so easy." I would shrug off these instances as best I could, but I walked into our room one day to hear her ranting to her mother about how she is struggling with her chemistry and biology classes and I was over there just coloring for my classes. Little did she know that me coloring was only a snapshot of what I had to do for that project and that there was a lot more to teaching than met the eye. She eventually dropped the pre-med co-major because it was too hard and she was flunking out of chemistry. She was sobbing, and as a good friend and roommate, I was there to comfort her. She told me that she had talked to her mom who had suggested that she switch her major to education. She told her mom not to joke around and get serious. The fact that both my roommate and her parents take my major as a joke leaves me without words. I feel no need to defend myself or the career that I have so passionately sought after since I was a little girl.

Times like that have me think back to the day on the bus. My parents told me that I could be anything I wanted to be. They raised me with the mindset that I can do whatever I put my mind to. I am no less than anyone else because my profession does not make a six figure salary. Experiences like the ones that I have described would have deterred some people from pursuing a career in teaching. Not me. I chose to stand firm in my drive and commitment to become a teacher, role model, and advocate for my future students. I know the world is not perfect and that there will be haters and people who criticize the way I choose to live my life. If I have learned anything from the experiences with my family and friends, it is that I have the power to see beyond these hurtful remarks and make a difference.

I have been able to change my mindset and outlook on life with one phrase my parents told me years ago. It is my hope that I will be able to transfer the effect my parents had on me to my future students.

—Lianna McDonald, preservice teacher

Creating a Teaching Platform

Autobiographical activities help set the stage for preparing a platform of beliefs about teaching. Sergiovanni & Starratt (1998) explain the importance of being open, specific, and detailed about describing beliefs that ground commitments to teaching, learning, students, schools, and curriculum. A teaching platform is a useful conceptual tool that aids reflection. An espoused teaching platform constantly bears re-examination, which often causes changes of mind or changes in practice.

> There is a floor of beliefs, opinions, values, and attitudes that provides a foundation for practice. These ... make up what has been called a "platform." Just as a political party is supposed to base its decisions and actions on a party platform, so too educators carry on their work, make decisions, and plan instruction based on their educational platform. ... Knowing *what* the platform position is, understanding the relationship between teaching practices and platform elements, perceiving inconsistencies between platform and practice, appreciating differences between one's own platform and that of another—these are the points of emphasis ... (pp. 158–159)

Sergiovanni & Starratt (1998) suggest eight general elements of the platform and provide several examples of written platforms in their book (pp. 158–171). Here I list several of their general elements of a platform below, adjusting their list for beginning teachers:

- *What is the purpose of schooling?*
- *What is your image of the learner?* This element tries to uncover attitudes or assumptions about how one learns. Is the learner an empty vessel, a blank slate? Or something else? What metaphors of the learner describe your ideas and beliefs?
- *What should be the nature and substance of student work?* What should students be doing in school? What should their work look like? What purposes should the work have?

- *What is your image of the teacher?* What is the teacher? An employee, worker, professional specialist, transmitter of culture, political and social engineer, change agent? Who is she or he?

- *What is your image of the curriculum?* What do you think are the nature and purposes of curriculum? What comprises the curriculum?

- *What is the preferred pedagogy?* Is discipline-centered or inquiry-oriented teaching most effective? What other approaches compete? Which do you prefer? Why? And to what ends?

- *What is the preferred school climate?* What qualities describe a reflective learning community? What qualities connote an orderly, predictable environment? What are your attitudes about discipline, school pride, faculty and community member morale?

- *What is the social significance of the student's learning?* Some teachers emphasize vocational learning or the utilization of learning for good citizenship, or the acquisition of a particular cultural heritage. What does a student's learning have to do with determining his or her place in society, fulfilling societal roles, or pursuing social justice and equity? (Adapted from Sergiovanni & Starratt, 1998, pp. 166–167)

Of course, just because someone says something is so does not make it so. As Kohlberg (1981, 1984) made so clear in his studies of moral development, we may say one thing and then do another when the time comes to act in real-life circumstances. No one can guarantee that an espoused position will be acted upon consistently and without variation. But this should not discount the importance of determining and revealing what it is you believe and what you are willing to commit yourself to doing since there is at least a connection between a predisposition to act and action, as well as a social obligation once the platform becomes public.

A moral question for teachers pursuing the ethical practice of their teaching craft is whether or not their stated assumptions match what they actually do in classrooms. In fact, one of the most important reflective activities of your professional life should be re-examining your platform ideas as you test your own practices in the classroom and school community against your espoused platform. Do I practice what I say is important to me about teaching and learning?

Write a Teaching Platform

Write a teaching platform following Sergiovanni & Starratt's format or create your own format. Write about what you truly believe in as a beginning teacher. What are your fundamental commitments? What core beliefs will drive your classroom and school decisions as a teacher?

Perhaps a goal is to create personal positions that are viable and then to live up to them on a day-to-day basis. This may be related to the most basic and essential activity of teacher leadership, which involves establishing the self as a reflective teacher in the classroom.

On the following pages are sample teaching platforms written by students of teaching.

A Teaching Platform

—Cassidy Conerby, preservice teacher

I believe that as a teacher I have the power not only to teach facts and information but to help students grow into bright, responsible citizens in society. I believe that I am not only a teacher but a learner and a leader. I believe that my passion for education and desire to teach in a way that interactively engages students will allow their learning to thrive.

I believe that **curriculum** should not only meet standards but surpass them, allowing students to become critical thinkers. Curriculum should provide students with the opportunity to be creative and touch on their personal interests. As a teacher it is my job to explain to students why their learning is important and how curriculum connects to life and the world we live in. Curriculum should be flexible in a way that allows students with different preferred learning styles to learn and participate in a way that works best for them.

I believe that the **classroom** should provide a sense of community and comfort for each and every student. It is important to construct the classroom into a safe place where everyone is accepted no matter their differences. There should be mutual respect between the teacher and the students, as well as between students and peers. The classroom should be a place where there is productivity and learning but also joy and excitement.

I believe that **learning** develops students' skills in different areas. As learners, students gain the ability to overcome challenges. Students can make thoughtful decisions based on what they have learned. Learning allows students to have a strong voice and share their beliefs and knowledge that could one day positively impact the world we live in.

A Teaching Platform

—Grace Olsson, preservice teacher

Tell me and I forget. Teach me and I remember. Involve me and I learn.

—Xunzi

Students are able to learn best when they are involved and engaged with the content you are teaching. School should not be about memorizing facts to regurgitate on a quiz or an exam, but rather about teaching students to think critically and to be involved in the world.

There are many items we assume can't be taught that will simply fade away if we don't teach them: manners, civility, good language, mature love, good art, self-awareness and reflection, intelligent reading, responsible travel, care of one's home and belongings, a sense of the beautiful, intelligent spirituality and empathy for our fellow citizens on the planet.

—Thomas Moore

Schooling, especially in the early childhood grades, should not only be about teaching the core four subject content areas. With such young children, it is equally if not more important to teach them the more abstract concepts about life, society, and the world.

Good teaching is more a giving of right questions than a giving of right answers.

—Josef Albers

Giving students all of the "right" answers will indeed create "smart" children who can ace a standardized test. However, these students will also be unable to think for themselves or to problem solve; they may be incapable of creativity, and they may lack an innumerable amount of other life skills.

Giving students questions that allow them to think critically, problem solve, and create their own answers will be infinitely more beneficial to students in the long run.

> If a child can't learn the way we teach, maybe we should teach the way they learn.
>
> —Ignacio Estrada

This is an approach that seems like common sense to me yet does not appear to be the opinion that the majority of teachers have. If a student is struggling, teachers need to adjust their teaching styles and differentiate their instruction instead of assuming that the student is inept.

> Making the world a better place is, or ought to be, the most cherished function of any school ....
>
> —Jim Haas

One of the most important goals that I set for myself in teaching is simple, but of the utmost importance, and that is to make the world a better place. I truly believe that if every human, not only teachers, strive every day to make the world a better place, then they can't help but have a positive impact on whomever they encounter.

References

Moore, T. (2011, November 17). Redefining Education: Cultivating the Soul. Retrieved from https://www.huffingtonpost.com/thomas-moore/redefining-education-cult_b_666019.html.

Xun Kuang Quotes (Author of Xunzi). (n.d.). Retrieved from https://www.goodreads.com/author/quotes/14098753.Xun_Kuang.

Albers, J. (2009). Interaction of color. New Haven: Yale University Press.

Haas, J. (2018, June 21). Question of Values: Are We Learning for Earning-or for Living? Retrieved from https://www.edweek.org/ew/articles/2010/09/29/05haas.h30.html.

A Teaching Platform
—Susanne Clements, preservice teacher

The purposes of schooling
- To establish a community in which everyone is constantly given the chance to learn.
- To provide lasting knowledge, valuable experiences, and opportunities.
- To excite students about learning.

The nature and substance of student work
- I believe that students should be involved in active learning. I think that students learn well through experience and teaching others.
- I believe that students should be doing work that promotes their creativity and individuality.
- I believe that students should be given the chance to work with others in the class.
- Student work should serve the purpose of furthering the students' knowledge, creativity, and social skills.

The social significance of the student's learning
- I believe that learning provides students with perspective.
- I believe that learning provides students with the ability to make well informed, thoughtful decisions.
- I believe that learning makes students want to be a positive part of society.
- I believe that learning helps students set future goals and plan for their role in society.
- I believe that a student's social learning will help to provide knowledge about different cultures and lifestyles.
- I believe that students should be exposed to diversity.

The image of the learner
- I believe that the learner is both a receptacle and a fountain. Learners need to be given information and the chance to give information.
- I believe that learners are much more than they are often given credit for.

- I believe that each learner has potential.
- I do not believe that students are blank slates. I think that there is something to be learned from everybody.

The image of the curriculum

- I think that the curriculum should meet flexible standards.
- I think that the curriculum should meet goals, but not limit them.
- I think that the curriculum should let teachers and students reach goals in a variety of ways.
- I think that the curriculum should provide teachers with the opportunity to be inventive.
- I think that the curriculum should involve interaction with the entire learning community.
- I think that the curriculum should promote active and creative learning.
- I think that the curriculum should meet guidelines, not give orders.

The image of the teacher

- I believe that the teacher is also a learner.
- I believe that a teacher is a coach.
- I believe that a teacher is a provider of opportunity.
- I believe that a teacher is a professional with a great deal of responsibility.
- I believe that a teacher is passionate about his or her profession.
- I believe that a teacher is a leader.
- I believe that a teacher is a contributor and receiver in a community.

The preferred pedagogy

- I believe that inquiry-oriented teaching is most effective.
- I believe that students should be given the chance to offer what they know as well.
- I believe that students should be given the chance to work with other peers and to build social bonds.
- I believe that the discipline-centered teaching style does not provide the best learning opportunities for students and teachers.

The preferred school climate

- I believe that the best school environment is a school that is a community.
- In the school community I believe that there should be responsibility and respect for all.
- I believe that high standards for all are important.
- I believe that a good school climate would include excitement for learning. It would be a community with members who were excited to be there.
- I believe a good school climate would include passionate teachers.
- I believe a good school climate would be a diverse environment.
- I believe that the school climate should involve high standards, but also flexibility.
- I believe that a good school environment should involve good communication.

A Teaching Platform

—Morgan Silinsky, preservice teacher

I have had countless memorable moments within my time in school, and it is because of those reasons and more that I am becoming an educator. I think that the purpose of schooling is to allow children the experience of learning and socializing and becoming better citizens throughout their many years in a classroom. I believe that each child, no matter what grade, has the capability to love learning and to love coming to school everyday. I may not get students in my class that already have these loves, but I believe that it is my job to either enhance or change their opinion of school through my actions. I believe a teacher is someone who was truly called to work with children everyday, not someone who thought it'd be an easy career option. I believe a teacher is someone who works tirelessly to create the best and most beneficial lessons and environment for their students. I believe a teacher is an advocate for students, someone who will listen to them and care for them each day of the school year—even when they are having a hard day or week. These are all characteristics I hope to embody one day. These characteristics are also the characteristics of past teachers I have had that created a lasting impact on my life, so I believe that if I can be that person for someone else, such as my future students, I will succeed. I think the school environment should be filled with happiness and excitement, so that each child who walks through the building doors in the morning feels those emotions as they enter. The school should absolutely never be somewhere a child is afraid of going and this isn't just a thought of mine because of the recent, violent events within schools. Children should not be afraid of failing or bullying within their school and that is why I want to be a part of a school climate one day that rivals all of the negative emotions students may be feeling. I want to be a part of a school climate whose main goal is to create happy and knowledgeable children.

Teaching Platform: My ABCs of Teaching

—Teria Fields, preservice teacher

Attend to the students' needs and ideas; you just might learn something as a result.

Be bold enough to take risks.

Courtesy; do unto others as you would have them do unto you.

Don't ever be afraid to ask for help or guidance from other faculty or staff members.

Encourage your students; even if they fail, you may give them a sense of hope.

Fun; a little laughter is always good for the soul.

Games help make learning fun for everyone.

Humanity; you will make mistakes, so don't ever try to be superhuman.

Interesting; without interest, you will be without student attention.

Justice; always try to be fair.

Keep a level head in all situations, even the worst ones.

Love each one of your students with the same love regardless of differences.

Manage the class effectively from day one.

Never give up on any student, you might be his/her only hope.

Openness; be open to new ideas.

Patience; for some the learning process takes longer than for others.

Question; find out if your students are paying attention and that they understand the work.

Respect goes both ways—respect your students and they will respect you.

Shut up is a phrase you should never use.

Teaching isn't easy, so when tough days come, don't give up.

Unique; don't be a copycat; the best person you can be is yourself.

Variety is a good thing; it helps shed boredom and taps unique motivations in students.

Work with students and with others, such as administrators, faculty, staff, and parents.

X-tra credit is only good when kept in good measure; that's why it's called extra.

You are the teacher, don't let the students walk all over you.

Zeal; bring this quality to work everyday.

Teaching Platform

—Katherine Young, preservice teacher

A teacher is defined in Merriam-Webster Dictionary as "one whose occupation is to instruct." This does not reflect the way that I see myself as a teacher. I will be more than an instructor for my students. As a teacher, I am an educator. I am a mentor. I am a friend. I am a resource. I am a leader. I am a provider. I am a role model. I am a scholar. I am a coach. I am a guide. I am an interpreter. As a teacher, I shape people.

I see it as my responsibility as a teacher to ensure that each of my students leaves my classroom better than they were when they entered it. My students will have a greater sense of self-worth, be more in tune with the world around them, and be ready to face the challenges that lie ahead, both in school and outside of school.

I believe that children are not blank canvases, waiting for teachers to design. It is not my right to try to change the unique values that make each child who he or she is. Rather, my role as a teacher is to create a nurturing environment in which children grow to appreciate the experiences and perspectives that they bring to the classroom, as well as to learn from the experiences and perspectives of their peers. In encouraging my students' appreciation of their peers, I will make it clear that our classroom is a safe place where students will be able to share their feelings, opinions, and stories without fear of retribution. Bullying of any kind will not be tolerated in my classroom, and I believe it to be my duty to ensure that my students not tolerate bullying of any kind outside of the classroom.

I believe that education should not be easy. It seems that it is becoming an increasingly widespread belief that a child's self-esteem will be brought down if that child is faced with a difficult problem and is not able to immediately come to a solution. Contrary to this, I believe that it is my duty as a teacher to present my students with difficult problems in order for them to learn how to conquer them. Through this practice, my students will gain a greater sense of their own ability and learn that they do not need to be "spoon-fed" answers.

My curriculum will challenge students. I will encourage students to question the ideas that they have always been taught. My classroom will be a place of discovery. Students will be asked to reflect on what they are learning, to dig deep into the material, and to not be satisfied with simply memorizing what they read in a textbook.

I will develop relationships with those who take care of my students outside of the classroom and foster effective communication between school and home. I will listen to and work with parents and guardians and see that they are informed and involved in all decisions in order to maximize their students' learning outcomes.

I will strive to constantly grow as a teacher, just as I expect my students to grow as learners. I will abide by my local, state, and federal laws, as well as the guidelines outlined by the Council for Exceptional Children, and I will speak up when these laws are not being followed in regard to other students. I will be informed about new developments in teaching and learning so that I can be a resource for my students and those who take care of them.

Teaching Platform: Students Come First

—Kelsey Browne, preservice teacher

Students should always be the center of the learning environment.

Teachers should act as guides to learning, not as task-masters; they should help the students acquire knowledge, not just pour out information to be soaked in.

Understanding the background of their students will help teachers teach more effectively and therefore help their students reach their greatest potential.

Deliver each lesson as if it is the most interesting lesson there is. Students are more interested when teachers are excited about the subject.

Environment of the classroom is extremely important in the learning outcome of the students. They must feel welcome and safe in order to participate in their learning.

Nothing should be more important to teachers than their students.

Teaching needs to be more than just providing students with more information; it should involve becoming a part of the students' lives.

Students should be encouraged to participate in the lesson; by being a part of the lesson, the students learn more.

Classes are all unique. Like students, each class will have its own dynamic and requirements. Teachers should be prepared to alter lessons and material class by class.

Online resources should be incorporated within the classroom, but they should not become the focus of the lessons.

Meeting the students' individual needs is a daunting task, but teachers must to be able to balance the lesson for the class as an entirety with reaching each student separately.

Every student learns differently and will have different challenges. Teachers should acknowledge these differences while adjusting their teaching to meet their students' needs.

Focus on each student's strengths and abilities instead of his or her weaknesses or deficiencies.

Invest time into students' lives.

Remember that the lesson won't always work for every student. Teachers must accept that they may not be able to reach every student every day, but they should try nonetheless.

Students should feel as though they are more important than the class or lesson. The lesson should never become more important than the students.

Teachers should care about their students as people, not just as pupils.

My Teaching Platform

—Ashley Martin, preservice teacher

I believe that the purposes of schooling are …
- To educate children and young adults.
- To instill knowledge in students and keep them interested in school content.

I believe that the nature and substance of student work should …
- Reflect their competence.
- Challenge them to work hard and think critically.
- Be collaborative and involve group work.
- Grab their interest and intrigue them.

I believe that the social significance of a student's learning is …
- To further his or her social skills.
- To further his or her knowledge of the content.
- To keep class from being monotonous and boring.

I believe that the image of the learner is …
- A student who enjoys learning.
- A student who participates in classwork, discussions, blogs, etc.
- A person who might need guidance and help along the way, whether it be through school issues or social issues.

I believe that the image of the curriculum is …
- Sometimes tainted by government mandates, but that teachers should do what they can to work with what they are given.

I believe that the image of the teacher is ...

- A role model for all students.
- A person with knowledge for students to question, even if she doesn't know every answer.
- Open-minded and willing to learn from her students.
- An approachable, trustworthy adult figure in each student's life.
- Always open to change if that is what the students, school system, or parents need.

My preferred pedagogy is ...

- Built upon an ethic of care; I want to do everything I can to show my students that I care for them.
- Based on social interactions; I believe that students should socialize in class and build a closely knit community among themselves and with me.
- Focused on respect. While I want my students to be able to interact, I want to maintain an orderly classroom that is always respectful.

I believe that the preferred school climate is ...

- One that feels safe for all students.
- One that values what anyone who enters the school brings to the table.
- A happy one.
- An intellectual one that fosters student learning.

Teaching Platform: Make Every Student Count

—Victoria B. Ellis, preservice teacher

Make the choice to recognize every student as a capable learner, no matter the circumstances outside of school.

Attend to the needs of every student, even if this requires many hours of work after the school day ends.

Keep up with "troubled" students; do not always expect them to come to you.

Every student has something to bring to the table.

Every student has a story.

Varied backgrounds are not a disadvantage; they help students bring different perspectives into the classroom discussions, which promote learning.

Every student has interests; pique them.

Recognize the students, parents, and administrators as a learning community.

Yearly progress can be seen far beyond standardized test scores.

Students' talents are focused in many different areas; recognize them.

Teaching to the test only prepares students for the test. Prepare students for the test of life.

Under no circumstances should you give up on a student.

Determine what works and what doesn't work. Don't be afraid of change.

Every teacher must reflect before, during, and after lessons.

Nowhere is there a perfect teacher, or a perfect human.

Telling is not teaching.

Connect the curriculum to the students' past and present life experiences.

Openness is key.

Understand where they are coming from.

Notice the lives that students are leading now. Pay attention to them.

Take every opportunity to learn more about teaching; it will help your students count!

All of these students of teaching have begun to think more deeply about teaching through the lenses of their own experiences as apprentices observing teaching for so many years. They have also examined their ideas in the field as they engage in early field experiences. After finishing her second draft of the platform at the end of the course on teacher leadership, Suzanne wrote, "I still firmly believe in my platform statement. In fact, after having firsthand experiences in two school settings this semester, I feel that I can live up to my beliefs and positions." Of course, teacher leadership requires a constant attention to the platform, as life and experience bump against the foundational commitments and beliefs of teachers.

Once you begin to situate yourself into a school setting as a teacher, your platform for teaching becomes more than a private matter. You can do this type of platform writing for a course, sure, but the true test of beliefs and positions held comes when you begin to interact with students, teachers, and schools in the field. The platform becomes a baseline for you to test your commitments, your foundations for professional work, and your moral core of beliefs. You may share your platform and encourage your colleagues to think about and create their own teaching platforms. You will become an advocate for certain positions, laying the groundwork for your work as a teacher leader in the school.

You will no doubt play a public role as you begin to define yourself as a teacher, participating in the great play that is public education and the great debates that surround teaching and education in our society. However, some preservice teachers in teacher education programs find that peers preparing for other fields hold teacher preparation in low esteem. People take positions such as "Those who can, do. Those who can't, teach." Others simply think of teacher preparation as easy and teaching as a second-rate profession, something to do for those without the ability or drive to do something more lucrative financially or more prestigious socially. Some preservice teachers report that their parents and even former teachers they hold up as role models discourage them from entering teaching. One student wrote a journal entry regarding the phenomenon of encountering others with a low regard for teaching. Her response is an example of teacher leadership in terms of her advocacy for teaching and her ability to situate herself and her teaching platform in her own real world.

Becoming an Advocate for Teachers and Teaching

Student Journal Excerpt

I have decided to write this week's journal entry for class on an issue that has been brought up a lot recently. It is the topic of our school, and specifically the teacher preparation program. Last semester, an article was written in one of our school newspapers about how the education program is an easy ride to a diploma. Here I offer a brief response to the article.

I cannot tell you how many times I have come across this same heated discussion about the education program for teachers. I am an education major myself and am constantly defending it. People are constantly laughing at the names of my courses and comparing them to the "hard ones" that they are taking. I laugh along with them while I secretly grind my teeth and clench my fists. "Math for elementary students? What's 2 + 2 equal? Ha ha ha!" or "Children's Literature? I read that book in 5th grade!" I hate these comments. "They are actually all quite challenging classes," I say, trying to defend myself. It is of no use, however. Friends say, "Yeah right. Try to take my business classes then you'll see what challenging is!" I never win because I can never make them see all the work that I do for my classes.

I have never had a class that has been an easy "A." If anybody would care to tell me exactly which classes everybody refers to as easy, I would appreciate it greatly and make sure to add a few of those into my difficult schedule. Every "A" that I have received I have had to do so much work for. Sure we don't have as many quizzes or tests as some of the other major's classes probably do, but there are more papers, more discussions, more projects, more field experiences, and with those come extra stresses and responsibilities.

But I can't wait to be a teacher. I want to be a role model for students. I want to set a good example for them as a person and as an educator. I know I will never have much money, but that is not what I want out of becoming an educator. If I did I would definitely be in the wrong profession. As I conclude this journal entry, it is 3:00 a.m. I have been up all night studying. My business major roommate, the pre-med major from down the hall, and the marketing major who lives next door have all been asleep for hours. I have been up trying to keep my head from sinking below the work in all of these education classes that are sure to give me a "easy ride" through college.

Then once again this weekend some people at a gathering asked me what my major was. I usually say "education" and sort of smile or snicker a little, making light of it myself, but not this weekend. I had spent the entire weekend typing paper after paper, reading book after book, and attempting math problem after math problem. When asked what my major was, I thought of all this work first. Then I thought of what all these books are really trying to tell us. We are more than teachers to our students. We are role models, mentors, tutors, and friends. Most of all we are leaders. I looked straight into the eyes of the people who questioned me. "Education," I said proudly. No snicker, no smile. "Oh," they responded, "that's cool." They sort of smiled at one another. "I know, I know what you are thinking, but I can't wait to become a teacher. It is really the job of my dreams." Silence. I loved it. Neither one of these people could say a thing. I could tell immediately that no matter what their majors were, neither one of them had ever looked past their titles and considered what it was that they are really going to become and if they were even going to like it. My sense of pride overwhelmed me. I had stood up for myself and defended a topic that I have so often just joked about along with *everybody else. There was no conversation about easy classes, or having an easy major. This may have been where they had originally intended for the conversation to go. Now I have taken what I consider to be a major step in truly becoming a leader in the field of education.*

—Anne Milbratz, preservice teacher

At a gathering of teachers and professors of education working in professional development schools, teacher educator and university administrator Nancy Zimpher spoke about the essentials of good teacher education programs. Her first topic was a call for those in education to make a commitment to the following perspective: "Teaching *is* rocket science." Her point? Teaching *is* a very complicated, challenging, and scientific art that requires deeply intellectual work. The public and teachers need people in the teaching profession who recognize this and foster the kinds of professional cultures in school communities where teachers are valued and supported. Equal responsibility rests on teachers: We must create professional norms that view teaching as a calling and support teachers who do "whatever it takes" to grow professionally and to serve students.

Last points here rest on the eloquent words of Eleanor Duckworth:

> The assumption seems to be that teachers are a kind of civil servant, to be "trained" by those who know better, to carry out the job as they are directed to do, to be assessed managerially, to be understood through third-party studies. In conceiving of teachers as civil servants, with no professional understanding worth paying attention to, we miss the enormous potential power of their knowledge … (T)o the extent that they are conceived of as civil servants, to carry out orders from above, teachers are deprived of the occasion to bring to bear on the world the whole of their intelligence, understanding, and judgment. To that extent, the students are deprived of those qualities, and the educational enterprise is impoverished. (Quoted in McCutcheon, 1998, p. 8)

I want to advance the point that teachers are capable decision-makers who provide leadership from the beginning of their careers. They do this by basing their best practices on effective approaches tempered and measured by experience, practical theories, local wisdom, and the wisdom of the field of education located in studies and research on teaching and learning. While this may seem daunting, it is only so because this is what the best teachers do. They seek, inquire, and successfully balance their lives, keeping in mind the key ends: to help students learn in classrooms and to make a contribution through those interactions to students' lives, communities, and society. One aspect of teacher leadership is to aspire to such ends.

The following case inquiry report by Todd Tracy has an autobiographical bend. In the case, Todd traces the genesis of his teaching career, helping others one-on-one.

Case Report: My Journey to Teaching

—Todd Tracy, preservice teacher

Case Background   I was a senior in high school, and my peers noted me as one of the "smart kids" in my math classes over the years. I was in Advanced Placement Calculus and had no problem understanding the material—some of my friends, though, were having a very difficult time understanding the material. Shortly after the year started I decided I would tutor my friends, at least help them understand the content we were currently studying in class.

Almost daily, my schedule would begin with AP Calculus, where we would go over the content for the day, and then in my study hall periods (I was in two study halls) I would essentially reteach any part of the content that my friends had trouble understanding. This quickly spread and by the end of the year, I was aiding at least half of my AP Calculus class, as well as several of my friends in lower level math classes.

I was feeling very confident in my abilities regardless of the fact that I had had no training in how to teach or properly instruct others academically. My tutoring was largely successful—no peer that I tutored received a grade lower than that in the "B" range over material that I had aided them with. However, the three peers that I most frequently reviewed material with (almost, if not, daily) all maintained grades above 93 percent.

This entire period of self-organized tutoring was performed at the high school from which I graduated. A majority of the content that I was essentially reiterating and re-teaching was at an Advanced Placement Calculus level—a class that was taught by a phenomenal instructor (my favorite high school teacher, in fact). My peers turned to me for aid first, even before the teacher himself.

The Events   There was a period of time during this school year, roughly a week or two, that is highlighted in my memory. In class we were learning about probabilities: the various sorts of probabilities, how to use them, involving variables, finding the probability of certain events occurring, etc. Before this time, when I thought of probabilities, the first thing to come to mind was not that they were a generally difficult topic. My mindset entering this unit seemed to be the consensus of my class. We were mistaken, as probabilities are something that almost everyone in my AP Calculus class struggled with, myself excluded (thankfully).

Per usual, in study hall, my peers asked if I would help them—they did not understand how to do any of the homework that was assigned on the probabilities we had just learned. As a group, we got permission to move into the hall where we could converse and not distract others. I quickly discovered that the topic of probabilities is one that is also very difficult to explain to others. This first day of probabilities, and the difficulty that I had making the information and explanations relevant to my friends, led me to reflect and brainstorm. This first day of trouble provided me with an innate wish to discover a way to make this information relevant to my peers. That night, when I got home, as I finished up my own work for Calculus, I continued to think about how I could help my friends understand. I couldn't find any direct solutions to how I would explain this content to them.

The next day I only ended up working with one of the three peers that I normally provided help to. I quickly discovered that the one-on-one experience was exactly what was necessary to make the information relevant. Working one-on-one with this peer helped me grasp an understanding of how to make the information real to her; I was able to make it something that she could see in her everyday life, which can be extremely helpful in the use of math content. I implemented the one-on-one tutoring style for one session with each of the three peers and was able to aid them very effectively. One student even showed an improvement of three letter grades on practice quizzes I had produced over the content.

Eventually, the exam on probabilities came about. The results were released, and among the group of my peers and myself, I performed at the lowest level. This was a trend that I was just picking up on—I was almost never the one (out of our group of four) to receive the best quiz or exam score. Reflecting upon this, it helped me conclude that I always rushed through the problems and made simple, stupid mistakes.

Discussion   Reflecting on this specific period of time, I've come to see multiple things. First, without realizing it (at the time), I spent time outside of school hours thinking about how I would go about teaching content to the peers who were acting as my students at the time. Not only did I spend time outside of school hours thinking and considering how I would go about teaching, but I remember it being an interesting, somewhat fun process. Second, this instance shows me that when I contribute time to it, I can discover ways to make difficult content relevant to the lives of students (though it may require some one-on-one time). Third, the results of our exam on probabilities and my score compared to the main group of students I provided aid to eventually led me to realize that I needed to take my time and attempt to be more careful in my use of simple math. Continuing to work with these students as they went through the math with me forced me to slow down my pace and actually helped me catch many of my mistakes before I would move on.

Overall this experience is the one that made me want to teach. The thrill of successfully helping students to learn was amazing. Reflecting on the times that I tutored, I've come to realize that they were imbedded in the times that were my favorite parts of high school and led directly to my interest in becoming a teacher.

Chapter 4, "The Teacher Leader as Reflective Agent," focuses on how beginning teachers can begin to view themselves as reflective agents while they build their own views of teaching and learning. You have begun the journey by laying out your assumptions about teaching through your autobiographical sketch and teaching platform. In transition, consider the following case and reflection.

Sam's Use of Praise

In his espoused platform, Sam made it very clear that he believed that all students were motivated by praise. He understood the power of hearing a teacher tell him "Good job!" during his own school experiences as a student. Yet, when Sam began to teach, his mentor teacher Colleen observed that he almost never praised the students. Colleen found this puzzling since Sam specifically told her that praising students was an important part of what he believed about teaching. When Colleen asked Sam if he still believed in the power of praise, he was surprised. "Sure, I do," he said. "I try to praise students at every opportunity." Colleen was a skilled observer who had scripted several of Sam's lessons. As they reviewed the transcripts together, Sam realized that no praise was evident. His lessons were going very well, and students participated in his class. But he was rarely praising students at all.

REFLECTION

If Sam takes a reflective approach to his teaching, what should he do about the apparent discrepancy between what he espouses about praising students and what he actually does? What are some of the pros and cons of using verbal praise in the classroom as a teacher? What is your view of Sam's "problem"? (Consult Brophy & Good's classic *Looking in Classrooms*, 1973, and Jackson's *Life in Classrooms*, 1968, for classroom-based discussions on the use of praise in teaching.)

4

THE TEACHER
LEADER AS
REFLECTIVE
AGENT

The protagonist in the following story is a successful veteran high school math teacher of twenty-seven years in urban schools. Gerald and I became friends when I began working with student teachers in his school, providing supervision from a university perspective. A student teacher was often assigned to work with him. Gerald's greatest gift and asset may be that after a long career in teaching he still had as much energy and spirit as a teacher just out of college.

I watched him teach and supervise all year, and I enjoyed working with him, talking about teaching, and learning from him. In the spring, he mentioned the school's summer school program and how much he enjoyed teaching in it, how much he was looking forward to it. "I've never actually heard anyone ever say they enjoyed teaching summer school until now, so please explain," I pleaded. He did.

A Case of a Reflective Agent

The story goes that several years earlier Gerald had been walking down the hallway back to his classroom after a guest speaker gave an invited address to his high school's faculty on multicultural issues. The speaker, an African-American female educator had said, "You can tell a racist school when you walk down the hallway and see all the white kids in the advanced classes and all the brown or black ones in the remedial classes. Try it some time.

You might be surprised what you find in your own school." This passage of her speech stuck with him, so he tried it. He walked down the hall, just looking in the math classrooms. What he saw and what he didn't see overwhelmed him. So few of the students in the classes for advanced math were African-American or Hispanic. Almost all of them were Anglos. How could this be? What was happening to make it so? He didn't think of himself or his colleagues or his school as racist, but the evidence seemed undeniable. His school somehow was systematically denying students of color access to classes in higher mathematics.

He began to inquire, and along with most of his other department members he realized that most of the African-American and Hispanic students came to the high school "unprepared" for Algebra 1 and often failed it. They rarely ever caught up with their Anglo peers, who almost overwhelmingly either passed Algebra 1 as freshmen or came to school ready for Geometry or Algebra 2 on the fast track to higher math courses, and of course, the benefits that came from high achievement such as college admission and scholarships.

So the math department tried several things. The first thing it tried was changing what got taught and the way it got taught in Algebra 1 classes, taking into account the differences in the learners and the variable background knowledge that the students brought with them to school. There was some success with this approach, but some teachers were slower and more reluctant to adjust their teaching to accommodate the differences in learners.

So the department decided to sponsor a special program during the summer school session for 9th graders who passed Algebra 1 to take Geometry in the summer. If the faculty could get more students through Algebra 1 and Geometry successfully, then more students would be able to pursue higher math, entering Algebra 2 as sophomores. Gerald led the charge along with university faculty and parents, helping to design the program and teach classes every summer the course was offered. Students would take Algebra 1 during the school year, pass it, and then take Geometry in the summer.

The success of the students in the summer program spread like wildfire through the community. Successful math students told their siblings and friends about the "cool" math class during the hot summer days. Attending to many of the National Council of Teachers of Mathematics (NCTM) curriculum recommendations, the course used hands-on methods and real world curriculum to connect with learners. Gerald found the students to be energized and excited about getting a head start on math, a subject with which they had success in middle school or junior high then typically found themselves failing in high school. But not anymore. Parents and community members coalesced around the program, offering scholarships for students whose parents couldn't afford the summer program but wanted to participate. First year teachers were often offered spots teaching the curriculum during the summer, and they were doing a great job.

To Gerald, it was about honoring the talent and ability in all students to excel when given the opportunity. It was about righting wrongs done over many years, wrongs dangling unseen or ignored by "the powers that be." It was about challenging a tradition in practice left unexamined and unchallenged. Gerald recalled that many of his skeptical colleagues said, "Kids won't come to summer school to get ahead in math." He takes pride that every year of the program has had four full classes. The bottom line was that no one had taken the time or energy to think about and reflect upon the problem critically and to come up with a viable solution.

"In a school where only half the students are white, shouldn't half the students in higher math classes be of color?" he asked, rhetorically, at the end of the story. We walked down the hallways together and looked in classrooms. We couldn't tell them apart.

Every year, preservice teachers begin asking, "What does a teacher leader actually do?" as they make their way through our course on teacher leadership. They start to get the idea in the class that the teacher leader reflects, thinks, and generates ideas. Students of teaching are becoming something in particular, readying themselves for a career in teaching, building themselves and their careers from the ground up. But, ultimately, the question persists, what do teacher leaders *do*? One of the points of this book is that reflection, thinking, and generating ideas *are* actions! Also, the teacher leader acts with clear purpose and resolve, working with others to choose or create responses that will address problems, right wrongs, correct injustices, or improve important programs already in place in their own classrooms and throughout the school. The teacher leader, like Gerald, is a reflective agent.

I want to caution you again against making an erroneous assumption with regard to the subject of teacher leadership and this book, already several chapters old. I'm not writing a recipe for the transformation of teaching or of public education. Instead, you will carry out the transformation in your own work with your colleagues in schools. Your best ideas in a certain context and moment will complement and transcend the ones that are laid out here. I put ideas forward and ask you to consider them and suppose what it might be like to realize the possibilities of the ideas in action. Your function as a teacher leader is to be reflective and to act responsibly in that reflective practice by challenging assumptions, engaging new ideas, and helping students and colleagues to learn in a just, safe, open, and democratic setting. This defines the teacher leader as reflective agent.

I want you to keep in mind that your teacher education is not meant to prepare you for some abstract future, but to ready you to meet the challenges of today and every day.

Some Initial Thoughts on Teacher Education and Building a Learning Community as a Teacher Leader

Teacher educators face two widely disparate criticisms about their work today. The first criticism is that much of what is done in teacher education is impractical, too theoretical, and disconnected from realities of schools. The second criticism is that our work is too practical, uninformed by theory, and has too much to do with the status quo, or precisely what goes on in schools today. Either one of these positions may ring true as you think about your experience in a teacher preparation program. William Pinar (1989) attempts to build a bridge between theory and practice in teacher education, suggesting that teacher education is something more than mere professional training; rather it is a balanced, intellectual, and moral pursuit of the professional craft of teaching:

> The cultivation of judgment and professional wisdom, provided they are grounded in serious study in the arts, humanities, sciences and in curriculum theory, is an appropriate aspiration (for teacher education). This general and important distinction between academic vs. vocational or technical curriculum is well expressed in the following catalogue statement, which was taken from the University of Michigan Law School announcement:
>
> > *The Law School is very much a professional school. But it is distinctly not a vocational school. Students are not trained to perform many, or even most, of the tasks that its graduates may be called upon to perform as lawyers, and should not expect to be fully prepared to deliver a wide range of legal services on the day of graduation. Students may acquire or begin to develop some practical or technical skills and*

may gain confidence in their ability to perform as lawyers. Our prac-
tice-oriented courses and clinics provide, however, only an introduc-
tion to skills and a framework for practice which can only be defined
through years of experience. The majority of our graduates join law
firms where numerous opportunities exist for skill development
under supervision of experienced practitioners who share with the
novitiate responsibility for the quality of service rendered. Michigan,
more than many other law schools, seeks to provide students with
the intellectual and theoretical background with which an attorney
can undertake a more reflective and rewarding practice. It is felt that
too much haste or emphasis on vocational skills, without a broader
and more critical view of the framework in which lawyering occurs,
runs the risks of training technicians instead of professionals. (p. 15)

Your teacher education experience should include practical aspects since you will be asked to teach and to teach well from day one in your first teaching position, but the main focus in teacher preparation should be on preparing you to think about, make decisions for, and reflect on key aspects of practice in a school community. Teaching is an intellectual practice, a moral practice, and a craft practice, requiring balance. An excellent teacher education program or experience should help you take and develop broader views and to consider exercising sound professional judgment situation by situation. These endeavors involve deeply intellectual and theoretical abilities. Beginning teachers must cultivate these abilities and view them as essential in order to be productive, leading members of the profession who are successful at teaching students. In my view, the beginning teacher can see the problems in classrooms and schools just as Gerald did in the previous case.

By extension, I suggest that teacher leadership involves initially, and in the main, the commitment by the beginning teacher to establishing a classroom learning community. I also delineate how the beginning teacher might exercise leadership in the classroom and on a more school-wide level by participating on curriculum committees, advising the school paper, coaching a sports team, or running a parent focus group on tutoring children in math, for example. These activities suggest beginning teachers' roles as teacher leaders lie somewhere in and beyond the classroom, and indeed, these activities are crucial for envisioning and participating in a more complete notion of teacher as leader in the school and community. But the primary concerns and focuses ought to be on the unique classroom situations charged to your care as the teacher. It is in these places that the beginning teacher builds a foundation for teacher leadership and exercises his or her essential thinking and work in the school with children.

In fact, being a teacher in the classroom and building a learning community with students create public opportunities for the teacher to have a profound impact on the present and future through student learning. In essence, *being* a teacher *is* leadership, the form that I want you to be most concerned with at this point. The primary units of change are the teacher and the classroom. Teacher leaders are agents of change, reflecting responsibly on their practices and building classroom and school learning communities at each opportunity.

Extending Your Autobiography and Platform: Toward Personal, Practical Theories of Action in Teaching

In her book *Developing the Curriculum: Solo and Group Deliberation* (1995), Gail McCutcheon describes how teacher leaders develop personal, practical theories of action as they practice teaching. Beginning teachers bring a platform of beliefs, ideas, and assumptions to teaching, but during their early experiences they begin to situate in their practices the theories that guide actions in the classroom.

> Practical theories of action are interrelated concepts, beliefs, and images teachers hold about their work. They guide the decision-making process before and during teaching and form the interpretive lens teachers apply to their post-teaching reflections. These reflections inform teachers' future decision making as well. (p. 34)

Teacher leaders constantly develop their personal, practical theories of action as they live and work in schools. The autobiographical sketch and the teaching platform serve as initial "interpretive lenses" as beginning teachers make sense of their teaching experiences in the classroom. The awareness and development of your personal, practical theories of action constitute an extension of the work you have begun in attempts to situate your autobiography and platform for classroom practice. However, your personal, practical theories of action may not take the tidy form of a written paper, as your autobiographical sketch and teaching platform may have. Instead, your personal, practical theories of action play out on the canvas of a life of teaching and learning in schools as you interact with students and schools over time as a teacher leader.

This notion of each teacher having a set of personal, practical theories of action gives legitimacy to the types of knowledge that form the foundation for actions teachers take on behalf of students, schools, and themselves day in and day out in classrooms. It gives credence to the practical, everyday realities and contexts that teachers affect with their decisions and actions. This also suggests that there is a moral aspect to teaching, given that what you believe and think has so much to do with actions you will take and the obvious and not so obvious effects they will have on others' lives. What I mean by moral is that teachers use their own and the culture/society's sets of beliefs to help them decide what to do and what not to do at every turn as they teach and live. Teaching and learning and the curriculum do not happen in a moral vacuum; they are not value neutral undertakings.

The reality of personal, practical theories of action and their seeming value does not necessarily make the positions teachers take and the decisions they make good in and of themselves, in other words moral and/or ethical. For instance, a teacher could hold racial stereotypes that suggest certain students can or cannot do classroom work because of their race. This type of personal, practical theory of action is wrong and immoral, and must be interrogated by the individual and the culture in which that individual teaches.

The National Network for Educational Renewal (NNER) is a national network of schools and universities that pays close attention to the development of teacher education, teaching, and the renewal of public education. The NNER's Agenda for Education in a Democracy (AED), founded by famed progressive educator and public school/teacher education advocate John Goodlad, builds its identity and its work from four moral dimensions of teaching that network participants adhere to in their varying levels of work as teacher leaders in the field. The AED focuses on:

- Fostering in the nation's young the skills, dispositions, and knowledge necessary for effective participation in a social and political democracy;
- Ensuring that the young have access to those understandings and skills required for satisfying and responsible lives;
- Developing educators who nurture the learning and well-being of every student;
- Ensuring educators' competence in and commitment to serving as stewards of schools.

Every decision we make in schools has an impact on students, communities, families, and ourselves. Our work as teacher leaders is enhanced when we frame teaching and leading as connected to higher ideals, strong theories, and steadfast focus on mining the best way forward at each turn in the complex business of teaching and learning today in schools with students and colleagues.

To learn more about the NNER and the AED, visit the network's website at *www.nnerpartnerships.org.*

REFLECTION

How do we as teacher leaders judge the moral worth of the theoretical positions and the actions we take?

Considerations of "Theory" for Teacher Leaders

For teacher leaders, theory is the bounded sets of ideas and images that form the parameters for thought and action employed in the daily work of teaching. I want to suggest here that your personal, practical theories of action can be developed professionally and reflect a reasoned, thoughtful, focused, open, just, and effective set of principles to guide your teacher practices in classrooms with students and that a fundamental commitment for teacher leadership is searching these assumptions out, testing them in practice, and reflecting vigorously on those tests in practice before, during, and after the fact. My goal is to arm you with ways to make informed decisions for teaching based on the theories and practices that seem justifiable and right given a certain set of circumstances. This will require self-reflection and inquiry, two hallmarks of effective teacher leadership.

McCutcheon's ideas suggest that "theory" is a crucial consideration for teaching, though many beginning teachers eschew educational theories at the beginning and throughout their careers. I think there are several reasons for this. Often, beginning teachers "try out" so-called "theories of instruction" they have learned in their teacher education programs, and these theories fail or don't live up to expectations in experiences with students in classrooms and schools. But this perspective clouds the distinction between a theory and an activity. If a theory is a "set of propositions derived from data and creative thinking from which constructs are formed to describe interactions

among variables and test hypotheses" and if theory "describes, explains …
predicts and leads to new knowledge" (Unruh & Unruh, 1984, p. 123), then
theory informs practice but does not constitute it.

Beauchamp (quoted in Unruh & Unruh, 1984, p. 119) notes that

> Theory is not what is practiced. A person cannot practice a set of logically
> related statements; he or she performs an activity. Theories of instruction,
> for example, might account for classroom discipline, grouping practices,
> lesson planning, and instructional materials as components of instruction,
> but the theories cannot tell teachers how to behave with respect to those
> functions …

Take, for example, the theories of teaching and learning that constitute
cooperative learning. Slavin's (1995) theoretical frameworks for cooperative
learning, for instance, are continuously misused by teachers who erroneously
think that cooperative learning is merely a technique or practice that can be
used sporadically, as opposed to a pervasive means of teaching and learning,
even a way of life, that must be used continuously and consistently over time
with great care and planning.

Slavin suggests very specific forms for cooperative learning and very
specific conditions for assessment that help make the activities distinctly "cooperative": (1) the presence of group and individual accountability measures
for student learning of the material and (2) the teaching of group roles and
processes along with the academic curriculum. If these conditions are not in
place, then one might have group work projects, but they do not constitute
"cooperative learning" activities.

Therefore, it would be erroneous to read Slavin's book on cooperative
learning, design a cooperative lesson, experience classroom management difficulties, then abandon "cooperative learning" as a failed educational theory
because cooperative learning doesn't "work." Worse would be to never read
Slavin and continue grouping students for group work, all the while calling
the practice "cooperative learning." But maybe even worse than badmouthing
a theory because it didn't "work" after one try or completely misunderstand-
ing it in the first place would be to return to the safety of lecturing and writing
notes for students to copy on the board or just handing out worksheets and
calling it teaching. All told, an activity in cooperative learning may have
failed, but the theory supporting cooperative learning did not. Impoverished
understanding or unsuccessful implementation might be the trouble, not the
soundness of the theory.

The distinction that must remain with you is that actions you take in the classroom are tied to theoretical perspectives in education but are not theories in and of themselves. In order to lead, you must understand the difference and work with and for colleagues to interrogate your teaching practices and the theoretical frameworks undergirding them through study and reflection. This study and reflection can reveal the theoretical assumptions you bring to teaching as well as how those assumptions do or do not inform the practices you carry on every day in the classroom. This is the most important, primary step toward teacher leadership and reflective agency.

I know teachers who publicly disavow being connected in spirit or in practice to any educational theory while they continue to theorize deeply themselves about their own practices and to use obvious theoretical frameworks in support of their teaching. Others support certain learning activities arguing that they simply "work," without acknowledging the theoretical bases of those activities, which they may not even support any longer if they understood the deeper theoretical grounds upon which they are based. The argument here is not to make a case for or against certain educational theories, but to show the difference between a theoretical perspective and activities loosely based on those educational theories. A teacher's platform should note the difference: you should commit yourself to defining the relationship between theory and practice, how theory deeply informs practice.

I believe that the application of sound theoretical positions advanced by research (many kinds, including action research, which is discussed later in this book) and practice in education is crucial for school improvement and enhancing student achievement, even given theory's bad name among many practicing teachers. I am more concerned now that beginning teachers become conscious that *theoretical perspectives inform everything they do*; the teaching practices you develop yourself have a theoretical basis. There is no such thing as "non-theoretical" practice of teaching or leadership. Every action taken by every individual in the classroom finds its basis on some theoretical assumption, adaptation, or discovery. Teachers don't live or work in a theoretical vacuum, and part of a teacher's professional development and commitment to leadership is to reflect upon, critique, and perhaps reconstitute constantly and with fervor the educational theories upon which practices are built. It may be the case, after all, that what we do does not match what we think or believe. In this case, theory and practice become extremely problematic considerations that teachers must try to understand and rectify.

The heart and soul of school culture is what people believe, the assumptions they make about how schools work, and what they consider to be true and real. These factors in turn provide a *theory of acceptability* that lets people know how they should behave. Underneath every school culture is a theory, and every school culture is driven by its theory. Efforts to change school cultures inevitably involve changing theories of schooling and school life. (Sergiovanni, 1996, pp. 2–3)

I want to suggest that the trouble with *theory* in education and in American public school practices has been its mandated, spurious, half-hearted, and incorrect applications to contexts through activities. And since the theoretical position often had no chance of proving successful in practice because the theory did not match the setting and its possibilities—that is, the activities did not give any indication of working early or late in their application, or a teacher charged with implementing the theory through activities did not support the theory or the activities fully and let the initiative flounder—the theory is proven "unworthy," or teachers say "that's just another theory." These hopeless situations for theory don't mean that theory is bad; they mean that it is fully understandable when teachers resist grand theories as cure-alls, especially when they show up in pre-packaged teaching or curriculum programs as activities, suggest that the curriculum is "teacher proof," and die on the vine with all of their attending promises and predictably short shelf lives. These "theories" will run their course in practice and appear only later on the radar screen as "fads." This is not to say that activities are bad; we do not do anything without doing activities. It is the unexamined activities and theoretical perspectives that may lead us to poor practices.

REFLECTION

As Sergiovanni notes, "theories of acceptability" undergird classroom and school norms. How do we interrogate, challenge, and/or uphold those theoretical foundations while we make our way as beginning teachers? What do we do once we establish new perspectives through reflection?

The Case of Mrs. Holder

Mrs. Holder, a fourth grade teacher, told her class to get out blank paper and remove everything else from their desktops. "On your papers, class, make a list of all of the reading skills you have." The class sat quietly. Only a few students wrote anything on their papers. And what they did write was rather vague. Do fourth graders have reading skills? Of course, they can define words in context, decode, use phonetics, and find the main ideas in a paragraph, among many other things. But are they conscious of these skills? Probably not to a great degree. And the same is true for those of us who teach. We have theories for teaching and learning, but we may not be conscious of them. Mrs. Holder's fourth graders can read without being conscious of the theories that undergird their skills. Teachers can teach without being conscious of the theories that form the foundations of their work. But can they lead?

> ## REFLECTION
>
> Go back and reread Teria's teaching platform entitled "My ABCs of Teaching" in Chapter 3. What theories of teaching and learning seem imbedded in her statement? What theories of teaching and learning are imbedded in your platform? What are Gerald's theories of teaching and learning? How would you describe his theory of teacher leadership?

5

CREATING A CLASSROOM AND SCHOOL LEARNING COMMUNITY

But leadership, it now strikes me, is not merely being forceful or gung-ho or simply operating where no higher authority tells one what to do. It is first and foremost being persuasive and determined about matters that count—that is, about learning and teaching and caring about kids and each other. (Sizer, 1996, p. 96)

Student Journal Excerpt

To establish a school community, I believe that teachers should genuinely care for students and help meet their needs. Teachers should also provide support and encouragement. This helps the student want to learn and to succeed with what she is doing in the classroom. School communities should believe that every child is capable of understanding and learning and that all students learn differently. In order to support this, teachers should use strategies to teach lessons toward different learning styles. In order to gain trust from students, teachers need to respect them, value them, and provide a fun and safe learning atmosphere in the classroom. Also, it is important to communicate not only with students, but also with their parents. This demonstrates that the teacher and the school care for the student, his or her family, and his or her education.

—Kelli Fox, preservice teacher

The Possibilities for Classrooms and Schools as Communities

When I think of classroom and school community, I think of how Tom Sergiovanni describes them in his books *Building Community in Schools* (1994) and *Leadership for the Schoolhouse* (1996). Both books build on a foundational premise: schools should look and act more like the communities that they are and can be as opposed to the mere organizations they have become in so many cases, especially in the public sphere. School communities should reflect the democratic values and activities that citizens value the most and not be mired in bureaucratic red tape, bound by rules, and tethered to the tightly controlled purposes of organizations.

I don't want to suggest that there is such a thing as a "pure" community or organization. Every community has "organizational" qualities, and every organization has "community" qualities. The distinction that Sergiovanni tries to make is more subtle and has to do with the qualities of a community or organization when the ledger is tilted out of balance, for instance, when a school begins looking and acting more like a business (an organization) than like a family (a community). If you believe a school should be run like a business (I understand that some people do and disagree with them, though I understand the importance of fiscal responsibility, of course), then you are dealing with a different set of metaphors, beliefs, and practices than you would if you believe that a school should act more like a sound family unit. How you view and interpret your surroundings and the systems with which they operate make a difference on a moment-by-moment, daily, and long-term basis and say a great deal about what you think the purposes of education and schooling are. I want to suggest that the metaphor of classroom as school community is richer, sounder, and more educational than the metaphor of classroom and school as organization.

For instance, people who live and work in learning communities base their lives on shared values, beliefs, and commitments. In organizations, people and the organization base their work on structures, roles, and rules (once again, as in the following examples, communities do have structures, roles, and rules, and organizations have values, beliefs, and commitments—the question is about the degree of value and focus).

Communities build and honor family ties, have a sense of place and memory through traditions and customs, and base their decisions on shared goals and directions. People have a say about what happens on a daily basis and long term, and share in decision making in communities. Organizations typically localize power among a few (a hierarchy) or build complex bureaucracies or production systems/processes in order to control others.

Covenants (promises, making commitments), situations and circumstances, and sharing roles shape the life of a community. Contracts (bartering, making deals), rules, and roles govern in an organization. Communities rely more on local knowledge, contexts, situations, and shared values in order to figure out what to do next. Carefully scripted systems govern the actions of an organization.

Relationships in communities are different from those in organizations. More familial and affective, community relationships are based on mutually shared obligations and commitments that have moral and perhaps even spiritual roots. Being bound to a "quid pro quo" that comes with formal agreements, bartered arrangements, and contractual obligations is typical in organizational relationships. (The previous paragraphs are based on Serviovanni's discussion of community in his book *Building Community in Schools*, 1994.)

REFLECTION

Consider the following passage from Codell's *Educating Esme: Diary of a Teacher's First Year* (1999) and discuss the interpretive lens (classroom and school as community or classroom and school as organization) that helped her decide how to respond to her student. Codell's book is written in the form of a diary kept during her first year as a teacher in the Chicago Public Schools.

April 15
I'm glad I didn't yell at Latoya today.

I almost yelled, "This is the fourth day in a row you're a half-hour late! You're missing important math instruction, and I don't appreciate repeating myself!" But then I remembered I promised myself to try not to single children out for public humiliation, which has been my modus operandi of late, but to talk—and listen—privately instead.

"Is there a reason you have been late four days in a row?" I asked her, alone in the hall.

"We are in a shelter this week, and I have to drop my sister off and take the train over. It takes longer than I thought. I'm sorry, I'll be with my aunt next week and then I can walk over."

"Don't apologize. I'm proud of you for coming each day. It wouldn't be the same here without you, don't forget that. And even though we can't wait for you, if you miss an explanation in math, just ask me or a classmate ..."

For the rest of the day I was glad I listened instead of yelled, but I still burned with shame at the thought of what I almost said and at all the occasions I have spoken harshly. (pp. 147–148)

The School as Community/ The School as Organization

Respond to the following case:

On a large urban, public high school campus, two friends, one Hispanic, the other Anglo, get into a shouting match during a lunchtime basketball game on the playground. Both boys attend a small magnet school housed in the larger high school; the magnet school is in an outlying building on the larger campus and serves about 400 of the school's total population of 2500 students. The "magnet" program in the small school offers a specialized curriculum and draws students from throughout the district; it acts like a smaller school within the larger one, with its own identity, culture, curriculum, teachers, administration, and students. The verbal exchange between the two friends turns heated when racial epithets are cast along with an errant punch or two.

A second fight erupts several minutes later, but the two friends aren't even involved in it. They, in fact, had made their way back to their own school building together, having "made up" and not even knowing that tensions had escalated elsewhere. The disturbance carries over into the cafeteria and onto the common courtyard in the middle of the school. Now other students from both the magnet program and the main high school are involved; these students don't even know about the primary disturbance. It takes an hour and the local police to quiet the crowd and get everyone back inside the building. The local news channels call it a "race riot"; some contend the TV stations fueled the disturbance with the presence of their reporters and cameras.

Three days later, local police still try to keep order at lunchtime. Fights still break out, violent threats are made, and students are carried away by police for interrogation. As tensions mount, the differences in reactions by people in the high school and by people in the magnet school are stark. Administrators and teachers in the main high school try to pretend as though nothing negative requiring further attention or education is going on, except for those perpetrators causing the disturbances. Inattentive, distracted, and disruptive students get in trouble in classes, and the attempts at conducting "business as usual" in classrooms is strained even further. In contrast, administrators, teachers, and student leaders in the magnet school immediately call a school meeting for school community members to air their differences, fears, reactions, and grievances regarding the incident. The magnet school's student body agrees together to a truce, under certain conditions among different student groups in the school. Several teachers incorporate student reactions to the "riot" in their classroom assignments, especially encouraging the students to critique through writing the media coverage of the event.

REFLECTION

Consider this case from the perspective of "classroom and school as a learning community" and "classroom and school as an organization."

The great American educational philosopher, pedagogue, and curricularist John Dewey (1959) (read his teaching platform, which he called his "Pedagogic Creed," found in Dewey, 1959, pp. 19–32) once wrote:

It is impossible to prepare the child for any precise set of conditions ... I believe, that education, therefore, is a process of living and not a preparation for future living. (pp. 21–22)

Dewey's assertion holds even more firmly now than during the earliest years of the 20th century. Indeed, education and learning should be about present life, about making all that we experience and learn in school meaningful and accessible for our students' current lives. We cannot fully prepare students for a future that is unclear, unpredictable, and that does not exist yet, or for a past time that is gone. Of course, this does not preclude the teaching of history, for instance, but the foundational question becomes "What does history have to do with us?"

All teachers can help students learn things that will help them lead their lives right now by creating a learning community in the classroom in which an adequate response to the child's question, "Why are we learning this?" cannot be "Because it will be on the test Friday." That's not good enough. Instead, teachers need to teach things that have to do with life and with building effective relationships among the school, community, student, and teacher. Maybe the bottom line is helping students to see how their present and future lives have to do with participating wholly in a democracy where individual and community opinions, positions, commitments, and actions matter to themselves and to others over the short and long terms (Postman, 1995). The reality is that effective teachers, ones not merely tied to the curriculum guide or the test questions as the only source of material, help students learn deeply so that they still score on standardized tests. The difference is that learning sticks longer, and the course is not dull-witted.

The starkly different reactions by the schools, the administrators, the teachers, and the students in the case above about the "race riot" are instructive regarding my position. Some of the best opportunities for learning lay at hand in the events of the day. Not to address in school the crucial, life-altering events that are happening inside and outside of schools, at least sometimes, misses such a valuable opportunity for learning and perhaps the whole point of schooling in a democracy. School can tie us to the most important lessons of life. And schooling can distance us as well, putting primary importance on things beyond the matters that concern and interest us, objectifying our existence and us.

Consider the powerful possibilities for learning and for building community when the curriculum and our teaching are not straight-jacketed by the textbook, for instance, or the worksheets we run off for class, or the test on Friday. What if we were open to attending to and dealing with the "real" issues of living and learning today as we lived and learned in schools with students?

Four Areas of Focus for Creating a Classroom and School Learning Community

The remainder of this chapter lays out four areas of concern and development for beginning teachers who are considering the possibilities of creating a classroom and school learning community as opposed to a classroom or school organization:

1. Setting high expectations for all students
2. Planning for teaching
3. Creating and nurturing a culturally diverse setting for learning
4. Teaching democracy

You may aspire to a mechanically sound, routine, controlled setting for teaching. Of course, some modicum of organization of a classroom is required. You should be aspiring instead, however, as a first priority, to build a place where interest, excitement, and passion for learning reside and grow along with an atmosphere of caring for students' and each other's lives. This type of place may not look like the learning environments in which you thrived as a learner. It is precisely the point that tomorrow's successful classrooms will be dreamed up and created by new teachers who never experienced different classroom settings. Dreaming, inventing, and planning new possibilities are primary aspects of teacher leadership.

I would like you to base your teaching decisions on factors that will help you create a learning community in your classroom and school. The considerations then are broader, not necessarily focused on narrow techniques, or rules, or recipes for success. Beginning teachers will attend to these concerns in a broad sense, finding specific answers and approaches as they develop habits of effective practice. By the end of this chapter, I hope that you will have built upon, challenged, critiqued, and expanded your autobiographical sketch and your educational platform for teaching into a beginning set of personal, practical theories of action by examining these four concerns.

1. Setting High Expectations for All Students

Student Journal Excerpt: *Reflections on My First Field Experience*

The thing that I have been most disappointed about this first week in the field with students has been my own low expectations for them as learners. I do not know why this was, but I was very upset with myself for having these thoughts. I would be surprised, for instance, if one of my students got an answer right. Why should I be surprised, when we just went over the material the day before? Yet, I constantly found myself saying, "Wow, they are really smart," as if I found this hard to believe. As terrible as this has made me feel about myself, at least now I realize that these kids are smart, and always were. After four days now, I expect them to know a tremendous amount, more than I ever had to know at their age. All kids are smart and have the ability to learn, and I need to always remember that!

—Michelle Welser, preservice teacher

Nothing is more anathema to building a learning community in a classroom than assuming that some students can and some cannot do academic work or that some cannot even function in a socially acceptable way in the classroom. Consider the crucial position of viewing each learner as capable, despite perceived or even diagnosed limitations. Philip Haberman (1995), esteemed urban educator and teacher education critic, suggests that some teachers have an appropriate set of perceptions of learners and their roles with them in urban schools that make them "star teachers" of children in poverty:

> When asked about the causes of at-risk children and youth, star (teacher)s ... first recognize the impact of the label "at risk" on all who use it. They then emphasize a wide variety of ways in which school curricula and teaching methods cause large numbers of children to be at risk. They make the locus of their explanation the school. They describe how irrelevant curriculum and authoritarian and boring instruction exacerbate the problems that children bring to school. Essentially, stars say, "Look, I have the most control over what and how I teach. I should be able to find a way to involve my children in learning, no matter what their out-of-school lives are like. That's my job, and that's what I work at until I find activities and projects that work—that turn them on to learning." This is not to imply that stars are insensitive to the problems and impact of poverty. They merely focus on their role as teachers. (pp. 52–53)

Perhaps the most pervasive problem among teachers who would lead today is that they perceive many of their students as incapable, and continue on with the same teaching methods and materials despite student failures and mounting discipline problems. Of course, students and their communities share responsibility for school success and failure, but certainly the responsible teacher leader focuses on that which he or she can have an impact, that is the classroom and the students he or she is charged to teach well by the school, district, and state.

Abby's Main Point

The problem that I have with stereotypes of certain schools is that they aren't true. Every time I tell someone that I did my last field experience in a certain urban middle school, they ask me, "How terrible was that?" All I have to say to them is that it wasn't terrible at all. In fact, I really enjoyed my experience there, and I wouldn't trade it for the world.

I guess most people assume things like, "A school doesn't have sufficient funding, so the school must be terrible … There is no point in teaching the kids there because they don't care … If the students aren't getting the love they need at home then there is really no point in trying to educate them … They will have no future in our society … They are all drug dealers and gangsters anyway." I get so frustrated because these are the things I hear every single day. I guess the reason why people perceive these things is because they have never been in an urban school. They do not know what goes on behind closed doors there. The fact is, most of the people who say all these awful things are too afraid to go into these schools. They have set in their minds that these schools are bad and that violent acts occur everyday. Granted some of the students I met are no angels, but that doesn't mean that they don't deserve to learn. This simply means that no one has gotten through to them.

I guess my main point is that the students don't choose to live the way they do. It is impressive to me that these kids are even coming to school in some cases. We should not criticize their environment; we should capitalize on the fact that they showed up. Whether it appears so or not, if they show up, they want to learn. These kids need the love and attention that every student needs. We cannot put them down because of where they come from or where they go to school. Society needs to not only accept these schools and these students, but they need to help in the improvement process. If everyone chips in, maybe there won't be so many stereotypes flying around ten years from now.

—Abby Gard, preservice teacher

REFLECTION

What prejudices or stereotypes do you bring to teaching regarding students and their communities? What do you think you can do to challenge your own positions?

The Case of Ms. Andrew's Class: Some Thoughts on Student Capability

While Ms. Andrews—a competent, capable preservice teacher—was doing her teaching internship as a high school English teacher, she realized how differently she had been teaching and treating the students in her "honors" (so-called higher ability) classes as opposed to those in her "regular" (so-called lower ability) classes. At the same grade level, covering basically the same material, she taught the "honors" classes with flair, and excitement, and engaged the students in activities that extended their thinking and skills in language arts. She debated with them, looked for deeper meanings in literary passages with them, and pulled out ideas from them for essay topics and material to include in their own writing. Two periods later she faced the "regular" students with dread, low energy, and boring "let's just make through this hour together" activities such as worksheets and answering the questions out of the book. Then one day a "regular" student asked her quietly after an extremely boring class, "Ms. Andrews, how come the other classes get to write a journal and prepare a video ending to the book and talk in class? We can do those things, too, you know. We're capable." His question and comments caught her off guard; she began to think it over deeply, and she decided to stop differentiating her practice for each class so distinctly. After several weeks of successes, including increased student achievement and improved classroom climate with her "regular" class, she began to wonder, "Why are these students tracked into 'regular' classes anyway? Shouldn't every student be given access to a spirited, challenging, enriched curriculum?"

Every teacher I have ever known (and this is true for my own teaching experiences as well, at both the school and university levels) experiences frustrations with students and classes at some point in his or her professional teaching career. Sometimes when frustrations set in, teachers vent those frustrations and slip into the discourse of despair and blame. But I know that to slip into the discourse of frustration and despair and blame is to lose sight, not to stay true to the purpose and calling of becoming a teacher leader. This purpose is to serve students by meeting them where they are, by finding interests and concerns that tap their internal motivations, ultimately for the purpose of leading them into activities that help them fulfill their potentials as students, activities that provide successful learning opportunities for them upon which they can build meaningful learning for life. This position holds no matter how students and the community respond. It is never someone else's "fault," and the process of trying to teach well is never "over."

Instead of venting their frustrations and laying blame, teaching peers who solve their problems with students, classrooms, and teaching successfully—alone and/or with the help of their peers—view teaching as leadership by asking, "What can *I* do to make things better? How can *I* change? How are the ways *I* am thinking and the approaches *I* use limited? How can *I* grow as a teacher and person? How can *I* adjust to meet the needs of the learners in this case? What can *I* understand about my students and their lives that *I* am missing?"

Student Journal Entry: *Around the World in 80 Days*
This past summer I taught a school age class—ages six to ten years old—at a child care center. Our theme for the summer was "Around the World in 80 Days." We would be "traveling" to many destinations around the globe, exploring different cultures, climates, people, etc. We would start our journey in the rain forests of South America. I had the maps all ready, the craft activities planned, and the books borrowed from the library. I was prepared. I would soon learn that we would not be following my well-planned script, however. These children had their own maps, their own visions of the destinations they wanted to see, and it was hard to do anything but give them an idea and let them run with it in their own direction.

I find it ironic that through my teaching them, they taught me. I underestimated the knowledge and experience that these children brought to the discussions and lessons and activities. When I look back on that experience, I see myself treating the children in a way that I've always despised in my own teachers—as blank slates. I wanted merely to give them knowledge, and at first I wasn't fully open to the ideas and knowledge that they already had.
                                            —Bethany Lawson, preservice teacher

Student Journal Entry: *Engaging All Students in "Higher-Order" Thinking*
Not only in this class on teacher leadership, but also in some of my teacher education classes, we have been talking about higher-order thinking curricula that incorporate higher-order thinking activities into student projects. In all of the discussions, the way "at-risk" students are being taught in the classroom has concerned me. From what I have read and understood up to this point, most "at-risk" students aren't being challenged in school.

I'm thinking first about the students who are labeled "gifted." These students get to take part in the higher-order thinking activities that are interesting and challenging. They do cooperative learning activities, laboratory experiments, inquiry activities, all of which are stimulating and allow them to go to another level of learning.

Now, what about how most "at-risk" students are being taught? They are often lectured to, given worksheets, and asked to look up low-level answers in the textbook. Group work is minimal, and labs are hardly ever considered. At-risk students should be given the same opportunity to engage their intellect in higher-order thinking activities. Teachers who present concepts through higher-order thinking activities have discovered that students retain the information longer. The use of higher-order thinking activities has also been known to raise the enthusiasm of students about learning. Finally, the issue of how a teacher can use higher-order thinking activities in the typical classroom, which consists of students with all types of learning disabilities and perhaps varying ability levels, has arisen. I understand how this could be a concern since students may comprehend information at different paces. The best suggestion I have come across is that higher-order thinking activities should be designed for partners or small groups. Working together in this way affords students a ready support system as they attempt more challenging, non-routine problems.

—Trista DiAngelo, preservice teacher

Sammi's Autobiographical Sketch

Just One Person

I grew up in a world of standardized tests, a world where I would ask my parents what percentile I was in for Math and Reading after the standardized test scores came in the mail, and a world where it wasn't enough to be in standard math or reading; a student had to be in accelerated math and reading to prove themselves as an intelligent student. Unfortunately, I was not that "standard" student, and it was clear to me, and everyone around me. It wasn't about creativity, or ideas and discussions throughout my school day: it was about how well a student could take a test, and how good or bad he or she would make the schools look on the standardized tests. I saw myself as less than my peers because while my friends received check marks, and later A's on their report cards, I received "X's" and C's, prodding me to try harder and focus more in class. My teachers criticized my intelligence and distorted my view on myself as a learner and as a person.

I was constantly embarrassed walking into my "less ready" courses. These classes labeled as "survey classes" during senior year explicitly stated that we were just learning a more comprehensive scope of the information, but still, we were seen as a deficient group of people, unable to be integrated into the "normal" or "standard" courses. We "survey" students were labeled, criticized, and mocked. When comparing my schedules with my friends, I would immediately white-out the word "survey" in my course schedule so no one would know the lack of competence that I and so many people felt we had. I did everything I could to get myself out of these courses, constantly studying and doing my best to excel in the classes, but once a student was on the survey track it was very hard to get out of it. I had became just another thread in the unraveling education system that was already failing so many people. The information was too easy for me, and I wasn't gaining anything from these "less ready" classes. However, I wasn't excelling on the tests and couldn't prove my knowledge. On top of this, I was already too deep into the survey classes to get out. I couldn't make any move until Junior year of high school when I had a fantastic math teacher, who finally showed me that I was smart and competent, and that I, too, could excel at the same level as my peers. This teacher represented lessons in several different ways, appealing to many different learning styles and different students. He introduced us to real life examples of math and had us doing hands on activities throughout our class periods. This teacher assessed us formally as well as informally, using observations and small group activities. This teacher helped me get out of the survey track. Despite resistance from the department chair, he worked with me hours a week and even assisted me with an online class in order to get me up to speed with my peers who were in the "standard" mathematical track. When I finally received my first high school schedule without any "survey" classes, I posted my schedule for the world to see.

It was then, when I finally figured out that the problem was not completely with me, but maybe the people I was surrounding myself with. This questioning began further when I stumbled upon a quote by Albert Einstein. It stated, "Everybody's a genius. But if you judge a fish by its ability to climb a tree, it will live its whole life believing that it is stupid." I was the fish in this example, and the tests I was being forced to take throughout my early childhood and into my later educational career, was the tree. I feel that if I was assessed in different ways throughout my educational career, and less emphasis was put onto standardized tests, I would have succeeded much more and much sooner both academically and personally.

This point in my life was the first time I realized that I was not stupid, that I just learned in different ways than other people. With a little extra help from some great teachers that believed in me, and a lot of hard work, I got myself out of the confinement of "lower level" classes, and got myself accepted into a university that a majority of my peers were not accepted to.

This experience taught me how truly flawed the educational system is. Despite how fantastic a school may look from the exterior, the individual students are what need to be focused on. Individualization is key, and if someone would have taken the time to individualize lessons for me, I would have gotten out of survey classes much earlier in my educational career than I did. This experience showed me that I wanted and needed to make a difference in students' lives and make sure they knew from a young age how truly capable they were, as students, and as people. I knew from early on that I would do this through working individually and in small groups with students.

I decided I would become the teacher who makes math and reading fun for kids. It would not be the experience that is thrown at students solely to be regurgitated out for standardized tests, but instead meant for overall learning and knowledge. Despite the fact that all teachers say they're going to be the ones who make learning fun, I truly feel that I have had experiences to become the teacher who can do that for students.

—Sammi Kushen, preservice teacher

What I want to suggest here is that each student is capable of learning, and that providing leadership in the classroom in terms of building a learning community means that all students, regardless of their so-called ability levels, should be challenged to learn. The ongoing challenge for a beginning teacher is to hold this position as a central tenet of the teaching platform and initial personal practical theories of action. It will take professional development, experimentation, experience, and effort to find the ways that work to engage all learners in a meaningful way beyond the often rote, surface level attempts too frequent in many classrooms. But it can be done, and it is an essential commitment for fulfilling our destinies as teacher leaders.

Consider the controversial research on student expectations such as Rosenthal and Jacobsen's (1968) book, *Pygmalion in the Classroom*, and Elashoff and Snow's (1971) response, *Pygmalion Reconsidered*. Rosenthal and Jacobsen "tested elementary school students and then picked out a few in each class that they told the teachers were late bloomers who should do well this year. In fact, these students were chosen at random and were of the same ability as their classmates. At the end of the year, when the students were tested again, those who had falsely been identified as late bloomers were found to have learned more than their classmates in the first and second grades, though this effect was not seen in grades 3 to 6. The teachers expected more from these students and transmitted those expectations" (Slavin, 1997, *Educational Psychology: Theory and Practice*, p. 362).

2. Planning for Teaching

Perhaps one of the biggest shocks to beginning teachers is the amount of time and effort it takes to plan for teaching day-to-day. I routinely coach beginning teachers that the work of preparing academic work for college classes as students is *next to nothing* when compared to the amount of time and effort necessary for planning and delivering teaching in a school setting, regardless of the subject matter or grade level. Preparing lessons and unit plans, doing the background reading and research necessary to have a solid base in the content area on any topic, preparing materials for student use or for presentations to students are continuous tasks, essential for good teaching, and bafflingly difficult, especially at the beginning.

But I am assuming that as beginning teachers you consider yourselves as learners, which may be the primary function of a teacher leader anyway, i.e., learning! It is impossible to avoid lifelong learning if you are teaching well or intend to teach well. In fact, one phenomenon I have noticed among successful master teachers is their unwillingness, typically, to use the same materials over again. They rather enjoy the learning process, and are always on the lookout for something more to read, new materials to gather and use, or another set of activities to explore or design for class. Of course, master teachers build a stash of "tried and true" lessons and materials; but they never stop filling their filing cabinets and computer files with "new" materials, either.

It is important, however, for me to draw a distinction between the sort of planning you will be required to do as a preservice teacher and the kind of planning you will see veteran teachers doing in the field. It is no secret that successful teachers plan, but successful veteran teachers plan differently than successful beginning teachers. As a function of experience, veterans often write less down on paper; they tend not to have a script or maybe not even a lesson plan for the day's activities. Instead, teachers often jot long-range notes in a plan book, knowing full well on a daily basis the status of the class and the activities that will help the class move toward goals. You may wind up asking yourself at some point during your early field experiences, "How did my cooperating teacher teach that lesson nearly flawlessly with nothing written down?" (See McCutcheon's discussion of planning in her book *Curriculum Development: Solo and Group Deliberation*, 1995, pp. 45–48.)

REFLECTION

Ask several cooperating teachers you have worked with during early field experiences how they plan for teaching. Report your findings in a short journal entry. Collect several different lesson plans from your teacher and compare them to your own initial attempts at planning.

It is no secret that some teachers plan poorly and that their own teaching and student learning suffer. One aspect of their poor planning is the lack of discipline these weak teachers show in thinking about and preparing for their day-to-day work. They breeze from day-to-day, paying little attention to their work and the importance of moving forward purposefully with their students. Having sloppy or underwritten lesson plans is often a symptom of deeper problems. Sometimes they just teach out of the book. But successful veteran teachers constantly plan by reflecting deeply on their work, while they are teaching and even while they are not! Although they may not spend as much time making lists and plans and notes for class as they once did, they are aware and open to new ideas, especially when they are outside of class and school time. They convert these ideas to plans "in their heads." They are planning while mowing the lawn, watching TV, grading papers, and brushing their teeth, and the skills they have acquired in teaching combine with experience and sound practical theories of action to inform the day's work.

In short, do teachers plan? If "planning" is considered as writing down in detail what is to be accomplished, the answer is no. If it is considered as developing a course of action, the answer is yes. The plan is a sketchy outline of events upon which teachers elaborate while teaching. Teachers consider previous lessons while planning current and future ones. They think about both the content and their students while conceiving of a plan. Although these plans do not focus upon instructional objectives as much as upon ideas about what to do, inherent in the lesson are aims. (McCutcheon, 1995, p. 48)

Let me make clear that beginning teachers should practice a very disciplined style of planning, even going so far as to support the rigor necessary to come up with instructional objectives (though I find this typically less than necessary for good teaching: see Eisner's discussion of behavioral objectives, problem-solving objectives, and expressive outcomes here later and in his book *The Educational Imagination*, 1994, pp. 108–124). You will be getting instruction from other teacher educators, most probably methods teachers in the content areas, concerning approaches to lesson planning. Almost invariably, they will teach you rather disciplined, perhaps even routine methods of creating lesson plans. This practice is crucial and essential for learning how to plan adequately and completely for teaching; but it is merely a beginning point in terms of method.

The deeper concerns for planning and teaching have to do with the types of questions you ask as you plan. The question is, which questions do we ask first? "How do I use the time?" No. "What cool activities can I do with students?" Maybe. "What do I want students to learn, and how can we learn these things together?" Yes. "What are the students' concerns and interests in relation to the material or topic?" Yes. The key to planning early in your teaching career is starting the process with a focus on learners and learning. This does not mean that a great lesson or teaching moment will not emerge out of an exciting, interesting activity or that activities that are attractive and engaging aren't important. Excellent activities are crucial to the learning process, and later in your career, teaching may be built primarily around activities and not around goals. What I am talking about here are starting points.

I consider several ideas to be crucial for your consideration for planning regarding pedagogy and assessment, including the organization of ideas for authentic pedagogy and assessment proposed by Newman and Wehlage (1995). Newman and Wehlage propose several standards in the areas of instruction and assessment that could help you to create an authentic approach to teaching.

They pack a number of crucial aspects of excellent teaching and assessment into their rather elegant and simple framework, outlined below. First, their notion of standards has to do with creating a usable, accessible template through which teachers can think of teaching and assessing student learning from three succinct categories: First, is the teaching, activity, and/or performance concerned with the *construction of knowledge*? Instead of merely teaching facts and information, does the learning event involve the learner in meaning-making, constructing knowledge from what is learned and what the student brings to the learning event? Second, does the teaching, activity, and/or performance engage the learner in *disciplined forms of inquiry*? Instead of merely allowing students to learn on a surface level, does the learning event push students into deeper and perhaps new modes of thinking, learning, inquiring? Third, does the teaching, activity, and/or performance, engage the learner in topics that have applicability, relevance, import, and *value beyond school?*

Standards for Authentic Pedagogy: Instruction

Construction of Knowledge

Standard 1. Higher Order Thinking   Instruction involves students in manipulating information and ideas by synthesizing, generalizing, explaining, hypothesizing, or arriving at conclusions that produce new meaning and understandings for them.

Disciplined Inquiry

Standard 2. Deep Knowledge   Instruction addresses central idea of a topic or discipline with enough thoroughness to explore connections and relationships and to produce relatively complex understandings.

Standard 3. Substantive Conversation   Students engage in extended conversational exchanges with the teacher and/or their peers about subject matter in a way that builds an improved and shared understanding of ideas or topics.

Value Beyond School

Standard 4. Connections to the World Beyond the Classroom   Students make connections between substantive knowledge and either public problem or personal experiences.

Standards for Authentic Pedagogy: Assessment

Construction of Knowledge

Standard 1. Organization of Information   The task asks students to organize, synthesize, interpret, explain, or evaluate complex information in addressing a concept, problem, or issue.

Standard 2. Consideration of Alternatives   The task asks students to consider alternative solutions, strategies, perspectives, or points of view in addressing a concept, problem, or issue.

Disciplined Inquiry

Standard 3. Disciplinary Content The task asks students to show understanding and/or to use ideas, theories, or perspectives considered central to an academic or professional discipline.

Standard 4. Disciplinary Process The task asks students to use methods of inquiry, research, or communication characteristic of an academic or professional discipline.

Standard 5. Elaborated Written Communication The task asks students to elaborate on their understanding, explanations, or conclusions through extended writing.

Value Beyond School

Standard 6. Problem Connected to the World Beyond the Classroom The task asks students to address a concept, problem, or issue that is similar to one that they have encountered or are likely to encounter in life beyond the classroom.

Standard 7. Audience Beyond the School The task asks students to communicate their knowledge, present a product or performance, or take some action for an audience beyond the teacher, classroom, and school building. (Newmann & Wehlage, 1995, pp. 14, 17)

I certainly want you to be aware of what teachers do in terms of planning as you enter the field. You should be constantly attending to planning and to the ideas that form the foundation of your teaching, no matter the form your planning and teaching take. The moral responsibility of the teacher leader rests in the commitment to being ready each day for class to the point of being "over-prepared." I want you to take seriously the notion that teachers are knowledgeable about subjects and are constantly learning more about the world, though I realize that one teacher can never learn everything about a topic or be able to conceive of every possible action that might inspire learning in a classroom.

As teachers, we are not computerized robots able to call up answers to questions related to vast topics of study. Better, as human beings we can, in addition to our thorough preparation and planning for teaching, allow for the possibility that students will ask about or know something that we do not know. This simply allows for the opportunity for you to become a co-learner, an inquirer for a lifetime just like your students. There is no shame in saying, "I don't know the answer to that, Michelle. Why don't we figure it out together?" In fact, these situations may hold the most potential for learning than any others in the classroom community you help create with your students.

A Case Report on Planning

—David Parry, preservice teacher

Background for the Case   Today was lab day in my field experience classroom. Students experimentally determined that land (sand) heats and cools at a faster rate than water (liquid). Before the lab, my cooperating teacher gave a lecture that took about half the lab time. I watched her teach the lesson first period, and then I taught the lesson second and third periods.

Materials: hot plate, 2 beakers, 2 thermometers, sand, and water

The Events   Second period was an experience I will never forget. Over half the class members have IEPs (Individualized Education Plans), designed for students identified with special needs, which means students have a variety of learning styles and difficulties. When teaching a class like this one, it is important to be prepared, which means creating a lesson that is meaningful to as many students as possible. This may mean creating a lesson that looks much different from the other classes that you teach. A single period just to watch how a lesson is taught is not enough for this type of class.

Since my cooperating teacher does not do formal lesson planning anymore but rather follows loose guidelines after so many years of experience, I was unable to be as prepared as I would have liked to be to teach the class. Because of this lack of preparedness, discipline problems emerged along with overall lack of class cooperation. I felt the class slipping away but did not know how to bring it back. I took care of the discipline problems the best I could, but the lab was not very successful. The students were not engaged and just did not understand what it was all about. Part of the problem was that I did not present the material in a way that they could understand. I had in my mind what I wanted to say and did not deviate from that when things weren't working. I just pushed through it hoping to come clean on the other side. I found myself looking at the clock wondering how much longer until the end of the class.

After second period I had about twenty minutes during which students meet in activity groups. This gave me a chance to review what had happened during second period and to make changes for third period. First, I designed a better lesson plan for me by outlining what I intended to teach and the order of the topics. Within this structure I left room to deviate, of course, if the class called for it. Then I wrote the new plan on the chalkboard so the students knew exactly what my plan was and could easily follow along (Review, Activity, Worksheet, Lab). For the third period I added an activity and a review that involved more of the class. The activity helped the students to understand some of the concepts better. If I had taught the second period with this plan, I believe the results would have been better.

Discussion   Third period went much better than second period, and the students experienced a much better learning environment. With a little extra planning I was able to do a much better job. I also found that being prepared for one class does not mean you are prepared for all classes. The same exact lesson may not always work with each class. It is important to know your students and to keep them in mind when planning a lesson. It is important to be prepared when you walk into the classroom because if you are not, you are doing a huge injustice to students.

REFLECTION

As you think about David's case, consider Newmann and Wehlage's (1995) *Standards for Authentic Pedagogy*. How does the lesson meet the standards? Where does it fall short? What deeper considerations for planning does this case suggest to you?

3. Becoming Culturally Competent

Following are several demographic characteristics of U.S. teachers: They are and will continue to be overwhelmingly European-American (85%), female (over 73%), and members of the middle class (Matczynski, Rogus, Lasley, & Joseph, 2000, p. 351). The stark contrast to these teacher demographics lies in the characteristics of students in our public schools. Of approximately 45 million K–12 students in public schools in 1995–1996,

64.8% were White, 14.6% African-American, 13.5% Latino, 3.7% Asian, and
1.1% Native American (*Education Watch 1998*, 1998). A significant portion
of students has less than middle class socioeconomic status and many live
their lives below the current poverty line.

> In most major cities, more than 70 percent of students are persons of
> color; and in some cities the numbers are almost 90 percent. Such trends
> are expected to continue; before the year 2050, more than one-half of all
> K–12 students in the nation's school will be children of color. According
> to Troy (1999), nearly six million public school students have disabilities,
> a disproportionate number of whom are African American. Two mil-
> lion students speak no English; and another 6.2 million are limited in
> English proficiency. An estimated one million suffer from the effects of
> lead poisoning, a leading cause of learning disabilities. More than a half
> million students are homeless. More than 14 million students live in abject
> poverty and come to school hungry; approximately half of these students
> are children of color. ...
>
> Despite increased student diversity, the workforce in U.S. schools is
> becoming less diverse ... as the number of students of color is increasing
> in schools, the number of teachers of color is decreasing" (Haberman,
> 1989; and Newman, 1998, cited in Matczynski et al, 2000, p. 351). "Our
> European-American youngsters need role models who promote multicul-
> tural understanding, just as our students of color need role models who pro-
> mote achievement and social justice concerns." (Matczynski et al., p. 351)

These demographic and cultural differences pose challenges for teachers, students, communities, and schools. I want to encourage teacher leaders
to recognize the differences between themselves and their students as well
as among the wider communities they serve and to be aware of the country's shifting demographics as they plan for teaching and teach. We want
beginning teachers to use difference to build community in the classroom.
We think that early is much better than late for considering differences. We
believe that recognizing differences will help teachers understand and utilize
the valuable richness of cultural perspectives in the classroom other than
their own and that this may very well enhance their teaching and raise their
expectations for student achievement.

Ray Terrell, longtime public school educator, college dean, civil rights
leader, and co-author of *Cultural Proficiency: A Manual for School Leaders*
(1999), lays out the theoretical and practical approaches for clarifying and

celebrating cultural difference in school community settings. He and his co-authors refer to stages toward cultural proficiency that teachers and schools experience in our society:

Cultural Destructiveness: Stage in which attitudes, policies, and practices are destructive to cultural perspectives, and consequently to individuals within different cultures.

Cultural Incapacity: Stage in which systems or individuals hold extreme biases, believe in racial superiority of the dominant group, and assume a paternal posture toward so-called "lesser" groups.

Cultural Blindness: Stage in which people believe that culture and color make no difference and that "all people are the same." The values and behaviors of the dominant group are assumed to be universally applicable and beneficial to all. An assumption that members of "minority" cultures do not meet cultural expectations of the dominant group because of some deficiency or lack of desire to achieve, rather than the fact that the system works only for those minority members most "assimilated" to the dominant culture.

Cultural Pre-Competence: Stage at which awareness occurs that there are limitations in cross-cultural communications and outreach. A desire to provide fair and equitable treatment with appropriate cultural sensitivity, combined with the frustration of not knowing exactly how to proceed take precedence. The danger at this stage is assuming that the accomplishment of a narrow set of goals fulfills the needs or obligation of obtaining equity.

Cultural Competence: Stage at which individuals and communities develop an acceptance and respect for difference. Members engage in a continuing self-assessment of cultural competence and attend carefully to the dynamics of difference. Members expand their cultural knowledge and resources and adapt their belief systems, policies, and practices to celebrate difference. (Lindsey, Robins & Terrell, 1999)

The stage beyond cultural competence is cultural proficiency: a stage at which teachers hold culture in high esteem, seek to add to the knowledge base on culture by conducting research and educating others about the dynamics of cultural difference, and become advocates for culturally competent policies, practices, and procedures in all communities.

Terrell believes that most schools and communities have moved past cultural destructiveness and incapacity, but that many are still mired in cultural blindness. One of the worst perspectives for teachers to take is that "All children are the same. I don't see my students' color or gender. They're just kids." This position devalues culture and other aspects of difference and diversity and typically assumes that the dominant cultural norms are good enough for everyone.

Moving past the notion that treating all children the same is somehow equitable, especially when it comes to considerations of cultural perspectives, is one of the most difficult stages to transcend, even for those who are aware and attempting to change. This does not mean that the grounds for unity and shared commitments among people are less important. Unity and difference constitute two unique characteristics of our American heritages and ways of life. The point is that aspects of unity and shared purposes become even more meaningful and important once we acknowledge difference.

● *Journal Response*

One important part of the school community in this urban elementary school is the culturally diverse setting for learning. Because the student body consists mainly of African-American students, the teachers must be aware and sensitive to the students' cultures. Most of the teachers are white, middle-class females, and during my visit I realized how expertly they handled situations and worked with the students. At first, I did not understand some of the things that transpired during my field experience, such as the ways in which students interacted with each other and how they responded to the teachers. I soon realized, however, that the teachers know where the students live, how they live, and that they understand the students and their lives very well. Differences are not discouraged or ignored in this school; instead, they are accepted and incorporated into teaching practices.

—Emily Hall, preservice teacher

As you consider building a learning community in your classroom, know that one of your greatest resources for building will be the differences in life experiences that your students bring from various cultural perspectives.

Remember, even in a seemingly homogenous school population, difference and diversity are prevalent and should be nurtured and celebrated. Your attention to these issues, beyond your preservice preparation, will constitute one of the most important aspects of your development as a teacher.

Student Journal Excerpt

I grew up in a rural school with other white kids who had middle or upper middle class backgrounds. There was only one student of another race in the school. This leaves me culturally incompetent in and of itself. Going to a college with mostly white students reinforces my incompetence as well. And I feel that I have so much more to learn in order to help all of my students develop and learn. I cannot continue living in a cultural bubble and teach well, nor do I wish to continue living this way.

Dr. Terrell's presentation to our class on cultural proficiency opened my eyes to my own cultural blindness. All people are different, and we as members of the human race need to acknowledge that we have more value as a community because we are different. It is a dangerous practice to blatantly ignore difference.

When I was in my last field experience in an urban setting, I found myself correcting students' spoken grammar. Now I know from Dr. Terrell's talk that they were probably speaking a form of Ebonics. And I know now that I didn't teach them well by correcting them. And I look back on that experience and feel bad. But I just didn't realize that their language forms are cultural, part of an actual language structure. I wish I had heard Ray's talk before I went to the school. I can see now how schools can be places of cultural destructiveness. If teachers are not knowledgeable about students' different cultural backgrounds, then they can destroy students without even knowing how or why.

I am about to finish my education classes, and I don't know if I am ready to deal with my cultural incompetence. I'm struggling with this. How do I become more educated on these important issues? If I want to become an effective teacher, I need to be able to recognize and deal with difference and the issues that surround difference.

—Deannah Bair, preservice teacher

Another important consideration in the area of diversity is the idea and reality of a multicultural curriculum. I introduce students to several basic questions about multicultural curriculum through the work of James Banks (1994), an eminent multiculturalist and curriculum scholar. Banks challenges teachers to move beyond the typically positive but surface response of appending culturally diverse materials and events to the curriculum. Adding an African-American author to the reading list during Black History Month or having a cultural feast day in which foods from various cultures are made and consumed by the school community treats difference, diversity, and multicultural perspectives as appendages to the "real" curriculum. These might be places for schools to start, but a truly multicultural curriculum and school community looks at cultural diversity pervasively, throughout the curriculum, as a part of what we "normally" do, not something that gets treated only in special cases.

> Teachers will need to partner with parents and leaders of the minority communities in order to understand the realities of the students' life world, both the different values and assumptions embedded in that context and the struggles involved in dealing with joining the mainstream while attempting to maintain and protect all that is good in their own cultural communities. Based on that understanding, teachers can build bridges between their students and the learning agenda of the schools. This will involve incorporating more multicultural components in the curriculum as well as creating reference points between the students' life world and the material under study. It will also mean supporting learning performances that use the life worlds of the students as an arena for legitimate research (e.g., the economics of the housing projects, the history of immigration in their communities [including the oral history of grandparents, grand uncles and aunts, etc.], the classical poetry of their language community, the art and dance of their cultural community, the political struggles of their communities, the geography of the country of origin of their forebears, and the contribution of women in their cultures). If the school is a community of learners, then teachers will allow themselves to be taught by their students and by their students' parents and will be able to reinforce the comparisons among the struggles and heroics of several different cultures. "Being different," then, becomes a way of contributing to an enlarged sense of community among people who are seeking ways to live in harmony, where differences as well as deeper unities lie. (Sergiovanni & Starratt, 1998, pp. 102–103)

Grant and Sleeter's Five Approaches to Multicultural Education

One of the most helpful and illuminating conceptual frameworks for thinking about Multicultural Education (MCE) for schooling comes from the work of Christine Sleeter and Carl Grant (1988, 2006). They began their work together in the late 1980s, constructing a literature review of historical and current school practices in MCE and then building on that work for the past two decades with examples of practice and studies in the field of MCE approaches in action. In their book *Making Choices for Multicultural Education: Five Approaches to Race, Class, and Gender*, they discuss five approaches to MCE that have taken shape in schools over the past decades, including "Teaching the Exceptional and Culturally Different," "Human Relations," "Single-Group Studies," "Multicultural Education," and "Education That Is Multicultural and Social Reconstructionist."

The "Teaching Exceptional and Culturally Different" approach attempts to honor students where they are, but the approach always foregrounds deficiency, with the end goal being to get learners in a position "to meet the traditional demands of the school and American life" (Sleeter & Grant, 1988, p. 35). As a means for delivering palatable and relatable content, learning, and achievement possibilities, the teacher and students work together to address cultural, language, learning style, or learning ability deficits with the main goal of incorporating the non-White students, the non-native English speakers, students from lower social classes, immigrants, and the disabled into the mainstream culture. This approach, however—although it was a starting place in the 1960s and 1970s for MCE—is criticized as assimilationist and as focused on difference as deficiency, not differences as simply differences. Also, the approach does not take into account the structural and institutional bases for oppression and "assumes that people do not succeed in life because they have not learned a certain repertoire of skills and knowledge that is the key to success" (p. 65).

The "Human Relations" approach attempts to create connections and understanding across different groups, to foster "tolerance," to help people and groups at "getting along," to create deeper "interactions between individuals and groups," and to "reduce prejudice and stereotypes" (p. 75). The hope is that advances in these areas and activities across groups in classrooms and schools will promote "unity and tolerance" and the reduction of stereotyping (p. 75). But the approach is too limited, focusing only on students "getting along" and "valuing diversity" across groups, while typically not examining social issues with any depth of purpose, including complexities regarding social justice and equity (p. 98). It is often perceived as assimilationist as well, leaving behind important considerations of poverty, discrimination, and the stifling impact on students of the status quo in terms of race, class, gender, sexuality, and disability (p. 99).

The "Single-Group Studies" approach, a term actually coined by Sleeter & Grant, refers to attempts by teachers and curricularists to foreground the group in question—for example, women, Asians, or the working class—thereby reducing social stratification and raising the "status of the group with which they are concerned" (p. 105). This approach attempts to broaden what counts as mainstream culture by studying a certain group. The goal is to "change attitudes and provide a basis for social action by providing information ... about the group and about the effects of discrimination on the group" (p. 105) and is usually implemented in the school through a teaching unit. Single-group studies became trailblazing attempts through the civil rights movements of the 1960s and 1970s, which began with Blacks demanding social, political, and economic rights (p. 126), and manifested itself in special courses and programs in universities focused on single-groups. But critics fear that single-group studies leave the "regular" curriculum uninformed, and that while well-intentioned, most single-group approaches end up not being inclusive of other groups besides the one being studied. Also, single-group studies are often only taught and consumed by the single-group in question, and they often focus merely on curriculum revision and not on changes necessary in the broader school environment (p. 129).

The fourth approach, "Multicultural Education," transcends the three previous approaches and embodies for the authors the "education policies and practices that recognize, accept, and affirm human differences and similarities related to gender, race, handicap, and class" (p. 137). Sleeter and Grant use this reflexive term to note how the previous three, often referred to as MCE, do not live up to their billing or to an accurate, more complete definition and practice of MCE. They cite Gollnick's (1980) five goals of MCE as central to the approach:

1. Promoting strength and value of cultural diversity
2. Promoting human rights and respect for those who are different from oneself
3. Promoting alternative life choices for people
4. Promoting social justice and equal opportunity for all people
5. Promoting equity in the distribution of power among groups

"The most severe criticism of this approach comes from outside of it, and argues that multicultural education promotes 'particularism' and weakens social unification and academic rigor ... Some scholars within the field of multicultural education point to the need for more attention to social structural inequalities and for teaching students the skills to challenge the disparities resulting from inequitable power structures" (Bode, 2013). In other words, while Multicultural Education approaches the ideal, both in theory and in practice, it does not go quite far enough.

Sleeter and Grant's preferred model, the fifth and last in their typology, is "Education That Is Multicultural and Social Reconstructionist." This approach goes a step beyond MCE, highlighting the need for students, teachers, and society to use educational means to transcend the status quo, to work for renewed schools, to produce societal norms privileging social justice and equity, and to eliminate oppression (p. 175). The curriculum should focus on social action and foreground difference and diversity as important means and ends.

As you think about your life as a teacher leader in schools, to what extent will you pursue MCE, and attempt to reconstruct the world with your students?

Reflection on Teacher Leadership: *A True Multicultural Education*

I am ashamed of myself to have taken so long to learn this, but it has been really rewarding lately to learn so much more about multicultural education and to incorporate it into how I think about teaching.

I grew up in a wealthy suburban area with virtually all whites and a little bit in a bubble. So I always heard about racism or how certain people (in other parts of the country, of course) could still be racist, even after the Civil Rights Movement; I honestly grew up believing that a multicultural education was just about trying to make people not racist. I was always told to not be racist so much that I started to get upset at the once-a-year seminars on African American History Month and trying to be less racist. I always had friends of a bunch of different races, even in my own barely diverse community, so I figured I had achieved the epitome of multicultural living. That is, I did not look down on other people for being of a different color than me.

But in retrospect, this is a totally mismatched way of viewing real diversity. So instead of getting mad at the system for beating into my head to not be racist, I should have seen the system as narrow for not promoting culture. When we become so paranoid of hurting everyone, we begin to run away from problems, instead of running to solutions. The way to really grow multicultural diversity, I am beginning to understand, is to embrace different cultures and give each of them power and value them for their differences. A multicultural view of life and a multicultural education were never just meant to combat racism. To be sure, they do, but they have a much wider scope on the world than just avoiding that one problem. The goal of multicultural living and education is to foster an appreciation of culture. I am learning to explore many different walks of life.

—Quentin Russell, preservice teacher

Reflection on "Critical Race Theory" Reading by Author Michelle Jay

Multicultural education is often times just seen as the "cultural food day" that schools have, the activities done for a week throughout Black History Month or on Martin Luther King Jr. Day, or highlighting a "hero" on a specific day. While all of these things may be important for students to learn, this is not the form of multicultural education that should be in schools.

I can look back upon all of my history and social studies classes and the content that I can remember learning was completely "white-washed"; there was little to no discussion of any other cultures or some of the true historical events that happened. It was not until my college years that I heard about so many pieces of Black history that were erased from the "American" history that is featured in textbooks and in curriculum.

"The ultimate goal of multicultural education is to move us towards the creation of concepts, paradigms, themes, and explanations that challenge mainstream knowledge, not help keep it in place" (Jay, p. 219). This goal is something that I do not see in schools today nor something that I have experienced for the most part in my own education. Multicultural education should interrupt the systematic racism that we see on every level. But when attempted to be implemented, multicultural education ends up benefiting those with white skin.

Whites end up being benefited because they are the dominant group in power. This group continues to see multicultural education as a threat because the empowerment of marginalized groups could potentially change the group in power, which would no longer be Whites. Which is why those who feel threatened by multicultural education are the ones fighting against it.

I believe that this struggle will continue into the years when I have my own classroom, and one of the most important things that I have taken away from this reading and from this class is that there is no time to sit around and stay silent, waiting for change to occur in schools. I need to be the agent of change in society and stand up for what is just and for what I believe in. This struggle may not always be easy, but it is most definitely worth it.

—Maddie Charles, preservice teacher

4. Pursuing Democracy in the Classroom and School

What I mean by pursuing "democracy" in classrooms and schools is not the notion of teaching democracy directly, as one might in a class on government or civics. These courses are typically important parts of the school curriculum in which democracy does, in fact, get taught and learned, but these courses typically are taught from a content standpoint, and may not, in fact, have much to do by way of structure or experience with the experience or practice of democracy itself.

What we mean by "democracy" in classrooms and schools at all grade levels is creating community structures and places in the curriculum for students, teachers, administrators, parents, and community members to develop a social conscience; to apply learning in school settings to real life situations in the world at large; to allow students to pursue and construct knowledge with guidance—or better yet on their own, and not just get knowledge handed to them by teachers and through their own passive reception. Classrooms and school-wide situations must be created for learning so students can inquire freely, test ideas, discover things, critique the status quo, question, make sound decisions, attend to the issues of the day that affect the nation, world, and local communities, and practice democracy by creating classroom structures that function democratically, thereby extending the power to contribute to decision making beyond just a few who hold positions of power and prestige through their formal roles (like principals, superintendents, and school board members, teachers and class presidents).

Ted Sizer (1996) calls the preferred orientation for a democratic citizenry "informed skepticism." The habits of mind necessary for approaching the world as an informed skeptic, wherein a legitimate, substantive questioning emerges as it is informed by knowledge of complex personal, social, and cultural issues, translates to an informed democratic citizen. The informed skeptic can be nurtured in school communities where the lives students bring to schools are valued; where students have some say in how the school day is structured, both in terms of how they spend their time and what they spend it on. Student learning must translate into meaning for students who live in a real world with real problems and issues. They should have the opportunity to address these issues in school with capable, caring adults and peers. School should help citizens to make well-informed choices and to learn the political, moral, social, cultural, and economic virtues surrounding the maintenance, protection, and nurturing of personal and collective freedom and equality (Noddings, 1999).

O'Hair, McLaughlin, and Reitzug (2000) describe the practices of democratic schools in their book *Foundations of Democratic Education*. Their approach is to contrast what they call "conventional" schools, schools that operate under traditional bureaucratic principles in the main, with democratic schools, schools that operate more like democratic communities of learners.

In conventional schools:

- Important classroom and school decisions are made hierarchically by superintendents, principals, and school boards.
- Decisions are handed down to teachers in the form of rules, policies, programs, and curriculum packages.
- Little emphasis is placed on teacher knowledge and expertise.
- For the purposes of efficiency, teachers teach primarily in isolation.
- Teachers rarely get the opportunity for extended professional talk with colleagues.
- Teachers are responsible for large numbers of students.
- Overcrowding creates situations in which students move from class to class with little interaction with teachers.
- Teachers' work, therefore, becomes more about controlling student behavior than about students' intellectual and social growth.
- Rather than building on and connecting what students already know, school is driven by uniform standards in state or local curriculums and often correlated with standardized tests.
- Instead of *teaching students*, teachers often have to *teach the test*.

(O'Hair et al., 2000, adapted from pp. 34–35)

O'Hair et al. are careful to point out that not all schools share these characteristics, but that many do, and that many fall between being largely conventional and being somewhat democratic. They contrast their images of conventional schools with schools they call democratic.

In democratic schools:

- The classroom and school climates are more personal, collaborative, and participatory.
- Respect for teacher and student knowledge is a norm.

- Teachers, administrators, and students share a collective sense of responsibility for learning.
- Teachers, administrators, and students embrace shared values and collaboratively develop learning principles that guide curriculum, teaching, and how the school operates on a daily basis.
- Leadership is shared among teachers, administrators, parents, and students.
- School and classroom decisions are based on critical study rather than on self-interest.
- Teachers learn from and with each other via discussion and critique of teaching and school practices, and by working collaboratively on initiatives related to curriculum and teaching.
- There is a concern for connecting curriculum with the world beyond school and especially in terms of exploring and addressing social conditions such as racism, sexism, poverty, and other forms of injustice and oppression.

(O'Hair et al., 2000, adapted from pp. 34–35)

While O'Hair and colleagues get very specific in noting the practices that help create democratic schools, they are careful to point out that schools don't ever become statically democratic, as if democracy is something to be reached. Instead, democracy is an ideal and a process to be experienced. As a result, a democratic classroom or school becomes a place that "respects all members of its community, a place where *all* children *and* all adults learn and grow" (p. 35). They continue their discussion by creating a table outlining the practices that help make a school more democratic. These practices are listed below.

In terms of democratic practices, democratic schools:
- Develop shared value systems.
- Practice teaching and learning using ideas about authentic pedagogy and assessment to guide their work.
- Conduct critical studies in order to make shared decisions.
- Use methods of shared decision making.
- Find ways of building internal and external support for teachers and students.
- Create a moral and professional community.

(p. 35)

These are essential aspects of a focus on democracy in the classroom community and school. Teacher leaders have a moral responsibility to pursue democracy in work with students, classrooms, schools, communities, and parents as they make their way in their personal lives and professional careers. Pursuing the democratic, committing oneself to achieving cultural competence, developing means for planning effectively for teaching, and setting high expectations are crucial principles for building a classroom learning community, and by extension, creating a school community.

So far in this book I have focused primarily on issues concerning you as a beginning teacher leader and your development of a sense of self within the functions of teacher leadership. I have already begun in these latest chapters to extend the discussion to important personal and professional considerations for expanding your notion of yourself as teacher and how you will fit within a wider learning community. But now the focus shifts to considering other deeply important issues that will affect you as you attempt to relate and function as a teacher leader in largely conventional schools, to broad issues concerning interacting with others and creating curriculum for teaching, and to the development of the teaching profession, of which you will be a vital and contributing member.

REFLECTION
What is teacher leadership?

Reflection on Teacher Leadership
In class I hear the words "Teacher Leader." About 20 minutes later I hear the same words again, "Teacher Leader." It continues again and again and again for about the next two hours. By the end of the lesson the words "Teacher Leader" are ringing in my ears. Since the beginning of the semester, we've heard this phrase countless times. Because of this, I've been thinking a lot about what the words really mean to me. After all, words are just words unless you actually take the time to think about what they're trying to get across. Words are meaningless until the listener or the speaker gives them meaning. I know that the speaker of these words clearly has a meaning for them instilled in his mind; however, it's about time I figure out what they mean for me.

Teacher Leader.

To those people who are not going into the field of education, it's a very simple concept. A Teacher Leader is one who teaches and leads. But to those of us who do plan to become educators, the words have to mean so much more. To me, being a teacher leader means that I have to be able to make difficult split-second decisions in my classroom and be confident enough in my abilities to be sure that I made the right choice. It means that I have to be able to see warning signs in my students, whether that is struggling with class work, issues with bullies, problems with friends, or a rough home life. I have to make sure that my students know that I'm there for them if and when they ever need me. I have to be up to date with the latest advances in whatever area of science I'm teaching so that my students are well informed. I have to be engaging in whatever way I can so that they have fun learning. Being a Teacher Leader means that I have to be the best possible educator I can for my students because with every lesson I essentially hold their futures in my hands. It is a tremendous amount of responsibility to place on a twenty-something, and I'm terrified and crazy excited about it all at the same time.

Teacher Leader.

—Sean Mormino, preservice teacher

Reflection on Teacher Leadership

To me a teacher leader is not the head of the history department, or the longest tenured teacher, or even the person who is vocal to colleagues about what she is doing in her own classroom. I would say overall a teacher leader is someone who creates a fair, non-biased, loving community in the classroom and who places the needs of all students before his own.

The community of a teacher leader's classroom is democratic, so that all students feel like they are in a safe space, and there is no bias in the classroom. These teachers want to learn about the community where their students live and bring the same values that students see at home into the classroom. Teachers are not just preparing these students for tests, but for how to operate in society. They are aware of diversity and do not back down from the challenges that come with integrating it into their class. Teacher leaders do not stand for any bullying or harassment and will never let it go undisciplined. Most important, a teacher leader is a person who cares deeply for and respects students, and wants more than anything for them to succeed in their lives.

Teacher leaders devote endless time differentiating their lessons so that every student can have the opportunity to be engaged each day. They are up to date with the newest advancements in their field and are willing to adapt their lessons to these advancements. These teachers reflect deeply over each lesson and how they can *improve their classroom to enhance learning. Teacher leaders push their students to achievements that they may not believe is possible at first. All teachers should strive to become teacher leaders. It may seem like a daunting task at first, but the benefits for students make all the difference.*

—Brian Veil, preservice teacher

Reflection on Teacher Leadership

As the semester has progressed, we have continued to read about and discuss in class some of these characteristics of "teacher leaders." One disparity between teachers and teacher leaders *that cannot be ignored is their willingness to support student difference, something I feel has a huge effect on classroom community. When students feel as though they are truly accepted despite their differences, they feel more comfortable and safe, which allows for a better environment and thus better learning.*

Though supporting student differences is easier said than done, it is definitely a focus of mine. "Student differences" includes everything from simply learning best through different styles to coming from varying backgrounds. Supporting student differences, as we often discussed in class, should not be an afterthought or some-thing solely added on to the curriculum. For a teacher to truly accept and support these differences, he or she must make it a priority to take the time and address any differences in a way that can actually foster learning. So much can be learned from adopting an open perspective of others and all students should understand the importance of this.

Extending past student differences, it also important to think about differences between the students and teacher. One thing that worries me is facing the challenge of students who value different ideals than I do. Of course, I want to encourage students to discover what they value, but when they go against something that I believe, what would I be expected to do? Ideally, if appropriate, I feel as though, similarly to above, I would take the time to acknowledge that everyone has different values and beliefs but then teach the lesson that we need to respect each others' own values in order to foster a good learning environment where everyone feels comfortable and welcome.

After our class discussion with visiting teachers, one quote still stayed with me. One of the teachers said, "You don't handle people, you handle objects. You work with people." These two simple sentences made me reflect about the dynamics between students and teachers. Though they are somewhat different from school to school, one thing remains the same: we cannot treat our students, who are human beings, as though they are objects that need to be controlled and handled. Once a teacher does this, she has established a limiting relationship that cannot be undone.

Teachers tend to be too worried about the problems students can cause instead of the good they can create. This mentality leads to the idea that teachers need to "handle" their students in order to properly manage their classes. Though students can't be distracting to the extent that they hinder learning, we must remember that in reality, they are people, too. They are human and make mistakes, and usually there is more going on than we may fully understand. Since this is the reality, we need to find a way to work with them and give them opportunities to grow despite the times that they make things difficult. By showing your students that you care enough to "work" with them instead of just shoving them aside, you are sending the message that your classroom is a place where collaboration is welcome.

Furthermore, I feel that issues with handling students and classroom management in turn lead to difficulties building a classroom community with students. How can we build deeper connections with our students when it's difficult to see past the fact that they are our "lesser?" We need to be able to understand that although we are in charge of "managing" our classroom, we are not supposed to manage the people in it. We are supposed to form a bond among each other and grow together, working towards success.

—Allyson Klovekorn, preservice teacher

Reflection on Teacher Leadership

To me, being a teacher leader is going above and beyond what other people expect a teacher to do. A teacher leader does more than teach in the classroom. Though some people might think this goes without saying, being a true leader is easier said than done. A teacher leader knows each of her students by name and is aware of their strengths and weaknesses. A teacher leader acts as a model for her students— not only when it comes to having a thorough knowledge of her subject—but also when it comes to respecting and accepting others.

A teacher leader does not go through the motions. A teacher leader is prepared with something new every day and is not bored with her subject matter. A teacher leader leads by example by letting her enthusiasm for her subject permeate her classroom in hopes that her students will be just as enthusiastic as she is.

A teacher leader never loses control of her classroom, nor does she lose control of her emotions. A teacher leader does not call out disruptive students in order to embarrass them, but asks them one-on-one what is going on after class has ended. She will show that student compassion and love in any circumstance and will strive to empathize with her student's situation.

A teacher leader makes herself available to her students in every way possible. Whether this includes coming to school early, staying late, or eating lunch in her classroom, a teacher leader is accessible to any and all students who need help with her subject or help with life in general. A teacher leader also says "yes" more than "no" and truly values her students' opinions. Finally, above all, a teacher leader loves her students unconditionally.

—Sarah Zaffiro, preservice teacher

6

Inquiry
for Teacher
Leaders

When I first started teaching, I had no idea that one vital function of teaching could be the production of knowledge about the world, or about some subject matter in particular, or about teaching itself. I never considered the possibility, as a beginning teacher, that research or inquiry into my own work as a teacher could make a contribution to the knowledge base on teaching and learning at a wider level. It wasn't until much later in graduate school that I discovered that for a century, teacher-scholars like Dewey had been calling for teachers to study their own work and to report their findings to colleagues as a means for understanding and improving education. The bottom line is that those who know the most about teaching and learning (teachers!) should produce knowledge about it! How rational and natural this all seemed.

And what seemed so reasonable and fascinating to me about the possibilities of researching my own teaching practices and then teaching other teachers to study their own settings was that inquiring into critical questions about teaching and learning is what good teachers do anyway. Good teachers always reflect, read, study, take particular actions, judge the results, and start again. Good teachers lead personal and professional lives that are examined (not lives unexamined!). They do this every day as a part of their teaching regimen. Perhaps they generate new ideas by testing old ones or come up with tried and true methods that work over time. Whatever the case, research in new forms like those being advanced in the field of education fit what so many good teachers already do in their heads everyday and perhaps share on the fly with colleagues as they grab a quick lunch. What if we taught beginning teachers to conduct research on their own teaching more systematically? How could their own research on practice contribute to their own and others' knowledge about teaching and learning, thereby enhancing their own and others' professional development? And if teachers improved through inquiry, wouldn't classroom learning communities improve as well? *What if teachers who inquire began teaching their own students to inquire, even to conduct research as they learned?*

—Author's reflection on inquiry

It should be no secret by now that I am attempting to challenge the status quo regarding what constitutes good teaching and how you should approach your work as a teacher leader. What I am really suggesting is that you, the people you will work with in schools, and school communities in general must make a commitment to seriously rethinking what makes for a good teacher and good teaching. I want you to consider that teaching well requires that you study your own work, like doctors, lawyers, and the clergy do, by conducting systematic research on your own teaching practices. In fact, studying your own teaching is as important as any other condition for teaching well, and the school community in which you work should support your inquiry activities by providing the time and the resources to do it well. You have started down this "inquiry path" by carefully examining your own experiences and the assumptions you bring to teaching. Testing your own platform as you teach is one means of conducting research on your own teaching.

Teacher inquiry (which I use as an encompassing term for all forms of reflective teacher inquiry including the case report and action research project more extensively described later in this chapter) is a crucial aspect of teacher leadership and the development of the profession of teaching. Therefore, the practice of teacher inquiry must become germane to the task of teaching to those who teach, to those who are entering teaching, and to those who prepare teachers. If teacher inquiry becomes rooted in our cultures of practice, a part of teacher preparation, and a part of the expectations that schools have for teachers, then teacher inquiry can become an integral part of teaching. Until then, some will find it to be an add-on, superfluous, even distracting. Learning to view research as an indispensable root of our work in teaching is an integral step, one that I am committed to taking and one I will encourage you to take from the beginning (Poetter, Badiali, & Hammond, 2000).

Over the course of my career, I have used many forms of action inquiry with preservice teachers as I worked closely with them during field experiences and student teaching. Early on I wrote a book about the experience and process of using action research in a teacher education program at Trinity University in San Antonio (see Poetter, Pierson, Caivano, Stanley, Hughes, & Anderson's *Voices of Inquiry in Teacher Education*, 1997). Most recently, Miami University faculty have been working with students and teachers in area partner schools focusing on teacher inquiry as a key component of teacher preparation. The experience of working with students of teaching and their mentors in the schools and using action research as a tool to advance the program and relationships has reinforced several crucial points.

First, students of teaching begin to view themselves and their work in teaching differently when they conduct action research projects while they begin teaching. Instead of viewing themselves as learning to perform a routine and technical service through teaching, they see and experience themselves as thinking, reflecting persons who create and critique outstanding teaching practices and curriculum from the beginning of their careers. Teachers who inquire become decision-makers and generators of knowledge with regard to teaching and learning.

Second, students of teaching experience the feeling of "efficacy," meaning they come to view their work in teaching as making a difference. Action research is a tool that helps them exercise some control over the setting, the problems that present themselves, and the solutions that might help improve matters (Costa & Garmston, 1994).

Third, students of teaching become part of the wider conversation about teaching and learning, sharing their insights and ideas with peers and colleagues in the school setting through public forums. They learn from the beginning about the power of sharing ideas and working together with colleagues and students toward engaging dilemmas and solving problems.

Above all, engaging in inquiry during preservice teaching creates a series of norms and expectations for teaching that are different from those that currently exist. These norms and expectations have the potential for transforming the profession of teaching and must be attended to by teacher leaders. Ultimately, engaging in inquiry radically challenges the status quo of teaching; I expect that teacher leaders will have an inquiry-oriented approach to classroom and school-wide practices, work to systematically address significant problems in the classroom and school, and share ideas and practices publicly with colleagues, students, and communities.

People who ask questions, test ideas, and inquire deeply can conduct research. Some people think that there are only a few, objective, legitimate ways to conduct a study that might be called research or scholarship or inquiry on teaching and learning. However, I believe that teachers can learn to conduct helpful and sound research on their own teaching, especially through the form of action research studies. In working with beginning and veteran teachers in schools, students and teachers who participate in professional development activities using action research complete productive studies. I describe action research and how to go about conducting your own study in more detail in this chapter. At root, action research has scientific aspects (its steps resemble the scientific method), but like Dewey understand that research (like teaching) is an artistic endeavor as well. This opens up so many interesting possibilities.

Action research activities can be folded into the activities that teachers engage in as a matter of course on a day-to-day basis. The systematic collection of data in an action research study in your own classroom can take the form of keeping lesson and unit plans, collecting examples of student work, collating minutes from faculty and team meetings, etc. These are activities that teachers engage in anyway. The act of keeping track of things and organizing materials might also serve the purpose of making you more organized as a teacher, let alone enhance your database for research. The work of producing observation notes and reflective journal entries about your experiences with students can be folded into the school day and could very well constitute assessment data that teachers would keep systematically on students and classes they work with in the first place.

Teacher knowledge and teacher agency challenge the power structures typical in schools. Knowledge, new ideas, and research are political entities; inquiry encourages political action among teachers and is therefore threatening to some. But the risk is worthwhile, and the benefits exponential.

You can engage in several forms of inquiry as a beginning teacher, many more than can be listed here. One form employed in classes on teacher leadership is asking students of teaching to keep a reflective journal regarding important issues, topics, problems, and experiences in the field of education. You are no doubt doing this right now as an aspect of coursework in your teacher education program, and perhaps you have been writing responses to some of the Reflection questions in this book. Another format that introduces students of teaching to inquiry is the case report that they themselves and peers write on some aspect of their field experiences. Field experiences can be an excellent source of questions, problems, and events to report for feedback from others. After several weeks of field experiences, students can use a case report format to describe an incident that happened to them while teaching. The case report format helps students of teaching divulge their own reactions at the moment, and then reflect on and speculate about their decisions and changes they might make if confronted with a similar experience again. Along with keeping a reflective journal, the case report is an excellent format for early work on inquiry into teaching. You might consult Huyvaert's format for case reporting in her book *Reports from the Classroom* (1995). Several of the cases written by students and shared in this text follow her general case report format: (1) provide background; (2) give a description of the incident, event, or case; (3) discuss/reflect on what happened; and (4) ask questions.

Student Journal Excerpt

To me, teacher leadership is most importantly a state of mind. It is the idea that there is no concrete answer to every situation. A teacher should be prepared for any event, and take each one as it comes. We had reflective experiences together around case reports we wrote for our teacher leadership class based on our field experiences. Some of the cases were positive and others were negative, but regardless, the incidents made us reflect on the decisions we made as beginning teachers in the field. This reflection was another step towards building our own sense of teacher leadership. We may have realized that there was a better way to approach the situation, and there is nothing wrong with that. As beginning teachers, we are starting the never-ending learning process that teachers must become comfortable with. If a teacher was to say, "Okay, these are my exact guidelines and rules for teaching, and I will not change them whatsoever," she would eventually become a terrible teacher. A productive teacher leader is one who stands her ground on issues, yet is open and receptive to new ideas. Having a closed mind as a teacher is a disaster waiting to happen.

—Kristina Moffo, preservice teacher

The following entries are examples of case reports, a form of inquiry employed in our teacher leadership classes. The case report is a very valuable tool for engaging students in deeper reflection about teaching and learning from the very beginning of their preparation experiences for teaching. The case report takes a step beyond the reflective journal, laying out particular experiences and dilemmas that require a public audience and discussion. However, the case report is not always a form of action research, a form of inquiry that will be explained in more detail at the end of the chapter.

Case Report: Teaching Huck Finn

—John Healy, preservice teacher

Background   For my first field experience I got placed at Bradds High School with Ms. Lines [all names have been changed]. She is a seven-year veteran teacher who has spent her entire career at Bradds. This incident occurred during first period, a sophomore English class. During the first week of the field experience, I got up in front of the class several times to conduct mini-lessons. On Thursday of the first week, I taught an entire lesson. By the time the following events occurred, I felt very comfortable with the class. I had established a solid relationship with the students, but I do not believe that I had effectively understood their positions on racial prejudices or stereotypes. Had I sought out this information by engaging my students in dialogue about these issues, perhaps the following incident could have been avoided.

Incident   On Tuesday of my second week in the field, the second period class heard an introduction to *The Adventures of Huckleberry Finn* by Ms. Lines. We watched a video about the book, the life and writing career of Mark Twain, and some of the controversies surrounding the text. Ms. Lines gave a short introduction about how some of the material in the book was controversial, especially the use of a racially charged word in the text, but she explained to the class that she intended on reading the material aloud the way Twain intended. She asked me to read aloud from the book for the remainder of that period. This did not bother me because the day before I had read from Steinbeck's *Of Mice and Men*, and the class seemed to like it. I had already read over the *Huck Finn* passage that I was to read aloud, and I saw that it included the word several times. I knew that Ms. Lines did not want to change the text, but when it was time for me to read it, I did not feel that the students had been given a proper introduction to his use of the word. I did not feel comfortable reading that word out loud to them, so when the word appeared in the text I said "Negro" instead.

After class, Ms. Lines and I discussed what I had done. She was upset with me because I knew that she had planned on reading the word, and since I didn't read it in the first place, if she changed back to reading the word later, she thought she would look like a racist. I sincerely apologized to her, but I told her I was adamant about not using the word. I expressed my opinion that even if that is the word Twain used in the book, it was my position that the connotation of the word had changed so much over the last 100 years that it was unnecessary to read it orally to get Twain's points across. We decided the only way to come to a decision would be to open the discussion up to the entire class.

The next day was the most interesting of my field experience. We got into a circle to discuss *Huck Finn*, and we had a very average discussion up until I brought up the use, or not, of the word. Then all hell seemed to break loose. The students impressed me with their knowledge that the word had a completely different meaning in the time that Twain wrote the novel. Although most of the class understood that Twain did not mean what we associate with the word today, there were still several students that felt we should not read the word out loud. I felt the need to support their side of the issue because Ms. Lines was supporting the opposite position. It was my belief, and that of several of the students, that you cannot ignore the history and evolution of the word, and therefore, we should alter it to say what Twain meant by it when he wrote the novel ("slave" was the general consensus of what he meant). This did not sit well with Ms. Lines at all; she felt that changing the word to be politically correct was wrong and the worst form of censorship. She and I got into a little verbal sparring match about what we believed in front of the class. The bell rang before we could come to a consensus as a class. But I felt that if we would have had 15 more minutes, we would have all agreed to read the word, and everyone would have understood that reading the word out loud from the book in the context of studying the book was not a racist act.

After class, Ms. Lines and I usually talked and prepared for the next period, but after the discussion she was visibly upset. She left the room and I did not see her until after the bell rang, and I had already gotten the third period class underway. When she walked back into the room, I asked her how she thought second period went and she said, "It was pointless; nothing got resolved." When we were talking some more about it later, she kept saying, "The whole class was pointless." I tried to point out to her that I thought the discussion was very good and that the class had discussed some very difficult material and performed beautifully.

She then told me that she had talked to several of her teaching colleagues, and they seemed to think, she said, that I had displayed very poor etiquette as a visitor, and that she should be upset with the way that I had acted. It took me some time, but I understood her point, and again I apologized to her. I felt bad because I know how I would feel if I were a teacher and a college student came in to teach with me for two weeks and I had told the class we would be changing the word to "slave" and the student read the word anyway. When I thought about it this way, I felt really bad, and I explained to her that I didn't mean to overstep my bounds. I had just felt so comfortable with the class and with her that it never occurred to me that I was not like a permanent fixture in the classroom. She told me then that she understood my position, too, and she challenged me to come up with a way to "fix" the problem. I told her that I thought it would take about 15 more minutes of dialogue for the students to come up with a solution. She agreed to give me another try.

The next day the students finally came to the conclusion about whether or not to read the word out loud. The students decided that they would not censor the book. Four of the students, though, were resolute about not saying the word in any context. They said that they did not have a problem with other people reading the word; it was just that they would choose passages to read that didn't have the word in it. I found this very admirable. They stuck to their positions even with all of the peer pressure to give in.

Discussion   At the outset of this incident, my thought process was that I did not want to perpetuate the use of this word in any way. Being subjected to the word, even in a school setting, may be upsetting to some students. Maybe using the word in school would make it seem okay to use the word outside of school. If the students had talked more about the word beforehand, I believe they would have been more comfortable from the beginning.

If I had to do it over again, I would do many things differently. First, I would have made my position known to Ms. Lines BEFORE I read aloud to the class. Second, I would have acted in accordance with Ms. Lines' wishes or reached some other agreement with her before starting; it wasn't right of me to undermine her in front of the entire class, when I knew, without a doubt, what she expected of me. Third, I should NEVER have had a verbal confrontation with her in front of the class; my emotions were running high, and that was extremely unprofessional of me.

I know I overstepped the limitations placed on me as a two-week field experience student, but I believe I did help fix the damage I caused, and in the process learned a lot from the incident. It was really a great experience because I learned about myself, too, and I gained so much new respect for high school sophomores. I told the students that I did not think that I would have been able to engage in such a stimulating and intellectual exchange when I was a sophomore in high school, and that I had underestimated their knowledge and maturity. In the end, I worked it all out with Ms. Lines, and we parted on good terms. I now have a better grasp on how to handle controversial materials in class. In the process, I had to learn some tough lessons about not underestimating students and balancing professional positions and egos with colleagues.

Take some time with peers to discuss the various nuances of John's case report. There are several starting points for this discussion and at least several layers to it, of course, including the actual experience John had and the meaning he attempts to make of it afterwards. You might consider the following while thinking about and discussing John's actions and reactions: What are the fundamental issues and concerns at stake in this case? What practical theories clash in the case? What would you have done differently if you were John? If you were Ms. Lines? What types of teacher leadership (or not!) do the people in the case enact? Where does deep learning take place for teachers and for students? In general, what should the role of a beginning teacher be in a school setting? What responsibilities for supervision do the school and mentor teachers share? You can apply these questions to the following case reports as well.

Case Report: *The Day I Almost Accepted Defeat*

— Ashley Kemper, preservice teacher

My class has eight different students who have multiple, different special education diagnoses. This normally makes for very chaotic days and an ever changing classroom atmosphere. I have students who need extra attention because after a talk with school psychologists, I learned many of them have been labeled as having experienced severe trauma cases. I knew that these students brought their home lives to school with them, and I had to ask myself, as Bill Ayers says, "Are problems within the classroom, the school, and the larger community part of student consciousness?" Are these problems that control my students' behaviors something they are allowed to deal with in school or something they must suppress? Throughout the week I felt as though I had gotten to know the needs of each student in my classroom. I knew which students needed extra attention and which students could not work well with other students. I had even gotten to the point where I knew what situations were going to set students off and the "tells" they had to show when they needed to take a break. When my teacher asked if I was ready to start my lesson, I felt more than confident in my abilities to run an hour long lesson.

As soon as I was working with my small group, an immediate switch flipped. They were out of control. There were students running off to the bathroom, students under the table, and students fighting each other for chairs. After 10 minutes of individually talking to each student, I finally got them all seated around our table. After about one minute of asking questions, a few students were off again. My teacher had told me that if any students misbehave, I was more than welcome to send them back to class. I felt that if I sent these students back, I was showing her I couldn't do the job and that I was failing as a teacher.

After many deep breaths and small individual talks, we made it through the lesson plan I had laid out. It took us an hour to give a pretest and then to go over vocabulary words they would need to know for the upcoming day. As I sent the students back to class, I sat at the table absolutely drained. In my head I had pictured that I would sit down to teach the lesson, and they all would be willing to participate and learn. These were the students I had grown to know so well and the ones I believed I knew what steps I needed to control their behavior. As I walked back to class, I walked slowly with my head down, defeated.

One of the ideas we have talked about in class, especially in Wheatley's chapter "Willing to be Disturbed," is the idea to be curious about how someone interprets things wo do or say and we have to admit we are not capable of figuring things out alone. In this moment I thought back to what we discussed and knew I couldn't and wasn't expected to do things alone; I had many colleagues and resources ready to help me achieve the goals at hand, mine and the students.'

After the day was over, I was able to evaluate and critique how the day had gone. I realized that I should have spent a few minutes going over expectations for the small group work and the layout of what the day would consist of so they weren't overwhelmed and surprised. These students needed more structure, and I had failed to provide that for them. I had introduced them to a new environment with new rules and had completely ruined their expectations for the hour. My biggest mistake was focusing all of my attention on the students who were running around in the hallway instead of on the ones who were ready to learn. By focusing on the misbehavior of students, I was giving them the attention they sought and was taking away crucial learning opportunities other students needed. The next day I came back with new tools, strategies, and a new mindset. The next time we still had some issues, but overall a more successful day. I became more confident in myself and my abilities and once again was reassured that being a teacher is what I am meant to do. I needed a reminder that the bad days will come, but when they do, they cannot overwhelm the mindset and drive I have worked years to achieve. Each day is a clean slate, and I have the chance to become more experienced and be the best I can be for my students.

Case Report

—Leslie Jason, preservice teacher

Sophomore year of college, I was in my first year of a program dedicated to learning about and enacting social change. My cohort within the program partnered with an urban elementary school in Cincinnati. We would be working alongside students in second through sixth grades. Our roles were not to enter these students' worlds and offer our insight and knowledge as older, more experienced college students with a "been there, done that" attitude towards school. As newcomers to these students' school and lives, they served as our mentors. They engaged with us about what was happening in their schools, what aspects they liked and disliked, and what they wanted to see changed in their community.

These student mentors provided us with insight as to what issues they recognized within their communities and how they wanted to change them. As mentees, we were to work alongside our student mentors to enact some form of community change. Our mentors selected their most pressing issues in their community for us to work toward changing, including racism, bullying and violence, poverty, and homelessness. Based on our own interest in each group, we were separated to work with different mentors. I was part of the anti-racism group, and we had three student mentors. Our project ended up being a public service announcement featuring our student mentors and some of their peers discussing what racism is from their perspective, how we can combat it, and why we have to combat it.

Over the course of the school year, our Miami cohort traveled to Cincinnati every other Friday to work with our student mentors after their school day. The community in which the school is located and many of the students live is facing large-scale development and gentrification. The student body primarily consists of students of color who live around the school in a working-class community. However, on one walk around the neighborhood, our student mentors shared that they did not feel comfortable visiting the newly developed areas and felt as if they did not belong. One student shared that he and his brother went to a new pastry shop along one block after school, and they were not even acknowledged by the person working behind the counter.

These students' willingness to share such personal truths with me and my fellow mentees during our work over the course of that year shows that the education process is not something that is transferred from teacher/adult to student/child. Education should not just be someone relaying facts and information to students for 50 minutes per day at the front of a room; education should be an empowering experience that encourages students to use their knowledge and abilities with one another in a productive way. This experience showed me that teachers are not the end all/be all of information. It was inspiring to see students take initiative and determine the issues they felt needed to be changed; students organized with their peers to divvy up tasks; students set up courses of action for the different groups to take. We mentees and the school teachers involved in the program simply provided resources and a channel for students to realize their goals. This collaborative process reinforced my belief that project-based and student-led work can be some of the most meaningful and impactful work educators and students alike can engage in. My experience also emphasized that teachers can work alongside their students in the trenches when working for the type of change students envision in their own communities.

Case Report: Making Music

— Angela Yingling, preservice teacher

Angela Yingling is the author of the following case, written about her experiences as a beginning music teacher in the preservice field. Read her case and discuss her message.

Background   While on a field experience at a high school, I had the opportunity to teach the high school's concert band. The concert band at this school was comprised of students who did not make it into the wind ensemble (the top group) after going through the audition process. This was the last class that I was teaching that day. I also had the opportunity to teach the elementary beginning band, the middle school band, and the wind ensemble that day. Since this was my first time running full rehearsals, I was nervous and doing whatever I could to please the directors of the bands I was teaching. Before the concert band class, I was talking to Mrs. Jane Doe, the director, and she told me that the concert band wasn't very good because the students weren't focused, they weren't good musicians, and since it was the end of the day, all they wanted to do was go home. She did not display a high set of standards for this ensemble and showed little interest in their potential. Unfortunately, I bought into what Mrs. Doe told me, and as a result, I lowered my expectations before I even saw the students and heard them play. It wasn't until I started directing the ensemble that I realized just how wrong and immoral these viewpoints were.

The Event   As the students were walking in and setting up, I noticed that the atmosphere of the room was filled with intimidation and insecurity. The students didn't seem to be excited to be there. At first, I interpreted this as what Mrs. Doe had said was their "lack of focus." I lost my excitement and some of my energy because I was unsure of how I could be energetic if all I received back were blank stares from the students. I started the rehearsal by doing a quick warm-up and as I expected, I heard timid and shallow sounds coming from the group. Still under the impression that I wasn't going to be able to get much more out of the ensemble, I continued on to the main part of my lesson plan. I wanted to rehearse the slow middle section of the piece that they were working on, which contained a trumpet solo. At this point, I was nervous about what kind of sound was going to come out of the soloist and whether or not I was going to be able to actually rehearse the group the way that I had intended.

I was losing confidence in the group. We started at the beginning of the slow section, and as I conducted, I was taking a mental note of the things that I was noticing as the group was playing. They were playing all of the notes and rhythms correctly, but there was something missing. The music wasn't being made into music. When I gave the downbeat of the trumpet solo though, my mind was suddenly blown away. The trumpet soloist played absolutely beautifully. I was shocked. This whole time, I let myself believe that nobody in the group had "real talent." I don't know why I let myself think that way, but I am glad that I was quickly proven wrong. I must have shown my shock on my face because once I cut the group off after a few phrases, a flutist in the front row said "Yeah, she is good, but the rest of us stink." I was quickly thrown off guard by this comment because it finally dawned on me what the cause was for the lack of confidence and musicality in the group. I was the reason that they were lacking these key characteristics in their playing. If I didn't show them that I believed in them, how were they supposed to believe in themselves? In response to my horrible mistake, I began to get excited, and I could tell that the more excited I became and the more passion I put into my conducting/teaching, the more excited the entire ensemble became. Rather than giving off the impression that I didn't have confidence in the students, I began to give them positive feedback and support along with tips and guidelines of what they could do to make the section more musical and outstanding. Once the students realized that I believed in them, it was like I had a whole different group of students sitting in front of me. Rather than working against each other, we were all working together as a team to create wonderful music. Of course they didn't sound like the winds of a professional symphony orchestra, but they were putting forth all of their effort to make the best tones on their instruments and to do the things that I was asking them to do. By the end of rehearsal, we had accomplished so much, and the music sounded completely different than it had at the beginning of rehearsal. Rather than just playing notes and rhythms, the students were playing *music*.

Final Thoughts and Reflections   Looking back on it now, I am embarrassed and ashamed of myself for believing that the students in the concert band wouldn't be able to do much. Just because they are the "lower" band at the high school doesn't mean that they don't deserve the best music education experience possible. They can do things just as well as the wind ensemble if you push them and motivate them to do so. It also makes me angry that Mrs. Doe has so little confidence in her students. It is as if she has given up on them and as a result, the students have given up on her (or whoever else is on the podium). I feel like too often in high school band programs, the director spends so much time and energy on the upper level band that they subsequently put the other band(s) on the back burner. What kind of message does this send our students? It tells them that they don't matter as much as the other students. The massive lesson that I have learned from all of this is that student success strongly depends on the dedication of the teacher. If the teacher is not confident in the students and shows little interest in them, then the students are not going to have confidence in themselves. I am glad that I was able to have the opportunity to teach at this school. Even though I may have made a huge mistake in the process, I learned valuable lessons that I will carry with me for the rest of my life and career.

Case Report: Tweaking My Test Review
—Kelsey Oros, preservice teacher

This particular incident occurred while I was student teaching at an area high school. I was in the classroom attempting to conduct a review session for the pre-calculus class before they had their chapter test the next day. This incident shows how my beliefs got pushed to the side because I was afraid of making other teachers mad at me.

My teacher was absent from the classroom this morning, and I prepared what I thought would be a fun *Jeopardy*-style review game for my students. The class split up into teams of five, and I decided the team that won would earn two extra points on the test. It started with the students appearing to be somewhat excited to be out of the routine lecture and notes that are associated with most math classes. I tried to do group work as much as possible while inside the classroom because the students seemed to really enjoy it. One student from each group had to come to the board and complete a problem correctly to earn a number of points for their team. It was a race, too, so whoever got the answer correct first won the points for their team. I informed them that they could not receive help from their peers because it would get too noisy in the classroom, and I was worried about having complaints from other teachers.

The game went smoothly for the first two rounds because the teams had at least 1–2 people who felt confident enough in their math abilities to participate. However, this trend stopped after the second round, and it was as if I had to pull teeth to get students to come to the front of the classroom. They complained that they were not good at math and that they knew they would not get the answer right. At first this really frustrated me because I was willing to give them pointers and critiques as they wrote on the board as a form of scaffolding. The atmosphere of the classroom changed from excited to fragile in a matter of minutes. I was too afraid to change my decision of letting their team members help the people at the board, though, because I thought it would get too rowdy. I turned what was supposed to be a fun and informative review game into a laborious and frightening task. In the end, the team that grouped together with the highest performers won the game, and they earned the two extra points on the exam. It was clear that the students who rarely struggled with the material benefited from the session, but the ones that struggled still remained at that state of confusion and the extra points went to the victors.

The reflection of this somewhat failed review attempt actually took place right after the class. I had this activity planned for my next pre-calculus class that took place after lunch. So, I had to make some quick decisions and took my lunchtime to talk to a teacher that was next door. I told her my dilemma, that I had made math scary for students, which was the exact opposite of what I wanted to do. I told her how the students did not want to perform on the board in front of the class because they were afraid of being ridiculed by their peers. Last, I told her how I was afraid to let them help their group member that was at the board because managing a loud class is harder than a quiet class. I thought the race would make the collaborative work more chaotic, and I was not used to chaotic noise in the classroom, especially without my cooperating teacher present. The advice that the teacher gave me has stuck with me for a while now. She advised me that the sound of students being on task is not always silence. She told me to at least try letting the students help their classmates at the board and see what happens. So, that's exactly what I did the next period, and it went much more smoothly. The students were not rambunctious because they did not want the other groups to benefit from their own suggestions. So the classroom management ended up not being a problem. Also, the students became comfortable rotating through their groups and taking turns at the board. It was not just the same few people from each group repeatedly volunteering. The atmosphere of the classroom became less heavy and more of a fun learning environment. I also changed the reward to two extra points on each student's homework who participated at the board. Many more students benefited from these tweaks, and I regret not initially facilitating the activity in this manner, but this experience taught me how to operate the next test review.

Case Report: Powerless

—Quentin Russell, preservice teacher

I volunteered to work in an area school's tutoring program in order to get experience in teaching and being around teenagers. This program grouped students who had failed one or multiple classes. The remedial programs were all online and designed so that the tutoring could happen side-by-side with the online work. The students whom we were to tutor were randomly assigned each week. I had been assigned to Joey once before and was assigned to be his tutor again, which was rare, but I was excited to have the same student twice so that I could build a relationship with him. Earlier I had him for math tutoring (the subject we were to tutor them in was also randomly assigned), but this time I was assigned to tutor him in science. Admittedly, I was a little bit frustrated with this tutoring program because I wanted to spend more time with the same student and tutor in English, since I am an English major, but I figured I would just help in any way I could and be cheerful about it.

I walked in and saw Joey working already. "Hey Joey! I am your tutor again today; science, right?"

"... hey ..."

I looked at Joey's computer and he was supposed to be taking a test through this online program. However, he was copying every single question straight into Google and picking the first answer he found to put into his test.

"Oh! Uhh ... Are you sure we're allowed to just copy the answers? What did Mr. Lewis say were the instructions?"

"... yeah ... he said it was fine ... he just gives us the answers anyway ..."

"Okay ... well ... I feel bad about just Googling every answer ... Can I help you figure out some of the answers? Is there any way I can help explain it?"

"..."

"Can I help out at all?"

"... I just need to finish this test ..."

I looked at the questions he had and none of them were really questions I could help with. They all seemed to be memorization type questions. I just did not know the answers.

"Okay, Joey. That one says we have to tell which ..." He Googled it and clicked past before I could even stop him. "Okay, this one here says we have to tell the density of a normal Gold molecule. Do you know what that is?"

"... No ..."

"Okay ... Is there a lesson we can go back and read or something?"

"... No ... it's supposed to tell me, but it doesn't ..."

I had no idea what to do at all. Before I could think of some way to help him at all, he finished the test and Mr. Lewis switched me over to tutor another student.

When teachers talk about feeling powerless in the system, I understand exactly what they mean. I had no idea what to do. It felt like the whole event was just a setup to make me fail. I felt even worse because if Joey goes through that on a regular basis, he is going to be completely unprepared to go to college or start trying to get work. I did not have a motivational, life changing speech to give to him; I could not even help with his test. I did not know if I should help him on a test to begin with. It brought up so many questions: What is the importance of testing? Are students being set up systemically to fail? Even if they pass the tests and the course, what do they actually get out of an online module? Can I teach within a flawed program? Can I reach students who don't want to listen? This early experience made me feel very powerless.

Case Report: Including Burt?

—Ashley Myers, preservice teacher

Background   The setting for this case report is an urban elementary school where I taught in a fourth grade classroom during a two-week field assignment. The school was full of diversity. African-American students make up the majority of the class I worked with. There were also Hispanic and White students. The teacher informed me that a majority of the students do not receive parental support for school. She told me the students rarely completed homework and that the students generally come from low-income backgrounds.

What Happened?   A student in the class had been diagnosed with Tourette's Syndrome. This is a condition in which a person cannot consistently control his/her behaviors, sometimes resulting in verbal outbursts. This student, Burt, had difficulties staying focused and on task in the classroom. The teacher told me about Burt's situation and explained to me that she does not feel it is fair to discipline him because he does not have control over his actions. Basically, the teacher dealt with Burt by ignoring him; for her, this seemed to be the best and easiest way to deal with him. I had a difficult time just ignoring Burt, especially when he became a distraction to the other students in the class. I constantly found myself reminding him to stay seated, work on his assignments, etc. It was a natural reaction, really, trying to keep some control in the classroom.

But the biggest concern I had was for Burt and his situation. One day during the two weeks, the students were taking a standardized test to measure the students' reading and writing skills. The same test is given throughout the district and is used as a diagnostic and placement tool. An hour into the test, I noticed Burt struggling and so I approached him to check his progress. I knelt down and looked at his test. It was blank, he had written nothing down, and he only had an hour left to work. I asked Burt why he had not started the test. He responded by telling me that it took too much time, so he didn't want to try. I explained that he still had an hour, and the sooner he got started, the sooner he would be finished.

I ended my talk with him by reminding him to review the story he had just read and to start retelling the important parts of it that he remembered. I left Burt's desk thinking that he had understood my prompts and was willing to start working on the test. I then approached the teacher and informed her that Burt hadn't written anything on his test. She responded, "You know he has Tourette's, don't you?" Her comment surprised me. I thought it was sad that it was okay for him to do poorly and not even try because he had Tourette's Syndrome. That's no excuse. Why couldn't we have made some modifications for him to take the test in a different way so that he could have had some success on it? I'm sure Burt overheard our conversation because he remarked, "I'll just take a zero on it." And the teacher took his paper and said, "Yeah, you'll just get a zero."

Discussion   This incident represents just one of many negative things that happened to Burt during my two weeks in his class. Burt's behavior was continuously poor, and the teacher's response remarkably consistent: She did nothing. To me, it felt as though she had given up on Burt and therefore did not want to put any effort into motivating or teaching him. Following along was hard for me to do. During these two weeks, I had trouble just ignoring Burt. He wasn't learning any of the material that was being taught in class. He was just sliding by, not passing any of his assignments or tests. But this was "okay," others said, because he has Tourette's Syndrome.

I decided to write this case study on Burt because I haven't been able to stop thinking about him. It saddens me that he is not receiving the kind of attention and discipline that he needs and deserves in the classroom. I feel as though Burt is being failed by the public education system.

REFLECTION

I have to be sure that you understand that Burt is not experiencing an inclusive classroom or "inclusion" in the case above. At best, you might call his situation "mainstreaming," whereby a person with special needs is placed in to the regular classroom with little support or aid and left to experience the classroom just like any other student might. In Burt's case, he is being included in the regular classroom setting, yes, but it is not inclusion because he is not provided with the supports, materials, or modifications, let alone the personnel, such as a well-trained teacher and an aide, who can deliver to him and to his classroom peers a quality educational experience. After reading Ashley's case study on Burt, comment on Ashley's position as stated in this sentence, "I feel as though Burt is being failed by the public education system." What things are missing in this scene that if present could help Burt experience an "inclusive classroom"? How could the teacher enhance Burt's achievement in the classroom?

Case Report: Re-Starting Teaching with Your "True Self"

—Rob Cron, preservice teacher

This experience comes from my time student teaching. I was teaching in a large urban district at a neighborhood school. I was an intervention specialist, and this situation occurred in the self-contained math class I taught. This class consisted of three fifth-grade students, one sixth-grade student, and five seventh-grade students. These students had a range of exceptionalities, were racially diverse (meaning there was an actual mixture of races, not the buzzword meaning they were not white), and split with four girls and five boys. I taught the class in the library. My students came from a variety of backgrounds: one was technically homeless, a few lived at home with their families, and the rest of my students were wards of the state who lived in a group home near school.

This incident happened about a month into the semester. I had just begun teaching the class full time. I was having some difficulty with classroom management, and this week I was "restarting" with my students. I was clearly laying out what I expect as a teacher. I am starting at this point, but this case lasts for the rest of the semester. At this point, I am in the middle of establishing my classroom expectations:

> If you are feeling too overwhelmed, anxious, scared, mad, or any other emotion to participate in class, utilize the carpet. It is there as a cool down place. All you have to do is say, "Mr. Cron, can I take 5?" and I will say "yes." I trust you to know when you need a break. I also hope that you will be able to collect yourself and come back to participate. This will not work, though, if you come into my class with a mask on. I am not asking you to pretend everything is ok in my class. I am asking you to *bring your true self to my class*. That means all of you. I am going to bring who I am, my true self, to class every day, and I ask you to do the same. Because if you are going to be able to take breaks and check in with yourself, your true self has to be here first.

This was part of my little speech to the class, hoping that classroom management would get easier. It had been difficult up to this point, with students arguing with each other and testing me. I knew I needed to reestablish and clarify my expectations. I meant what I said about the students' true selves, though. I felt it important for my students to know there was one place at school where they did not have to pretend. There were days where I could see it took all my students had to get through the day. Many times this ended up with blow-ups at other students, or disruptive behavior in the classroom.

For the rest of the semester, I believe my students responded to my request for them to bring their true selves to class. Did this mean that everything was always lovely and perfect? No. And it should not have been. That is not the reality the students were living. That is not the reality in any student's life. But it meant that the students knew they had a place in the school to relax. Sometimes this meant a meltdown, or a "take 30" in the back of the room. Mostly it meant an overall reduction of tension in the classroom, as well as fewer students getting sent to the office. My students showed an amazing ability to recognize when they needed to step back and rarely misused the carpet. The reality of my classroom was complex. Students were dealing with difficult situations both inside and outside of school. There is no particular incident I can mention to prove that this approach worked. It has more to do with an overall feeling that the classroom environment improved.

I asked my students to bring their true selves to my classroom because I believe you have to start from a real place as a teacher. This can be a scary thing to do, but I am not about surface-y interactions. Marginalized students especially have to put on a mask to protect themselves at school. Safety is hugely important in the classroom. If students do not feel safe enough to be who they are in the moment, to not check their feelings and personalities at the door, is that classroom really safe? As I look back on the rest of the semester, I want to emphasize that this request was not a magical cure for classroom management. I asked for my students' true selves, and my students delivered. I had to step up and be ready to accept their true selves. My students felt safe enough to be vulnerable in my classroom, and it was my job to maintain a safe environment so as not to shatter their trust. As a teacher, you have to be up for the struggles and the difficult times. That is where you find out who you really are. That is when your students find out who you really are, and hopefully, who they really are. Do not stray away from those moments of difficulty and struggle. Walk through them with your students, using your true selves as the guides.

There are several excellent sources that define and explain action research for beginning teachers in this next section of the chapter. I attempt to define action research and how it can be used with beginning teachers, but any further work you do will help you understand its purposes and functions even better and more completely. Complete references for the following sources are given in the reference section in the back of the book.

Anderson et al., *Studying Your Own School* (1995)

Cochran-Smith and Lytle, *Inside/Outside* (1993)

Dana and Yendol-Hoppey, *The Reflective Educator's Guide to Classroom Research* (2008)

Gitlin and Bullough, *Becoming Students of Teaching* (1995)

The Holmes Group, chapter on inquiry in *Tomorrow's Teachers* (1990)

Sergiovanni, chapter on inquiry in *Leadership for the Schoolhouse* (1996)

When introducing student teachers to the notion of conducting an action research project during their student teaching experience, students typically ask several questions: What is action research? How do I do it? What will I get out of it?

What Is Action Research?

Action research is a form of inquiry typically done by teachers in school settings. Professionals in different fields conduct action research, too, but the energy and work on action research in education has become significant over the past three decades. Action research is usually focused on studying a problem or question or issue that is prominent in the classroom and upon which specific actions may be taken. Data for an action research study are usually qualitative, as opposed to quantitative (though using quantitative data should by no means be excluded from the work, if necessary). The goal of the researcher is to portray the qualities of the scene and not necessarily to measure something in order to prove some significant, quantifiable change (such as "in response to behavioral prompts, students raised their hands 50% more often"). The point is to actually affect change in the classroom in order to enhance the learning of students and to tell the story of that process.

What teachers who study their own classrooms do is conduct a cycle of action inquiry in four stages, typically (the following description of an action cycle comes from the excellent description of the action research cycle in Anderson et al., 1995, *Studying Your Own School*):

- Identifying and understanding a problem, issue, or question that is of immediate concern in the classroom setting
- Designing and taking actions to address the problem, issue, or question directly in the classroom
- Observing what happens as a result of the actions taken and collecting "data" to document what is happening
- Reflecting on what happened and determining new courses of action, conclusions, and implications.

Related to the question "What is action research?" is the question "Why engage in it in the first place?" and the associated question "Isn't learning to teach and teaching itself hard enough without adding more to do?" Well, teachers should have a predisposition to critically engage the decisions they make on a daily and moment-by-moment basis. Acting and living personally and professionally requires people to exercise a certain form of personal, intellectual discipline, even from the beginning and perhaps especially from the beginning, with regard to the decisions they make when acting on the behalf of children as teachers. And action research, when done efficiently and smartly, shouldn't be considered an "add-on" to teaching. It should be a normal part of what we do as teachers, and we should build it into our daily routines—as much as planning, paperwork, and eating lunch with friends— as an acceptable and normal use of time by teachers. The moral grounding for action research by teachers is that professional development and improved teaching practices that can benefit children can come when teachers carefully and systematically examine what it is they do and why they do it.

How Do I Do Action Research?

Perhaps the first and most logical step toward answering the question "How do I do action research?" is finding out what interesting questions and concerns emerge from your initial experiences as a teacher in the field. This is often the most difficult stage of the action cycle for beginning teachers. At the beginning of student teaching, so much is happening. Just trying to keep up with the pace of planning, teaching, and assessing student work is difficult. Some students of teaching are so caught up in trying to master the technical, routine matters of teaching that they are unaware of some of the deeper issues, problems, and questions at hand. It is essential to engage in action research for precisely this reason: the act engages you from the beginning in the deeper questions of teaching. It's not that taking roll and keeping order aren't important, but they aren't the crucial matters for teaching.

What I suggest to students of teaching who will be conducting action inquiry is that they keep a reflective journal from the beginning of student teaching, part of which they should plan to devote to noting observations, questions, and problems that arise in the classroom. Perhaps one of these initial observations will yield issues, questions, or problems that will give rise to a topic for study, action, and reflection during the semester.

I also ask that students of teaching attend to several criteria for choosing an issue, question, or problem to study more closely. First of all, is the issue, question, or problem *substantial?* What I mean by substantial is that the issue, question, or problem merits deeper study. And, can the study be sustained? Is it meaningful, potentially, to the teacher, the students, and to a wider public, including peers and colleagues in the school site? Also, is there enough that is interesting about the topic to warrant taking specific actions to address it in the classroom?

If the answer to the question raised seems incredibly obvious, or technical, or inane, then perhaps the topic isn't worth the time and commitment. Perhaps recognizing that seniors have "senioritis" is important, but can an in-depth study of the issue be defended, and if taken up, can it be sustained? What might we possibly learn from the inquiry beyond the fact that many seniors have senioritis? Of course, one could argue that the most mundane question is crucial, and that the study of it would make a substantial contribution to the teacher's development and his or her teaching and student learning in the classroom. But it is difficult to argue cogently and persuasively for some topics, and therefore they should be discouraged and avoided.

Second, is the issue, question, or problem *consequential?* What I mean by consequential is determining early whether or not taking action in some regard will have any observable, or particularly scene-altering impact. Does addressing the topic with action stand to yield significant consequences in the classroom? For instance, will adjusting the size of groups engaged in learning activities have a significant impact on your teaching and student achievement? Of course, we don't know the answer unless we conduct an action research project on the problem, but before we even start, do we have a sense that addressing the topic will have consequences in the classroom that we can defend in terms of focusing on student achievement and teacher development?

And third, though there are other vital considerations beyond the three discussed here, does the action inquiry have the *potential to yield principles for curriculum and teaching?* If the topic is potentially substantial and consequential, can the topic yield principles about teaching and learning that can inform a beginning teacher's conceptions of teaching practice *and* be shared with a wider pubic? Does a study of "making parental contacts" have the potential to yield principles about the role of such contacts in student learning, in community involvement, or in teacher agency for student achievement, for instance, and what might those conclusions be? If the answer of an extensive inquiry is that parental contacts are a good thing and we ought to have more of them, then the topic, either in its own right or because of the inquirer's lack of depth, ought to be avoided. Bottom line, consider conducting a study that will have an impact on you, students, and the school in some substantial, consequential, and principled way, or keep looking for a topic. An excellent one is waiting for you right inside the classroom.

Sample Questions for Action Research from Preservice Teacher Projects

- How can I more completely engage "quiet" girls in my language arts classrooms?
- How can I best group students for enhanced academic achievement?
- What are the best methods for using technology and manipulatives in math?
- How do I teach/reach students who are seemingly "unmotivated" to learn?
- What role does alternative/authentic assessment play in student achievement?
- How do we make classrooms more "inclusive" for students with special needs?

REFLECTION

Consider how each of the previous questions might constitute a substantial, consequential, and principled action inquiry.

Once you have identified a topic for study, it is necessary to carefully plan how to take action to address the question or problem. This stage represents the day-to-day engagement in the question and involves the focused brainstorming of possible solutions and approaches to taking actions that may help in answering the question. I suggest that students write a short proposal laying out what they intend to do in the study. The proposal typically has four parts: (1) Describe the question, problem, or issue for study; (2) Describe the specific actions you anticipate taking to address the question, problem, or issue; (3) Describe the means by which you will collect data on your actions; (4) Speculate on what you think might happen during the study and how conducting this research will help make you a better teacher.

Jenn Reid's action inquiry proposal illustrates the four parts of a successful proposal.

Case Report: Speak for Yourself: Encouraging Girls' Voices in the Classroom

—Jenn Reid, preservice teacher

Problem   After a summer class that focused on gender issues in schools and classrooms, I began to discuss the matter with mentor teachers and students at school. Based on my early perceptions of the classes I am teaching in which so many quiet girls rarely participate in class discussions and other activities, I believe it is important for teachers to defy cultural norms and create a classroom environment where all students feel comfortable speaking and actually have the opportunity to do so. My initial goal for the project is to find practical methods to elicit girls' voices in the classes I teach.

Action   After struggling somewhat with the transition between recognizing and understanding the problem and taking action, I decided with my mentor teachers to begin engaging students in our classrooms through some specific teaching approaches designed to bring out more voices in the classroom. We will design more personal journal prompts for students to relate and share their reactions to text; we will create more small group discussion opportunities; we will call on students to share and read their journal responses to the literature; we will call purposefully on quiet girls to speak during class time.

Observation   I will keep a journal recording observation notes on events and perceptions of the planned actions during class; I will collect artifacts, primarily student work consisting mainly of journal entries; I will elicit specific reflections from students and teachers about what is happening (or not) with regard to student participation in class; I will observe my mentors teach, focusing on gender-related issues for teaching; my mentor teachers will observe my teaching and coach me on how to help students participate more; and I will interview quiet girls in my classroom.

Reflection and Revision   I plan to analyze all of my data and tell the story of the class, in writing, through the voices of quiet girls. In retrospect, after completing the project, I find that my inquiry informs everything I do as a beginning teacher, and perhaps the interactions on the topic with faculty and students in the setting had a long-term impact on the assumptions and practices surrounding teaching and learning in the school.

Because classrooms, teaching, and students are dynamic, I recognize that a proposal, a beginning place, may change as an action study progresses. In fact, a project might change completely when the student realizes that the question that is most pertinent in his or her experiences as a preservice teacher is not reflected in the chosen topic. I always allow students to shift, though, because learning will happen as a result. There is form to the process of action research and recognizing and understanding it helps, but the processes, the rules, and the forms don't rule all. Instead, individuals in context decide direction, focus, and depth as he or she encounters the topic, teaching, curriculum, and students all firsthand.

Having said this, the next step is the careful and systematic collection of data that will be used to analyze the results of your action on the question at hand. There is a myriad of ways to collect data that fit the work of teaching on a daily basis. One common tool used by teachers who conduct action research is to keep a daily reflective journal that most teacher education programs already require as an essential activity during student teaching. You might simply gear this assignment toward the action question, issue, or problem at hand. In the journal, you might keep track of observations of classroom scenarios or events, transcripts of conversations and interviews with selected respondents, reflections on particular artifacts such as lesson plans or student work.

Cooperating teachers might keep detailed observation notes on your actions focused on addressing your question, problem, or issue. They might also conduct interviews with students and colleagues who might help you understand your work better. You might collect student work, keep a detailed bank of lesson plans and reflections on how they worked, and/or talk to students and note their comments yourself. All of these things are activities that teachers do; your charge as a teacher researcher is to keep track of them. I recommend that students keep everything they do for the action project in one central location; this makes dumping data in one place less time-consuming and organizing materials for analysis later much easier.

At some point, usually near the end of the student teaching experience or other field experience, you have to quit collecting data and analyze the results of your actions. At this stage, organizing your materials and preparing a report of your findings and experiences are critical steps. Student teaching interns report the experiences and the findings of their studies to their teaching peers and colleagues in the school site. The idea is that beginning teachers have something to contribute to the knowledge base of teaching.

Their inquiries about teaching and learning improve the work teacher leaders do when colleagues engage in their inquiries with them and hear the results of their inquiries.

What Can I Get Out of Action Research as a Beginning Teacher Leader?

Before giving an answer to this question, a case study may serve to make several points.

Look Who's Talking: Learning from Student Teachers
(*Badiali, 2000*)

Perhaps one of the most interesting and powerful examples of inquiry was an investigation by Jenn Reid, who interned in senior English with DJ Hammond at Madeira Jr/Sr High School in Cincinnati. Jenn was interested in the issue of gender equity in high school; more specifically, she was interested in the way in which senior girls participated in their classes. She had read widely on the subject as part of a senior project at the university, including books like Pipher's *Reviving Ophelia* (1994) and Orenstein's *Schoolgirls* (1995). Jenn had attended an all girls' school where participation was never a problem. Why, then, she asked, were girls silent, or silenced, in schools of mixed gender?

DJ was interested in this issue, too, because she observed girls in her classes who were bright and articulate but unwilling to say much during class discussion. As part of their teaching together, Jenn, the intern teacher, and DJ, the 25-year veteran, devised a plan to collect information from the senior girls in several of their classes. They interviewed girls at regular intervals during the semester. They solicited journal responses that asked how the girls felt about speaking out in class, about expressing their views, and about their "air time" compared with the boys in the room.

Instead of the typical superior/subordinate relationship that often exists between mentee and mentor, Jenn and DJ were full partners together in the research and the results of the inquiry proved profound. The data Jenn and DJ collected surprised them both. Girls spoke and wrote about feeling inferior in discussions. They were afraid of the social consequences of saying something "dumb." They worried about what boys might think about their comments. Jenn was confirming for herself what she had read the semester before. She and DJ began devising classroom strategies to encourage more active participation from the girls in their classes. They discussed the issue with the classes. The two of them had deep and meaningful conversations about teaching, about curriculum, and about the nature of girls' socialization.

At the end of the semester, there is an opportunity for all of the interns to take 20 minutes to report their findings from their inquiry projects to the entire faculty. Jenn made her presentation to about 25 Madeira teachers, university professors, and several visitors from other schools. She presented data in the form of quotes from the interviews, girls' writing samples, and anecdotal accounts of classroom events. The teachers, especially those teaching senior girls, listened intently. The presentation was powerful, sometimes tearful. At the end of her presentation, the head of the math department stood up and said, "That's it! Every female in my class will participate tomorrow and from now on! I will find a way to make that happen."

Later, then school superintendent, Michelle Hummell, who was in the audience for Jenn's presentation, said that she was stunned at the powerful response to Jenn's report. She said, "I could have spent thousands of dollars on a staff development program about gender equity in the classroom and never would have gotten such a response from teachers. They have read the studies. They know what the national data show. It's just that this report was about us. These are *our* girls. They have names and faces and we know their parents."

Jenn's inquiry project was the talk of the faculty for days, even weeks. Several teachers acknowledged that they saw senior girls in a new light. The wonderful thing about making these projects public is that they create discussion among the faculty. Interns enjoy a sort of political immunity with regard to their findings. Veterans can always write them off as just superficial investigations by a neophyte discovering the craft of teaching, or they can learn from what they discover. But it is obvious by their questions, during and after the presentations, that teachers are willing to learn from interns who can provide them with observable data about the workplace. And interns feel pretty good about being able to give something back to the setting that hosted them for a semester.

Beginning your career as a reflective teacher and as an action researcher gives you a lease on a long life as a teacher leader. As a result of engaging in action research:

- You enter the teaching profession aware that teaching is complex and difficult, but deeply engaging and exciting.
- You engage the process of finding and taking reasoned approaches to problems and answering questions while systematically determining if, how, and why the approaches and answers work with students.
- You learn to discuss with colleagues and your students the deeper questions surrounding teaching and learning, far beyond the routine questions of teaching.

Jenn Reid has the last word about the impact of action research on her development as a beginning teacher.

Response

I always knew that I was destined to be in school for the rest of my life. I love school; I love classes; I love learning. However, I had absolutely no idea of the incredible learning that goes on in the life of a teacher. I enjoy learning when I have a desire to learn or understand something in particular. This inquiry project helped me focus that desire to hear girls' voices during my first teaching experience. With so much to absorb, I was still able to focus on the many lessons I was learning from my students. I learned how to listen, not just to girls, but to what all students are trying to teach me. I learned to listen to my cooperating teachers; I could not have found more supportive women to guide me through this semester.

This student teaching experience would have been incredible even without the inquiry project because my cooperating teachers are exceptional mentors. But without the action research component, it would just not have been as rich. My teachers made me feel like a professional teacher while conducting this research. The interest that the faculty at the school and university expressed in my research made me feel like a professional. Because of the incredible knowledge I have gained from the girls in my classrooms, I feel like a professional. Conducting an inquiry project while student teaching distinguishes this learning experience as unforgettable. I met countless young women whose voices have changed the way I'll view teaching forever.

—Jenn Reid, preservice teacher

7

SCHOOL REFORM AND TEACHER LEADERSHIP

Defining School Reform

I use the term "school reform" reluctantly here, feeling as though it would be more responsible and accurate to use the term "school renewal," a concept coined by John Goodlad to refer to the inside/out developmental work that all communities and organizations, like schools, need to do to keep their purposes and mission in focus and to do good work for the benefit of society. The term "school renewal" stands in contradistinction to "school reform," which almost always refers to a top-down approach foisted upon unwilling actors by outsiders, outside/in. "The main difference between reform and renewal is that reform comes from the outside; renewal is a cultural process from the inside" (J. Goodlad, personal communication, March 2011).

But because the term "school reform" is so pervasive in the literature and discourse of public schooling and teacher education, I use it while hoping the reader understands throughout the conversation that my hope is for a softer, more professional approach to change in schools, teaching, and learning, which all should take place over time with the collaborative leadership of parents, students, teachers, and administrators. Educational renewal is a process of inquiry and professional development that builds upon the best of aspects of community or educational processes already in play in a setting. I'll use the terms "school renewal" and "educational renewal" whenever the story more closely approaches this stronger, sounder notion of school change that I'm thinking of, but for the most part will stick with the term "school reform" in order to deal with and reflect the current reality.

The key transition here is that as a teacher leader you will be practicing and inquiring all the time. Vital will be combining a local perspective and self-knowledge with at least a fledgling understanding of what is going on in the wider world of schooling and education practices. Knowing more about the "bigger picture" is an important aspect of teacher leadership, and it ultimately will help you toward having a positive impact on the curriculum, teaching, and learning in your own classroom and school.

A Historical Perspective

Phillip Schlechty (1990), a well-known school reform expert, asserts that today's schools do a better job of what we used to want schools to do than in any period in our history. The problem is that we don't want them to do most of those same things anymore. In previous eras, schools served very different purposes than they must serve today. As society changed, the purpose for schools changed. In early America the purpose of school was to enculturate the young into the values and ideals of the religious traditions of families as well as into the ideals of the republic. Teaching was thought of as a "sacred" profession because society entrusted the future of youth with the teacher. The typical school curriculum was based on reading the classics, studying Greek and Latin, and learning mathematics. White Anglo-Saxon morality was promoted. Bible stories were used to teach elementary reading.

As the country was being settled and the American frontier moved west over and through native peoples and communities, civic literacy became important. Of course, civic literacy was important only to a select few within a small racial and social segment of society. Black slaves and Native Americans had little to no access to schooling, or to basic literacy for that matter. This was the case as late as the first years following the end of the Civil War, a period during which "county schools" emerged for Blacks in the South (Anderson, 1993). The history of denying opportunity for education runs throughout American history, from the lack of attention to freed slaves in the Jim Crow South and in treacherously oppressive Northern towns before, during, and after this period to the culturally destructive practices of moving young Native American children from their homes to government schools.

Thomas Jefferson, rather ironically in retrospect and regardless of the social inequities of the time, said that a democracy could not be both ignorant and free, therefore schools were charged with inducting the youth into pursuing a responsible civic life. During the eighteenth century, America was a rural, agrarian, Christian, and largely white country. With the rise of the industrial revolution, however, the country changed dramatically and so did the purposes of schools. Waves of immigrants from Europe brought myriad customs and religious beliefs with them throughout the 19th and 20th centuries. Immigrants sent their children to schools often with the expectation that they would be Americanized. Schools were faced with the task of attending to the needs of widely diverse student backgrounds and somehow preparing them for life in America.

Schools, desperate to find an organizational pattern to accomplish such a daunting task, turned to successful models used by industry and business. Assembly lines, hierarchies of bureaucratic control, division of labor, and other efficiency models influenced if not dictated how schools would be organized. School structures soon began to mirror their industrial counterparts, factories, and offices. The purpose of schools changed from promoting civic literacy to sorting and selecting students for various kinds of work in an urban, industrial society or a rural, agrarian one. (For strong overviews of the development of public schools in America, see Kaestle, *Pillars of the Republic*; Cremin, *Traditions of American Education*; and/or Tyack, *The One Best System*.)

America's schools commonly created divergent curriculum, and tracking students by academic ability (or academic promise as "assured" by IQ tests beginning in the early part of the 20th century) became the apparatus for separating young children into groups according to their perceived capacity to do certain types of school work. Teachers during this era shed their sacred garb to become technicians who employed something that did not exist in the era before—student failure. Curriculum became "teacher proof," deskilling the profession and emphasizing a narrow band of intelligence through which to differentiate among student "abilities." If you look at schools today, you can still see the legacy of the industrial revolution in school structures and in behavior patterns. No wonder Schlechtey and others argue that schools organized in this way no longer serve our society very well.

Contemporary society is very different from any bygone eras. Children today have very different needs. America is no longer mainly rural and agrarian, nor is it going through the throes of building industries that need cheap labor to work on assembly lines. Schools today cannot simply *identify* a student's capacity; they must *develop* a student's capacity. Although many would cling to a simpler time when the task of teaching was much easier and clear-cut, today's teachers have to deal with the preparation of students for the information/technology age. Today, America is for the most part multi-ethnic, multi-religious, multi-lingual, and urban. The information age demands that all students think, inquire, and solve problems. Teachers must be leaders who are wise enough and creative enough to develop curricula that engage student interest, while at the same time preparing them for the complexities of today's fast-paced way of life. Indeed, teaching is so complex that it makes rocket science look like two-digit addition.

At the beginning of a new millennium, schools can no longer afford to attend to the purposes of old. The problem is that we have been left with schools organized to serve yesterday's students while the schools we need must serve today's and tomorrow's citizens. We still have a school calendar based on the agricultural calendar. Those two months off in the summer that most schools still give originated to allow for children to be home working with the planting and harvesting. We have a curriculum that still tries to determine what capacities students have so they may be sorted into various career paths instead of a curriculum designed to build capacity of all children to use their minds well and exercise democratic citizenship. Superiors in schools typically hand down decisions for workers to carry out. Shared decision making is still mostly theoretical in schools today. Today's schools, even the best schools, operate using a structure that no longer fits the needs of society or its children. School organizations today are a result of a patchwork legacy from bygone eras on the one hand, and an effort to emulate efficient businesses on the other.

It is precisely because we don't fully understand our history and the fact that we try to emulate business organizations that efforts to reform schools have failed. Most people conceive of schools as bureaucracies arranged hierarchically from the school board to the superintendent, to central office personnel, to building administrators, to teachers, to students. When schools are not performing well, many people think it has to do with some breakdown in the hierarchy, some breakdown in the bureaucracy and its promises of efficiency and competence.

The Current Reform Agenda

And so we have the current, massive school reform agenda that is driven by test scores and the pursuit of them by school people and school wannabes, from the federal government's chief executives in the education field, through national and state legislatures and governors' offices, to wealthy billionaire businessmen, and ambitious, obedient school leaders who advance because they cater to the status quo. The billions being pumped into schools by the federal government and by businesses and philanthropic foundations have certain things in common. All of the approaches ignore the realities of how teachers and schools work, how communities behave, and what matters most to people. Check out the annual Gallup/Phi Delta Kappan poll, called the Public's Attitudes Toward Public Schools, for a more realistic and accurate view of what citizens and parents think of public schools today, about key issues, and about what they want out of them as citizens experiencing them today (*http://www.pdkintl.org/kappan/poll.htm*).

As a result of seeming malaise propagated by powerful outsiders and the media, the lament over a lack of achievement and commitment rambles on, all the while picking up steam and leading to the forced judgment of teachers merely through test scores and the ultimate ignominy, closing schools or reconstituting staffs because scores don't go up enough. All of this madness, some say, is about the money. If only the public's money could be administered privately, some powerful people say, through vouchers and private charters, schools would improve. Besides the very evidence that suffices as the "coin of the realm," test scores, showing that this is almost universally not the case, the constant banter about privatizing education and "reforming" it carries with it this hidden, but obvious underside. Who stands to benefit if public schools close, if test scores "reveal" a lack of acceptable achievement, if leaders see only one sign of academic progress as telling the whole story about children, their families, and communities, as opposed to just a significant part that could be used effectively for diagnostic purposes, as most tests were originally conceived for?

All of this is fodder for critics like Gerald Bracey—who spent the past 20 years working to help expose the problems with this technical, top-down, standards-based and high stakes testing approach to school reform that is winning the day—to suggest a different agenda for public education renewal. Unfortunately, before his recent book, most of his words fell on closed minds and hearts in the field of education. To look at his latest work, check out a copy of his last book, *Education Hell: Rhetoric vs. Reality* (2009). The biggest problem is that no one is paying attention to Bracey and other critics (see Poetter, *The Education of Sam Sanders*, 2006). And this opens the door to wealthy billionaires who are not interested in addressing the root causes of underachievement, such as poverty, but instead treat schools as symptomatic of the nation's ills, such as laziness, inefficiency, lacking goals, lacking control, etc. (Dillon, 2011; Beamish, 2011).

Ultimately, their reform efforts turn out to be unsuccessful, pointing to the decades and centuries-long disconnect between the notion of reforming a system from the top down and outside/in, as opposed to dealing with situations and people where they are, on a local level, from the inside/out. There is no doubt that more top-down reforms are coming, as the government and businesses seek to increase their control over the agenda of public schools and the ends that matter. The Common Core State Standards Initiative has rumbled through the states and is leading inevitably to new tests, new assessments, and new curriculum; but the entire movement has proceeded uncritically, with little teacher input. Corporate interests and control of teachers lie at the center of the movement, leaving the larger purposes of schooling underserved as well as the deeper issues of public education largely unexamined and under-addressed (**http://www.corestandards.org;** Tienken, 2010, 2012). Billionaires are reloading for more reform efforts even in the wake of unsuccessful ones (Dillon, 2011; Beamish, 2011). When will the madness end? Can it? Where will schools, teachers, children, and parents be when the dust settles?

Mindscapes for School Reform

Sergiovanni suggests that people have a certain notion of school organization—a mindscape—that is erroneous. They see schools organized rather like the inner workings of an old wind-up clock with wheels and gears and springs all aligning to run efficiently. When schools do not work, these people see the problem as one of realigning the inner workings, fixing a gear, tightening a spring. However, Sergiovanni points out that this mindscape is false, that schools are not at all like clocks, not at all like hierarchies. Sergiovanni claims that schools are more like small communities. There are no gears, no springs, nothing to align. When you think of schools like machines, you approach school change with inappropriate assumptions. Schools are social sites where individuals interact and relate in complex ways more similar to the interactions found in some small towns or neighborhoods. Schools are more like communities and families, and when thought of as communities and families, strategies for change must be compatible with that mindscape.

Many elementary schools and PreK education settings have used the "community" approach for years to organize themselves and to function effectively. Some of the best early childhood education environments create a sense of togetherness similar to a large, democratic family. Secondary schools are less likely to think of themselves this way. Faculties there tend to be arranged along subject area boundaries that define independent departments. At least one description of the difference between elementary and secondary school mindscapes is that elementary schools often think in terms of teaching "students," and secondary schools often think in terms of teaching "subjects." One strong hope for reform and reorganization of secondary education exists in the middle school movement, which values the notion of integrating curriculum and instruction across subject areas and building human capacity among teachers and students. This movement is having an impact on middle childhood education as well as on the education of younger and older students (see *Turning Points*, 2000).

Recently there has been an emphasis on regarding the school as a learning community where all people—students, teachers, administrators, and parents—think of themselves as learners. People learn individually, but they also learn as a group. Teachers, in this way of thinking, become responsible not only for the welfare of children in their own classroom, but also for the welfare of the entire school. John Goodlad would call this idea "stewardship." Teacher leaders are stewards of their whole school; this responsibility becomes a moral dimension that accompanies teaching.

REFLECTION

Keeping in mind that you were one of the people for whom schools have worked very well, what is it about the present structure of schools that does not permit the best learning for all children?

Linda Darling-Hammond, an eminent scholar in the field of school reform, says: "The new model of school reform must seek to develop communities of learning grounded in communities of democratic discourse" (in Goodlad, 1994, p. 195). The new model of school organization that relies on notions of democracy at the core not only creates a space for teacher leadership, it sets an expectation for it. The new model of school organization not only promotes democratic discourse, it regards it as the fundamental grounding for it. Teacher leaders, therefore, will have to have a deep understanding of and commitment to the democratic ideals underlying the American way of life.

Considering School Reform

Very few people who care about public schools would argue that what we do in them across the board is always good and effective. It would be erroneous, as well, to argue that public schools are in ruins, in both concept and in practice. Instead public schools fulfill many valuable functions in our society and democracy, and schools do an enormously vital and often thankless job fairly well across the board and in many cases very well. For a description of the public school system's successes see the report "Do You Know ... The Latest Good News About American Education?" published by the Center on Education Policy (**http://www.cep-dc.org**) and the American Youth Policy Forum (**http://www.aypf.org**).

However, there is always room for all sorts of improvement in schools. At least one prominent scholar in the field of school reform points to the cases of schools where dissatisfaction *among the faculty* with regard to the status quo of teaching and learning in that site constitutes in itself evidence that good things are probably happening there for students and learning. Complacency is certainly an enemy of change and reform. People who are edgy in terms of looking for better ways to get the job done, searching for answers, inquiring, and adjusting practices responsibly pursue the kinds of reform in schools represented by teacher leadership (Glickman, 1993).

That being said, teachers hold the key to school reform, and without them, any new process or program is doomed to failure. We don't get anywhere as caring citizens or as a society in terms of education if teachers aren't willing to at least consider moving. You, as a beginning teacher, are key in constituting a teaching force that looks reflectively and critically at current practices and makes the needed adjustments across the board in education, including changing typical classroom pedagogical practices as well as curricular and structural reforms across a wider spectrum. Teachers must see the need for change and commit themselves to shifting their practices, and perhaps more fundamentally, their conceptions of the purposes of schooling, teaching, and learning altogether.

This can be a difficult task for veteran and beginning teachers alike. The challenge for the veteran is that the call to reform from outsiders, even the internal recognition of the need for reform by the individual him or herself or other insiders, sounds a chord that may in his or her mind discount or disapprove of all the supposed good work that came before. For a teacher who used thoughtful lectures and carefully prepared tests for twelve years in an award-winning biology program to shift gears in order to develop all new lessons and assessments utilizing hands-on, laboratory-based lessons in her classes takes a monumental recognition of the need for change despite the seemingly sound results of previous efforts.

For the beginning teacher, there may be little recognition or understanding of the point of changing or reconceptualizing teaching practice when a baseline of practice hasn't yet been established. "How do I change something I haven't yet experienced?" But this question discounts the wealth of experience that student teaching, early field experiences, and an apprenticeship of observation represent in a teacher's early life in the profession. Beginning teachers can and must be able to judge the worth and effectiveness of certain commitments to particular teaching practices. They can judge and support conceptions regarding the value and worth in certain types of educational programs before they enter teaching. You must be aware of the need to be able to do these things and actually be able to do them in order to be a teacher leader. You no doubt will be asked to provide leadership in this area, perhaps being appointed to a committee to examine the worth of a school-wide reform model or even to create a new model with others.

Considering Varying Conceptions of School Reform

Let me be clear that school reform or "restructuring," as it is often referred to in the educational literature, doesn't merely have to do with building new buildings or reconstituting governance structures in schools or changing the school schedule. These are all very common concerns that exist in the subject and literature of school reform in schools these days, but I'm not primarily concerned with them specifically as roads to reform that we might bank all our hopes on or even spend much of our time with. It doesn't mean that these and other concerns aren't important; teachers and scholars have devoted their whole lives in pursuit of positive answers to technical questions and concerns in these narrower areas.

I'm not talking either about the current wave of school reform movements in the area of school vouchers and school choice. In general, school voucher programs are politically charged "restructuring" movements in which constituents attempt to set aside public moneys to be used for schooling by citizens at their own discretion, most likely to pay for or offset the costs of tuition in a private parochial or independent educational institution. Programs of this sort can be found in experimental sites all across the country, and they are gaining ground as the walls between church and state, in some cases, come tumbling down. The jury is still out on whether or not these movements will be "successful" in and of themselves and whether or not they will proliferate as a result.

School choice programs are related to the discussion of school vouchers, but getting a voucher isn't the only way to exercise school choice. Many school districts across the country are making it possible for students and their families to choose alternative forms and locations for their public educational experiences. Students are no longer always tied to the school they should attend by geography, but may qualify or may be chosen at random to participate in a school program that is more appealing or appropriate for them in a different part of town (see Poetter & Knight-Abowitz, "Possibilities and Problems of School Choice," 2001).

These choice options might be "magnet" programs, specially designed, thematic programs meant to draw students from many areas to the school (thus the term "magnet) such as a fine arts or science magnet school. Another set of choice options exists in "charter" schools, new public schools chartered with a district or a state (other chartering entities exist in different locations, such as universities, for instance) that typically focus on innovative curriculum and instruction and typically exempt from many state controls, including testing. In general, I support the general notion of school choice, as long as students are not chosen by so-called "merit" or "achievement" to attend public institutions of choice, but are chosen randomly. I do not support under any circumstances the movement to support private, K–12 educations of citizens with public funds through school vouchers. Both the notions of awarding public moneys to some students K–12 based on "merit" and the use of public moneys for private use tear at our democratic fabric, separate us out further, distance us from each other.

Three Prominent Conceptions of School Reform

Several other conceptions of what school reform is today besides the ones previously mentioned dot the landscape of educational thought and practice. Again, this list and exposition are not exhaustive, but constitute beginning points. I will highlight a few of the conceptions in order to familiarize you with the terrain and to help in making several points for you to consider strongly about the challenges of school reform for teacher leadership. What I am more concerned with here is why and how persons and professional groups purport to change the overall nature and structure of schooling to serve new constituencies and new sets of purposes and reasons for schooling over and against long accepted purposes and reasons embedded in school systems and educational practices.

Intensification Reforms

The first conception is that what we do in schools and have been doing in schools for nearly a century isn't flawed in terms of teaching or curricular practices, and that the key to reform means "intensifying" what we are already doing because we know it works if we could just do more of the same better. We can rectify, "intensifiers" argue, the supposed sorry state of student achievement in schools (a position certainly contestable) by intensifying the rate and quality at which the transmission of knowledge to students takes place and by holding students and teachers accountable for learning through scores on standardized tests. We can increase the time that students are in schools during the day, spend more time on subjects that are included on the tests, have students go to school year round, and/or make it more rigorous for teachers to get certified, for example. Intensify.

The intensification approach to reform is wrapped up in efforts such as mandated statewide achievement and proficiency testing, especially when those tests are used for more than diagnostic purposes and they become high stakes hurdles, publicized by the media, and constitute barriers to promotion and graduation for students as well as access to funds and programs by schools and school systems. (See Fullan, 1992, for a discussion of "intensification" and Bracey, 1998 and 2009, for a discussion of the inaccuracies in the pronouncements of doom in public education. In terms of academic achievement, Bracey contends that we are doing better today across the board in nearly every way in public schools and that reform approaches, while still ongoing, of course, have worked to achieve these ends.)

I don't want to give the impression that everything about American public education needs reforming by talking extensively about reform in this chapter. For so many students of teaching, like you, their experiences in schools have been good. I am glad that students had good experiences in school and that they have a positive viewpoint of the schools they will soon enter as teachers, but I want them and you to have a realistic view of the terrain and to realize that your work as a teacher leader requires more than reproducing the status quo or the images of schooling experienced in the past. I believe in the public education system, and defend it at nearly every turn. But I definitely don't think that doing more of the same with more intensity is the answer to the fundamental questions that are important to ask and answer as teacher leaders.

The perspective of those who support intensification rests on the importance of competition, and viewing the school as a field upon which the game of accumulating knowledge is played. The primary measures of success are test scores; they constitute the tickets by which citizens have access to goods such as higher education and jobs. I don't dispute that there is some truth to their claims; what I do dispute is the centering of an educational system on them. Perhaps an aspect of teacher leadership is to redefine the purposes of schooling and create practices to support them that have a great deal of worth. Maybe the worth will be more than a ticket to a good college or job (this doesn't eliminate the possibility that a different set of reasons for schooling and good schooling experiences under different conditions will mean increased access to certain goods like education and jobs). School reform should not be viewed merely as an intensification of the approaches that are already in place.

Local, Grassroots Reforms

The second conception is the notion of local reform, or grassroots efforts at changing the basic purposes of an education and the practices that support them in a local context. Local efforts at reform respond to particular sets of problems and issues confronting smaller communities of citizens. Some of the most exciting and worthwhile attempts and results for reform happen in local situations.

The case of Gerald's work, depicted earlier in Chapter 4, which focuses on providing more opportunities for students of color to have success in mathematics, is an example of reform at the local level. His efforts surpass intensification. The point was that students needed more than increased homework and hours of instruction in mathematics; they needed to experience a whole new approach to mathematics and to be given their rightful opportunity to show their ability and skill in the subject matter without being subject to practices systematically eliminating them from competing with others in the regular classroom. Their ability to achieve in an alternative setting did not preclude their ability to come back to the regular classroom during the school year and succeed in more advanced mathematics courses with the same teachers who would have failed them before. The new program, instead, made it possible for them to experience multiple layers of success that the former system had all but eliminated for them.

This local reform movement no doubt included aspects of thought and practice that originated outside the local context. University faculty members brought knowledge from academia to bear on the situation as did ideas from professional journals and organizations such as the National Council for the Teachers of Mathematics (NCTM), for instance. But the locus for change, the original impetus for reform, is local, and the response is local. Others could appropriate the program Gerald helped design and deliver in his school into another school system or school situation, but like so many other local programs that get transplanted to other contexts, it may not work and often doesn't, especially when we think of "work" to mean that there is a long-term, positive impact on the setting that fundamentally changes how people go about their business. Local reforms often rely on the particularity of the scene and the unique passions of those working on the problems close at hand for success and long-term sustainability.

I also would hold up as examples successful local reforms like the ones undertaken by reformer Deborah Meier. Meier, famous for starting progressive public schools in Harlem such as Central Park East Elementary School in the 1970s and 1980s and for shepherding them through difficult political and economic crises over the years, began with the notion that all students could be taught and that teachers, if given the opportunity and the support of parents and administrators, have the knowledge and the power to run schools effectively in any community. Her work is eloquently portrayed in her own book *The Power of Their Ideas* (1995) and in accounts such as Bensman's *Quality Schooling in the Inner City* (1986). Meier has also been integral in national reform movements such as the Coalition of Essential Schools (*http://www.essentialschools.org*) and the Fairtest Organization (*http://www.fairtest.org*).

School-Wide Reforms

The third conception of reforms is called "school-wide." These reforms represent "wider" or "national" reform efforts that have come to be used in a variety of locales and have a profound impact on local and more widespread levels. Several networks of schools that represent particular ideological/educational points of view have sprung up around the country. Most of them emerged out of the wave of despair that clouded public education and public opinion in the wake of (1) published reports such as *A Nation at Risk* (1984) and *A Place Called School* (1984) in the mid-1980s that pointed to severe problems in the public education system, and (2) ongoing research and grant moneys supporting a search for changes to the nature of public schooling, and new conceptions of learning, curriculum practice, and pedagogical change.

John Goodlad—founder of The National Network for Educational Renewal (NNER)—focuses on the simultaneous renewal of public schools and institutions of higher education in partnership; Robert Slavin—founder of the Success for All and Roots and Wings programs—focuses on basic curriculum in the subject areas delivered using cooperative learning techniques; Ted Sizer's movement—*The Coalition of Essential Schools*—focuses on reshaping the American secondary school through nine essential elements; Henry Levin—founder of Accelerated Schools—focuses on the acceleration of student learning as opposed to remediation, and shifting the governance of the school to democratic means and co-inquiry by all member of the school community into educational problems and solutions; James Comer—founder of the School Development Program—focuses on reorganizing and refocusing urban public education to serve students and their families in communities better; E. D. Hirsch—founder of the Core Knowledge Program—focuses on a core curriculum composed of classic and basic subject matter that all Americans need to know to be "culturally literate." These reform-minded programs, among others, have founded substantive reform movements that have spread into thousands of schools during the 1990s and beyond.

In the mid-1990s, the federal government changed its rules regarding the use of Chapter I/Title I moneys, large federal grants meant to serve students in underprivileged and underfunded schools (Fashola & Slavin, 1998).

The money was typically used to support remedial programs and earmarked only for certain segments of the population in certain schools. But new regulations permit the use of Title I moneys for school-wide reform efforts in elementary schools utilizing school-wide reform models, including all of the ones listed above and several others on a list approved by the federal government. All of the school reform programs that were a part of the New American Schools design consortium were eligible for public funds. What the school-wide reform models offered were varied models of reform that schools could study, see in action, and choose to implement. Initial research on implementation of the reform models showed generally good results, even so far as raising test scores in certain locations (though many of the reform movement programs carefully avoid making promises about raising test scores or even suggesting at all that raising test scores is a concern or focus in the reform model). I have three specific concerns regarding school-wide reform models that teacher leaders should consider deeply as they enter schools, and since they will no doubt be asked to scrutinize or implement a school-wide reform model, most likely one associated with the Common Core, in their first years of teaching.

One concern is the notion of importing an outside model into a local school or district. There are several questions that must be vigorously addressed by people in any locale thinking of adopting a school-wide reform model created by someone else. To what extent does the faculty and community support a new program, especially if it stands to change drastically the kinds of things we do and how we go about making decisions? How does the new model reflect or extend the values evident in the school site? Recognizing that no model can be imported without it changing along with the reforming site, how will we go about making the aspects of the model that we want to implement our own, and how will we deal with the aspects that fall away because they are unappealing or don't seem to work? For instance, is it possible to join the Coalition of Essential Schools and stay a member and not adopt each of Sizer's nine elements that guide the reform? Or, can we have an Accelerated School while eschewing Levin's call to inquiry by essentially ignoring the structural reform in the program of creating cadres to address school problems through systematic inquiry?

The advantages of these school-wide reform models, however, are also considerable. As Fashola & Slavin (1998) noted:

The advantages of adopting these "off the shelf" instructional models are clear. School staffs need not reinvent the wheel. Organizations behind each of the school-wide models provide professional development, materials, and networks of fellow users. These reform organizations bring to a school broad experience working with high-poverty schools in many contexts. Unlike district or state staff development offices, external reform networks are invited in only if they are felt to meet a need, and they can be invited back out again if they fail to deliver. Their services can be expensive, but the costs are typically well within the Title I resources available to high-poverty school-wide projects. (p. 371)

The second concern, referred to above, is the cost of the programs. Costs vary, of course, and some programs are more costly than others. Title I moneys haven't always covered the initial start-up costs and the long-term investments needed to do selected school-wide reform models well in a school or school district. This makes it possible for schools to start and stop when they run out of money, or for schools and districts with great need being unable to afford to get started. Some schools are successful at raising other outside money to complement existing funds, but others are not. Some schools that might be ready to move don't qualify for Title I funds and can't get the monetary support needed to make bigger, deeper change from other outside sources. In the long run, careful planning and moderately aggressive financial leadership can lead to a prudent and effective expenditure of funds in a school-wide reform effort if the funds can be attained in the first place. Another related concern is the cost of what is lost because of investment in the expenditures supporting a school-wide reform model. Perhaps professional development activities for faculty get paid for but not new books for ninth grade English classes.

A third concern that needs to be firmly kept in mind is how the expenditure of money is having an impact on student learning. If the money is being spent almost exclusively on faculty development, how does such spending translate into benefits for students? If the money is being spent primarily on materials, how are the materials benefiting students, teaching, and learning? Is it enough for new materials to be available? What responsibility do we have for ensuring the effective use of the materials in the classroom? In many cases, large amounts of money have been granted to assist in reform efforts, and soon after the expenditure, the school site or district has nothing to show for it other than an empty bank account. Certainly, no one can ever guarantee that an expenditure of funds will make any difference at all. But the teacher leader's task as a reflective agent is to closely monitor the appropriate expenditure of funds, to be sure that activities being supported reflect the overall goals and purposes of the learning community, and to guard the bottom-line question, "How will our efforts benefit students?" Inquiring into this important question and being sure to document and report the results are tasks for teacher leaders and can make the efforts of reform and continuing opportunities to change and grow possible.

Preparing to Lead: What You May Be Asked to Do as a School Reformer

Many students taking this teacher leadership course who go on to teach in area schools are often asked to participate in school-wide and local reform efforts. Almost all of them get caught up in the intensification frenzy, focusing with teachers who are mentoring them on raising student test scores while learning how to teach. Some of them experience early field placements or student teaching in a reforming setting. Students of teaching get placed in all kinds of programs, those implementing national reform models and those working with and toward local reform efforts. Locally developed and model school-wide programs cannot be avoided. For instance, students who work in local middle and high school placements encounter aspects of the school-wide program High Schools That Work and Making Middle Grades Work, sponsored by the Southern Regional Education Board (**http://www.sreb.org**). When they encounter the routines and practices of teaching and learning in school sites, these frameworks have an impact on their work, and they should be aware, as teacher leaders, of what they are and how to make the most of them with students and colleagues.

People in American public schools are changing, and in many ways for the better. It is important to be aware of several pitfalls and of several promising aspects of school reform for schools and for you as a teacher leader.

There is much to learn and understand about school reform, and as a recent college graduate or current college student, especially as one who has at least been subjected to this topic through discussions of a book like this one, you will no doubt become one of the resident experts regarding school reform when you enter the school! School cultures do look for expertise when they consider change, and it so happens that your proximity to a college education in the education field may make you more aware and more conversant in the field of school reform than many of your veteran peers (this may be true in other areas as well, even in the subject areas you are licensed to teach, for instance). This is a good thing: an opportunity for you to participate in the intellectual and cultural life of the school and community from an early date in your tenure as a teacher, of course, without acting like a "know it all."

There are several productive things you can do in this regard. You can conduct inquiry on various reform models if several are being considered for your school site. You can participate on a visitation team looking at how different sites are implementing certain reform efforts. You can be an advocate for certain approaches and build support for those approaches among peers by supplying information to them and encouraging them to learn more. You can pilot certain approaches in your own classroom and/or school. These approaches might reflect those inherent to particular reform ideas and provide a baseline of data on practice in your own school with regard to a prospective reform package.

You might also be appointed to or volunteer for a faculty/staff committee interested in examining a model program more thoroughly. Or you might be asked to participate on a selection or design team. In these cases, your understanding of and skills in deliberation may make invaluable contributions to the change process. These are wonderful opportunities to participate in school reform initiatives at the grass roots, and perhaps to build professional development bridges for your own work as you consider alternatives and reflect on possible changes you can make to enhance your own teaching and/or build learning community in your classroom and school.

What you ought not to do is sit on the sidelines, just letting things happen to you without exercising your voice and intellect with regard to these matters. You may find yourself thoroughly against a reform movement taking shape in your school; teacher leadership requires that you state your case and argue against change if it is unwarranted, or if other measures haven't been given their full due to work, or if the changes proposed are immoral and will damage people or learning processes immeasurably. The point is that the teacher leader, as a reflective agent, participates in the wider and the narrower conversations regarding the direction of the school program and the conceptions of what appropriate and good teaching and learning are. Teacher leaders do not sit idly by, with so much at stake, so much professional development to gain, and so much to teach and learn. Teacher leaders participate in school reform.

Also, teacher leaders often work within organizations, such as teacher unions, to advance their work and the purposes of public education. The next chapter explores what teacher unions are, and how they can provide opportunities for teacher leadership and productive change in teaching.

Reflection: *School Renewal and Teacher Leadership*

I have been challenged a lot this semester to think about the bigger picture when it comes to teaching, as well as of the curriculum in general. In teacher leadership, it is important to think about this bigger picture because it will ultimately help you towards having a positive effect on the curriculum, teaching, and learning in your own classroom and school. I think my biggest goal as an educator is going to be forming a personal relationship with each of my students to the best of my ability and making school a positive environment for them to feel safe and welcome. This is why I think school reform (or educational renewal) is so important, because this process of professional development builds upon the best parts of a community or educational processes that are already working.

I believe there is always room for improvement in schools. Looking for better ways to get things done, adjusting practices, and inquiring are all kinds of reform that are represented in teacher leadership (something I'm taking in stride right now in my classes). It is going to fall upon me, as a recently-graduated teacher, to help other veteran teachers see the need to change and commit themselves to shifting their practices to better the educational experience for their students. This can be really difficult to do, and it has been something I've been thinking about since I've begun taking these block classes. How can I change and reconceptionalize teaching practices when I haven't even developed my own lines of practice yet? How do I change something that I haven't experienced yet? I often forget how much my experiences with field placements and student observations have taught me, not to mention all I will learn when I'll be student teaching this time next year.

Something I *can* do, however, is be a judge of the worth and value of educational programs before I enter the teaching profession. Doing this allows me and gives me the tools to be a teacher leader. I've mentioned this before in my first writing installment a couple weeks ago, but my mom has told me time and time again that one of the major points of college is to teach you how to think and ask questions. It's been a rewarding experience, especially in this class, to be able to read from texts and practice questioning and thinking about them. I am preparing myself to question and change curriculum for the better when I become a teacher and provide leadership in these areas when I enter the field.

—Nicole Geygan, preservice teacher

8

Teachers' Unions and Leadership

By Kevin M. Talbert, with Dustin Hornbeck

When I began my teaching career, fresh out of college, I was hesitant to join the union. Most of my knowledge of the form and function of unions at that time was superficial, based on perceptions largely propagated via media images of teachers' unions—think picket lines, bullhorns, and catchy chants. I was also turned off by unions' political activities and affiliations, or my perceptions of them, at least. I thought of my teaching as apolitical (though I proudly identified as a "conservative"). I knew that I would not be a "boat rocker," and thought that, ultimately, as long as I was competent, I would avoid controversy and have no need for the union or its protections.

My assumptions aligned with the dominant narrative of unions—that they were only interested in protecting teachers' jobs, working to secure "cushy" contracts and "perks," but really did not concern themselves with broader interests, especially the interests of students and their families. It did not take long, however, for me to begin to change my mind once I began to experience the day-to-day life of a teacher. Over the course of my eight years as a high school teacher, I became increasingly involved in my local

---

Kevin Talbert is the first author of this chapter, speaking from the first person point of view as a former public school teacher and union member/leader. Dustin Hornbeck, also a former union head, comments on the most recent public events driving change in teachers' unions.

teachers' union. Only then did I gain a more accurate appreciation for what the union was actually about. For starters, it was one of the few formal avenues for leadership without becoming an administrator. More important, I began to see its value in terms of a deliberative space for teachers to work toward solving issues having an impact on the district.

Admittedly, when I signed my first teaching contract, I did not fully realize what my contract even was. The document I signed was a single page that verified my acceptance of my position as a high school social studies teacher. What I came to learn, however, was that the actual teaching contract was dozens of pages long and had been negotiated long before I was hired, through a process known as *collective bargaining* that I will explain in a little more detail later in this chapter. The contract is negotiated between the union and the school board and outlines a range of "bread and butter" issues like the pay scale, medical insurance, retirement plan, and so forth. It also outlines a number of policies and procedures for the district and its professional staff, such as the plan for evaluating teachers, the length of the workday, and even class size. Of course, many of these issues (e.g., class size) may vary from district to district, but nearly all contracts contain quite similar pieces, especially because law sets so much of their contents anyway, such as the number of school days.

Later in the chapter, I will discuss some of the more well-known yet controversial parts of union contracts, particularly seniority and tenure policies, "RIF" (Reduction in Force) lists, and "fair share" dues. Also, I will offer a brief history of teachers' unions and describe how they are organized and how they work. I will explain some of the key issues that many teachers' unions address, especially on the local level. I will also discuss some of the recent conflict over unions in the context of educational reform and try to disentangle some reality from the prevailing rhetoric. Finally, I end with a discussion of unions in the context of teacher leadership and curriculum deliberation, a core theme of this book. Throughout, I weave some of my personal experiences as a union member to provide a "first-person" context to the topic.

Union Organization, Structure, and Issues

There are two major teachers' unions in the United States, the American Federation of Teachers (AFT) and the National Education Association (NEA). The AFT generally represents teachers in larger urban districts; it has a strong connection to the AFL-CIO (American Federation of

Labor-Congress of Industrial Organizations) and is much more of a traditional "union" as a result, in that it tends to focus primarily on the bread-and-
butter, labor-oriented needs of its members. The larger of the two unions,
the NEA, was founded originally as a professional association for teachers;
it did not become a union until it was pressured to do so in the mid-20th
century, largely to keep up with the American Federation of Teachers.
Typically, the NEA is considered the more progressive of the two organizations—more "liberal," in today's vernacular—although both unions tend not
to take stances that are too politically risky, as a matter of self-preservation
(Weiner, 2012).

Each of the national unions is also composed of state and local chapters.
Unions are supported by their members through membership dues. When
a teacher joins the union, she joins at the local level, usually the building or
the district. She is automatically in the state and national union chapters as
a result. Lois Weiner, union activist and educational scholar, notes that the
AFT tends to concentrate more of its power in the national union and its activities, whereas the NEA tends to locate its power at the state level. Most of
the state and national activity of the union is advocacy—lobbying—engaging
policy makers but also influencing conversations about educational practice
(Weiner, 2012). However, the local union is much more likely to be where the
nuts-and-bolts issues that most directly impact members (who are teachers,
remember) are engaged, or at least where the most local decisions about how
to exercise state and federal educational mandates are made.

A union contract outlines the many policies and procedures protecting
teachers' (union members') workplace rights. While the union and its contract are often perceived to be only focused on teachers' narrow self-interest,
the conditions under which teachers teach are also the conditions under
which students learn. In instances where a teacher feels the administration
has acted contrary to the contract, the teacher may ask the union to file a
grievance on her behalf. Often, even when decisions or actions violate the
contract, they are resolved through discussion and/or negotiation without
filing a grievance. For example, the district where I taught would occasion-
ally pull teachers from their planning period to cover the class of an absent
teacher, especially for very short-term absences (like a doctor's appointment).
Often, the same teachers kept getting selected, sometimes multiple times a
week, typically because of when their planning period fell (say, right before
the lunch hour). Contractually, our teachers were guaranteed a minimum
of four planning periods a week, meaning that they could be asked to give

one up. As a union, we raised the issue with the administration and noted that not only was it a contractual violation to repeatedly give up the period but, more important, the same teachers were repeatedly asked and therefore were giving up their planning time regularly, which is not good for them or their students. We acknowledged that it was often impractical, and not cost-effective, to hire a substitute for those situations. The union and the administration worked informally to find a better process to cover classes internally and no grievance was necessary. The contract provided a framework for solving the situation fairly.

Below, I explain some of the more common, and often confusing and controversial, aspects of a union contract. Of course, these are not nearly everything that a union contract might include. You should be aware that many of the items in a contract are established through legal mandate—especially state laws. I encourage you to investigate the district from which you graduated, or the nearby district in your hometown if you didn't attend a public school, to see what specific items are covered in that contract. What I list here is intended primarily as a way to understand some of the "hot topics" in current debates about the merits of unions.

- **Collective bargaining:** As I mention previously, collective bargaining is the process in which the union and management, in this case the school board, negotiate a contract. The reason it is called "collective" bargaining is because the union negotiates the contract on behalf of all of its members (and non-members—more on that later) collectively, which relieves them from having to negotiate on their own. Historically, individual workers had little power over their work lives; but if they pooled their power, they were able to exert much stronger influence. Collective bargaining has been rather controversial throughout its history, though recent years have seen intensified criticism. Several states have attempted or enacted what are known as *Right to Work* laws in an effort to disestablish unions' collective bargaining power.

Right to Work laws are enacted to forbid requiring union membership as an employment mandate—hence, protecting an employee's "Right to Work" without joining the union. In states that are not Right to Work states, the law affords unions the right to require all employees to join the union or, to at least pay an agency fee, sometimes called a "fair share" fee. Because even non-union members are covered by the contract bargained by the union, the "fair share" fee requires non-members to pay a certain percentage of the regular union membership fee to compensate for the per-employee expense to the union of the bargaining process. Many Right to Work states are now prohibiting this fee, arguing that it violates workers' rights because it denies their choice whether to pay for the union support or not.

- **Tenure & seniority:** Tenure is arguably the most misunderstood issue of teacher contracts. People typically define tenure as the guarantee that a teacher cannot be fired. Even the recent Hollywood movie *Waiting for Superman* capitalized on this incorrect assertion. In fact, though, tenure is simply the establishment of firm due-process protections based (most of the time) on a combination of years of experience, also known as *seniority*, and qualifications such as an advanced degree. Tenure qualifications are negotiated as part of the collective bargaining process. In the district in which I taught, as in most districts, tenure was not guaranteed; the school board decided which teachers would receive tenure. In practice, tenure does make a teacher more difficult to fire than a non-tenured teacher, but only because the administration must follow due-process protocols established in the contract for the teacher's removal. In some instances, tenure meant the teacher earned a permanent contract (sometimes called a "continuing contract") rather than a year-to-year contract; still, the teacher could be removed according to contractually established due-process procedures. What many people don't realize is that non-tenured teachers can be fired without any cause at all, short of legal prohibitions such as sexual harassment, which can be difficult to prove, of course. In cases of suspicion that a law is broken, the union often provides legal counsel.

Critics argue that this combination of stringent due process and permanent contracts means that tenured teachers are *de facto* unable to be fired, even if they technically can be fired contractually. They further assert that tenure reduces teacher quality because it removes the teacher's incentive to improve—they become the stereotypical "lazy, out of touch," older teacher who simply reuses the same lessons year after year, never moves from behind his desk, and out-sprints his students to the parking lot after school. Of course, this supposes that, in essence, teachers only act in their own narrow, economic self-interest and are not motivated to do well without a measure of surveillance and the constant threat that they will be fired; in other words, they have no professional integrity driving them to do their best work.

The concept of tenure developed in universities as a protection of professors' academic freedom. In particular, tenure protections emerged as a reaction against the arbitrary firing of professors whose teaching and research conflicted with the tenets of the university for which they worked or were considered too controversial. The American Association of University Professors (AAUP), organized in the early 20th century, issued a statement in 1940 formally advocating for academic freedom for the first time:

> The common good depends upon the free search for truth and its free exposition. ... Academic freedom is essential to these purposes and applies to both teaching and research. ... Freedom and economic security, hence, tenure, are indispensable to the success of an institution in fulfilling its obligations to its students and to society. (Quoted in Lucas, 2006)

Tenure afforded a measure of job security to professors as a vanguard for them to do their work as public intellectuals. The same underlying idea is transcribed for PreK–12 teachers, since they, too, do public intellectual work; teachers are "idea workers," as education scholar and union activist Lois Weiner calls them (Weiner, 2012, p. 22). Of course, throughout history, the notion that professors (and teachers) should be free to deviate from the prescribed curriculum and its underlying ideology has been widely and hotly contested. Many people still argue that the teacher's role is merely to reproduce the dominant values of society and to directly inculcate those values into children. Therefore, many critics argue, tenure coddles "radical" teachers, those who "indoctrinate" children with their radical ideas.

Tenure, as a protection of academic freedom, buttresses the English teacher who wants to teach a piece of literature deemed controversial, perhaps one that has been banned. It safeguards the biology teacher who teaches evolution, or the health teacher who teaches comprehensive sex education in a district where the predominant cultural context would render those academic choices controversial and, therefore, risky.

An underlying assumption of the criticism of tenure is that it has no value to the district—that it is merely a "perk" negotiated by the aggressive union. In reality, though, districts may also benefit from having tenured teachers. As I've describe, tenured teachers typically have both experience and some advanced education, which often translates to higher quality. Of course, not every experienced teacher, and not every teacher with a master's degree, is "high quality" (whatever that even means—also a contested idea in this high-stakes era). But one would assume that an administration would not grant tenure to a teacher they did not consider worthy. It is in the administration's interest to offer a bit more job security to their more experienced and competent teachers so that these teachers don't move to another district.

Most districts want to be able to invest in a teacher's long-term success; they do not want to have to re-invest yearly in hiring, training, and supporting a new employee. This is also an example of how unions, working in teachers' best interests, also have a positive impact on students. Tenure is one way to try to ensure that students have competent, experienced teachers.

Finally, some people argue against tenure protections for teachers simply because jobs in most industries do not provide such protections; most jobs do not guarantee any sort of procedure to protect employees from being fired without any reason. So, this logic asks, "Why should teachers get these 'extra' protections when no one else does?" Two reasons: (1) Teaching, as public intellectual work, opens teachers to criticism in ways employees in most industries are not. Tenure emerged because of specific conditions endemic to the work itself; given that those conditions haven't changed, tenure is still necessary; and (2) This "why do you get it when I don't" sort of mindset is symptomatic of larger structural issues in the labor force, namely that most laborers have very few protections or assurance of their economic security. A more democratic solution would be for all workers to join together to fight for economic protections for all workers instead of fighting against each other. I will discuss this in greater detail later in the chapter during a discussion of *social movement unionism* (see Weiner, 2012).

• **RIF (Reduction in Force) list:** One of the more surprising (when I signed my first contract, anyway), and troubling items in the teaching contract is the RIF list. The RIF list describes the process for non-renewing teachers when a *reduction in force* is necessary. Typically, a reduction in force occurs when a district's financial situation is strained, and it must cut costs. Labor is the largest operating cost in a school district, so cuts in this area can yield the most savings. Generally, teachers are organized on the list in reverse order of seniority. The person most recently hired is at the top of the list. Typically, the list is also arranged by grade-level and content-subject area. For example, when I was hired, I was the most recently hired of five social studies teachers, so I was at the top of the RIF list. Had our district had to cut teachers, and chosen to cut a social studies teacher, I would have lost my job before anyone else in the department. Of course, tenure puts you at the bottom of the list and therefore the last to be fired.

Some critics of tenure refer to this RIF process as *LIFO*, or "Last In, First Out." They argue that LIFO protects bad, experienced teachers at the expense of new, better teachers. Their argument has a kernel of truth to it, at least in specific contextual circumstances, but should not be generalized. That is, one might argue, for example, that I was a better teacher than someone lower on the RIF list and so, if we are concerned with quality, I should have been retained and the other teacher fired. But in order to generalize that LIFO is categorically bad, one must accept that new teachers are always better than experienced teachers—that, in essence, experience does not matter—a highly contestable assertion, to be sure. Of course, it's also important to remember that new teachers generally cost less than experienced teachers, at least as contracts are currently constituted. Consequently, if districts only think about what is most cost effective, they would fire all of their experienced, and therefore expensive, teachers and replace them with new, inexperienced, but cheaper teachers. The conundrum for many districts is that, while this might be the best financial decision, it is not the most educationally sound (assuming, of course, that experience matters). Unfortunately, many poorer districts are consistently left in exactly this situation.

- **Teacher evaluations & merit pay:** Another of the more controversial issues in education today concerns the best way to evaluate teachers. Guided by state policy, teacher contracts establish the timing and manner in which teachers will be evaluated, as well as the criteria by which they are measured (for example, "Limited," "Proficient," or "Accomplished"). Contemporary "accountability" discourse has increased the stakes for many teachers as policies linking teachers' performance to students' achievement, and especially test scores, have become more prevalent. The argument for *merit pay*, by which teachers are rewarded with higher pay if their students are high achieving, is built on the idea that we must find ways to incentivize teachers who are otherwise low-performing, to motivate them through competition. Of course, that is predicated on a number of highly contestable assumptions, including: (1) There is a direct link between teacher effort and student output; and (2) Teachers are motivated primarily by competition.

One of the uncertain issues of intensified emphasis on teacher evaluation is whether districts will be able to actually follow through on evaluating every teacher regularly. Many districts simply do not have enough resources, in people or time, to do so. Consequently, one additional criticism of merit pay proposals, and any high-stakes teacher evaluation, is that it will necessarily mean teachers may well be judged only by a single hour's (or less) observation or a single measure (test scores). Critics also counter that teacher evaluations must be focused on improving teaching and not merely punitive, and therefore schools should provide professional development, opportunities to improve skills, and so forth to teachers who receive poor evaluations.

It is important to understand issues in context. For example, when unions in many financially strapped districts advocate for more job security, they do so in response to their specific circumstances. That is, they are responding directly to situations in which the district has eliminated teaching positions and fired teachers as a cost-saving measure. Yet, these same districts often have very high turnover (largely as a correlate to the poor funding); they are advancing a position governed by the specifics of the local circumstances. Despite what many people opposed to unions claim, unions are still necessary because the historical circumstances are still so similar that render them necessary, even if the specifics have changed. In some respects, joining the union is a little like an insurance policy for workers: You often don't notice it or realize its value until you need it, and then it becomes invaluable. Unions are the only way for teachers to (collectively) assert their authority with the administration and school board.

Unions and the Reform Debate: In Whose Interests Do They Work?

If one believes today's dominant rhetoric, teachers' unions are inherently and vehemently interested only in narrowly protecting the interests of teachers rather than students; by extension, one may assume, administrators are therefore the ones that protect students' interests, rather than merely the school's or district's interests. Or, perhaps no one in the school actually attends to students' interests (a troubling notion, to be sure); only parents do. This either/or dichotomy is problematic, of course. More reasonably, both unions and administration work in their own interests, sure, but they also work in the students' interests. That sometimes students' (and parents' and communities') interests are secondary is a reasonable critique, but one that reveals the undemocratic nature of schooling, especially its tendency to put educational stakeholders at odds with one another rather than in cooperation.

As I mention at the beginning of this essay, what I discovered was that the union was one of the few places where we as teachers could come to deliberate, discuss, and yes, sometimes just merely gripe, but also to work to solve issues relevant to our work lives. Indeed, many times, the discussions centered primarily on "bread-and-butter" matters like health insurance, pay increases (or, more recently, pay freezes), and other compensation issues. Still, there were plenty of discussions that more directly connected to the daily teaching experience and that benefitted students, even if indirectly. Particularly, these discussions often occurred in response to administrative decisions that we felt interfered with our ability to do our best teaching work. In these situations, one may see that matters of "working conditions" and being "student centered" are, in fact, interconnected rather than mutually exclusive, as is the prevailing criticism of unions.

Many people who claim the title of Educational Reformer (or have the title put upon them), like Bill Gates and Michelle Rhee, tend to see unions as obstacles to educational progress. Rhee, for example, founded an organization called Students First, which implies that she and reformers like her are interested in students' success, but that most teachers, and especially their malevolent unions, are unconcerned about students. Reformers have, by and large, successfully claimed the mantra of "progressive" education away from unions. The irony is that "reform" is equally conservative, in its own way. That is, it may well be in the interest of reformers to reproduce the status quo, rather than actually reforming, because it justifies their existence. Many so-called reformers capitalize on anti-union, anti-teacher rhetoric to advance a reform agenda that increasingly aligns itself with neoliberal forces of privatization, an agenda that profits from high-stakes tests for students and high-stakes evaluations of teachers and has decayed our country's commitment to free and equal public education for all students. As I will argue in the next section, unions are one important avenue by which teachers may mobilize in support of public education and work with parents, students, and communities in opposition to the privatization agenda.

"Right to Work"

Political backlash to teachers' unions has intensified in the last decade, mainly through state legislative proposals or ballot initiatives known as "Right to Work" laws. These proposals seek to change state laws that require all teachers who benefit from a collective bargaining agreement to pay union dues. When local teachers' unions negotiate a collective bargaining agreement (contract) for teachers, they use resources paid through union dues, often covering legal expenses and fees for negotiations.

Many states have laws that require anyone who benefits from the agreement that was bargained by the local union to pay "fair share" dues to cover their costs for bargaining and representation during the process. Those who contest these laws argue that it is unjust to require someone to pay union dues which may go toward causes that they do not personally support. In fact, in 2018 The United States Supreme Court heard arguments in the case *Janus vs. AFSCME*, where it ultimately ruled that the long practice of "fair share" is in violation of the constitutional right to free speech, which will significantly change the way in which teachers' unions operate in many states.

Teachers' Unions have been impacted by "Right to Work" laws, which often make going on strike illegal in states. Yet, in 2018, teachers in several states with low wages—including West Virginia, Colorado, Arizona, and North Carolina—ignored rules and organized statewide teacher marches, rallies, and strikes. West Virginia, Arizona, and North Carolina are all "Right to Work" states, yet teachers collectively organized and received wage and benefit raises in each state. It's difficult to know what role teachers' unions will play in the future considering the changing dynamics of teaching in the twenty-first century, but unions of teachers will remain powerful actors as long as teachers continue to collectively organize.

Unions, Teacher Leadership, and (Curriculum) Deliberation

Although there is much to critique about unions—their structure, how they operate, and where they place their interests (see Weiner, 2012, for example)—there is also the possibility for unions to become a place for teachers to exhibit leadership for the field. Unions hold the potential to be democratic, deliberative spaces within a system that is predominantly undemocratic—at least, undemocratic in the sense that top-down directives, often emanating far from the individual teacher's classroom, have such disproportionately high influence over the everyday expectations and practices that happen in classrooms.

Educational scholar and activist Lois Weiner, who has written extensively about teachers' unions, makes a distinction between "business unionism" models (or, "service model" unionism) and "social movement" unionism (2012). She notes that traditionally, teachers' unions, as with most unions, have acted in accordance with the service model. They have functioned largely to provide service to their constituents, their members. They provide members with contract negotiations, legal advice, pension advocacy and protections, and even discounted auto insurance or other associated "perks." And because they behave similarly to a business, they tend to be hierarchical and, therefore, prone to "top-down" decision-making that is disconnected from the rank and file members. Interestingly, the business union model also tends to be rather conservative, despite common media depictions of unions as "radical," in that the union's objective (as with most organizations) is to perpetuate itself and protect its members, which often means working largely to protect economic interests. However, it actually works against the union's interests (even if not really to the members' interests) to support positions that are too politically controversial because to do so might threaten the union's very existence.

Social movement unionism is quite different, as Weiner (2012) notes, and may actually be more consistent with the spirit of inquiry-oriented teacher leadership outlined throughout this book. Social movement unions, as you might guess from the name, have a different arrangement and different objectives. Instead of being hierarchical and top-down, they are much more horizontal and grassroots in their organizational structure.

They also act like other social movements, organizing and advocating across a range of social justice issues pertinent (directly or indirectly) to education.

> In social movement unions, members' self-interest is defined broadly, as much more than immediate economic and contractual concerns. The union struggles for its members' stake in creating a more democratic, equitable society, and the union allies itself with other movements that are working for justice, peace, and equality. (Weiner, 2012, p. 36)

Social movement unionism is issue transcendent. It engenders unions as participants in the larger deliberative sphere, with teachers exerting their influence as idea workers committed to democracy. Teachers (unions) are equally yoked with others who labor for sustainable democracy. As issue transcendent, it works with others to deal with a range of issues that frame the context of students' and their families' lives such as poverty, inadequate health care, environmental degradations, and so forth. One of the benefits of teachers' unions acting as social movement unions rather than business-model unions is that the social movement union would help teachers reclaim agency and power over many of those very issues that currently undermine the success of their students and make teaching and learning much more difficult.

Over the years in your teaching career, you will probably have the opportunity to come in contact with and no doubt become a member of a teachers' union. Knowing how teachers' unions work and what they can do is an important starting point. But also being aware of what the possibilities are, and how you can exercise teacher leadership within teachers' unions and other teacher organizations, constitutes a move toward teacher leadership. Ultimately, you will have an opportunity to transform organizations, functions, perceptions, opportunities, and possibilities of teacher groups during your career, and the function of teacher leadership is to move those groups toward just and democratic practices for students, teachers, schools, and society.

9

CURRICULUM PERSPECTIVES

*There is no such thing as a simple, basic curriculum. All curriculums
are complicated and involve deeply held assumptions and positions.*

There are strong parallels between writing a chapter about curriculum and
preparing curriculum for teaching. In both cases, decisions have to be made
about what knowledge is of the most worth. And how will or should the
teacher go about deciding what is important to teach? And who should be
included in the decision-making process? These are classic questions in the
curriculum field given any curriculum question or problem, and they affect
the text here, of course, in terms of deciding what to put into this short space
and what must be left for you to learn later during your professional lives
and experiences. Those who teach and work within the field of curriculum
realize that we ourselves only know a little bit of what is out there to know
about curriculum. So, this chapter and those following it constitute a starting
point with regard to the study of curriculum and its importance for teacher
leadership. After all, on the heels of chapters regarding inquiry and school reform and unionism as critical aspects of teacher identity and schooling today,
curriculum seems to me to be a clearly critical lever for making a difference as
a teacher leader. I hope this becomes clearer in the coming chapters.

In terms of this chapter, first I want to engage you in an effort to define
what "curriculum" is and means. Please realize up front that there is no single
definition of curriculum that is universally accepted. This doesn't make the

exercise fruitless. What this realization does is reinforce the notion that teacher leadership with regard to curriculum work has to do with addressing the following questions.

- Given a particular set of personal and community-oriented values, norms, and beliefs about the nature of knowledge and the social, cultural, economic, and political factors at hand, what/whose knowledge is of the most worth to teach and learn?
- Who will decide, and how will constituents decide what that knowledge is and how to teach it?
- How do standards imposed upon the teacher and school have an impact on the curriculum and what is actually taught on a daily basis in the classroom?

Second, I want to introduce several curricular concepts that will aid you in the process of making classroom decisions about curriculum and for participating in wider discussions regarding curriculum. Teachers make decisions each day, each hour, and each minute regarding the curriculum. However, teachers never act with complete autonomy regarding the curriculum. The curriculum is always shared in a community, created and implemented by many, and interpreted by students as they learn. Hopefully, students will learn things of value that you intend for them to learn through your teaching of the curriculum. You must realize that they will also learn things of value (and perhaps of not so much value to you) that lie outside your intentions. Perhaps the curriculum truly exists at the place where students make sense of it or not, creating personal meaning from it for themselves, not necessarily beforehand in its creation, or while it is being taught or implemented, or even during assessment activities at the end. We want teacher leaders to keep in mind the experiences of students with regard to the curriculum. After all, students are the reason for curriculum in the first place.

Last, I want to build a foundation for and relationship between this chapter and the next chapter, "Curriculum Deliberation and Teacher Leadership." Teacher leaders must understand that since curriculum is almost always a community endeavor, conflict and disagreement will arise while it is being developed and probably during its implementation. In many public forums where teachers come together to discuss curricular issues, people disagree about ideas. Of course they do. But they don't have to develop personal dislikes for each other, or take those differences personally. They need instead to understand where those differences exist and why.

But people do have different ideas about the things that matter the most to them. We live in a pluralistic society. So teacher leadership requires that we each understand what our positions are and what others' positions are before we make blanket judgments that will affect children and their learning. There is a certain level of consciousness, a meta-cognition about what we are thinking and doing that is necessary for leadership. We cannot ignore our differences and acquiesce to the one with the loudest voice out of fear and/or spite. We cannot avoid the hard work of understanding others with different points of view and making the commitments to finding common ground, compromise, and perhaps, if democracy can truly be had, consensus.

Reflection

Frankly, I have been confused my entire college career about what curriculum exactly is. I had never taken a class where the definition was explicitly defined, although the topic of curriculum was brought up constantly. I was paranoid that there was some major concept I was missing, and that because of this, I was going to be an inadequate teacher. When I began reading Chapter 9, I was relieved to read Dr. Poetter's words that there is no concise, magical definition of curriculum that I had been missing out on. Rather than simply being a collection of lesson plans or Common Core standards—like I had previously thought—curriculum is much more involved and complex.

Furthermore, curriculum is not created by the state or textbook company. The teacher leader is the one who creates and implements the curriculum in its entirety. She is the one responsible for what is taught and how it is taught. However, she does not make these decisions in a vacuum. She takes into account what is relevant to students' lives, the community around them, and students' interests. I think this concept is quite intimidating for teachers, and I freely admit that I am a little intimidated. However, I also am very aware of the fact that a classroom that only discusses mainstream topics, does worksheets all day, and does not welcome discussion or innovation offers little opportunity for learning or growth.

I often hear professors and cooperating teachers use the phrase "reinvent the wheel" when talking about curriculum. Whether these educators want to reinvent the wheel or not is their prerogative, but I find it interesting and kept coming back to it while reading this chapter. On the one hand, I see the benefits of using strategies that are effective and have worked well in the past. However, I am cautious because I know that each group of students is unique. If there was one sentence I could say to describe curriculum after reflecting upon this chapter, it would be "Curriculum is not one size fits all."

—Allie Skorcz, preservice teacher

One of the best things in a course on teacher leadership is engaging students in a project in which small teams of preservice teachers (4–6 people) deliberate upon and create a new curriculum, of varying sorts, together. One reason the activity is usually so successful is that the project captures several aspects of teacher leadership. Yes, curriculum development happens on an individual level with teachers deliberating alone about how to go about teaching a certain subject or topic on a daily basis or even long-term. But much curriculum work also takes place in small groups—especially in middle school teams, or grade level teams in early childhood settings, or in departmental or interdisciplinary groups in high schools—as schools move forward to create, adjust, hone, and integrate curriculum for classroom use. What could be better than bringing numerous teachers to the table to invent curriculum together? It is challenging, fun, and crucial because teachers creating curriculum must skillfully "read" the local context and understand students' needs together.

More than one head focused on a task is usually better than just one. A committee deliberating at a high level can sort through conflicts and reach agreements and solutions for the curriculum that increase student learning in ways exponentially better than an individual might be able to accomplish alone. Therefore, curriculum work requires certain forms of leadership, involving complex relationships and interactions. I spend some time in the next chapter explaining the idea behind a deliberative curriculum development project and what you might consider about the curriculum at beginning stages of thinking about teaching (see McCutcheon, 1995, for a discussion of curriculum deliberation, especially Chapters 2 and 5 on solo and group deliberation).

I often hear from practicing teachers that they wish they had a better knowledge of curriculum—beyond the basics of lesson planning taught in most teacher preparation programs—before they entered teaching. Comfort with curriculum work and the issues surrounding defining "the curriculum" often only come later, if then, in graduate school classes in curriculum. In my opinion, graduate school is too late for this. This chapter is an attempt at providing some curriculum background for students of teaching and leadership.

REFLECTION

Before you encounter the substance of the chapter, please discuss or reflect upon two critical ideas about curriculum: (1) curriculum is essentially a philosophical matter and (2) context matters.

Curriculum and Philosophy I hope that you have begun to recognize and challenge the position that leading involves not so much an attention to technique but to purpose. Sure, attention to technique comes with the territory of teaching; at some point it will be nice to know how to make a certain curriculum product in response to a particular curricular situation. But asking why, challenging the philosophical underpinnings of ideas, actions, and decisions constitute the starting points of teacher leadership and curriculum action. The first question is "why?" not "how?" The hows of teaching and curriculum work will come after careful consideration of the whys and with experience. People who reflect think about the reasons for things, who challenge knowledge claims, who wonder about moral commitments and responsibilities, and who learn to articulate their positions ... lead.

Context Matters There is no one right answer for any curriculum problem, except for the one that makes sense, morally and practically, for a given situation in a given context, at a given time. Perhaps the best response to any curriculum question at any time is "it depends." The learners, the place, cultural differences, politics, economic realities, values, norms, beliefs, and cherished ideas all matter, among other considerations, all at once and all the time. Leaders attend to complexity, ambiguity, tension, conflict, and the situation as it takes shape, emerging out of experience.

Everyone has and shares positions that influence decisions in context, though they are often latent, tacit, unstated. People don't just chuck their values; they typically defend them, and I want you to be able to do so as well, along with understanding and valuing others' positions. I like to think of the position of valuing context as a sort of "reflective eclecticism," which Posner (1995) says is a position wherein

> What curriculum decision-makers need is an understanding of the myriad curriculum alternatives. But to avoid the trap of garbage-can eclecticism, they should understand the dilemmas that underlie each curriculum decision and be able to unpack the tacit assumptions behind

each alternative. When they can do this, they will have gained the ability to assess critically the alternatives and the claims their proponents make. (Schwab, 1971, cited in Posner, 1995, p. 4)

The Curriculum Defined?

The word *curriculum* comes from the Latin word that literally means, "the course to be run":

> This notion implies a track, a set of obstacles or tasks that an individual is to overcome, something that has a beginning and an end, something that one intends to complete. This metaphor of a racetrack is not altogether inappropriate. Schools have historically established "courses" of study through which a student is to pass. (Eisner, 1994, pp. 25–26)

Regardless of how the curriculum is presented to you as a beginning teacher—in the form of a syllabus for a course you are to teach, or a textbook, or a thickly bound curriculum guide filled with instructional objectives, suggested activities, and worksheets, or in some other form, such as a wide open charge from the principal to "use your best judgment to engage the children in learning"—creating and adapting "the curriculum" is something that beginning teachers and veteran teachers do every day of their lives spent in schools. Therefore, curriculum is not static, set in stone, or irreversible, even if it is put to paper with ink. When push comes to shove, no matter what the curriculum says or looks like, teachers translate it, shape it, and adapt it for classroom use, alone or in groups, perhaps even into forms that are unrecognizable from the original curriculum. Teachers are the great arbiters of the curriculum (Connelly & Clandinin, 1988).

> ● **REFLECTION**
>
> Consider the following definitional statements about "curriculum" and discuss them. Write your own curriculum definition and share it with peers. Is there any consensus about a "best" definition?

● "The curriculum of a school, or a course, or a classroom can be conceived of as a series of planned events that are intended to have educational consequences for one or more students." (Eisner, 1994, p. 31)

- "The transformation approach (to curriculum) changes the structure, assumptions, and perspectives of the curriculum so that subject matter is viewed from the perspectives and experiences of a range of groups ... This approach can be used to teach about our differences as well as our similarities. Teachers can help students understand that, while Americans have a variety of viewpoints, we share many cultural traditions, values, and political ideas that cement us together as a nation ... It brings content about currently marginalized groups to the center of the curriculum. It helps students understand that how people construct knowledge depends on their experiences, values, and perspectives. It helps students learn to construct knowledge themselves. And it helps students grasp the complex group interactions that have produced the American culture and civilization." (Banks, 1994, p. 6)

- "Left to itself, a child will not grow into a thriving creature; Tarzan is pure fantasy. To thrive, a child needs to learn the traditions of the particular human society and culture it is born into. Like children everywhere, American children need traditional information at a very early age ... We will be able to achieve a just and prosperous society only when our schools ensure that everyone commands enough shared background knowledge to be able to communicate effectively with everyone else." (Hirsch, 1987, pp. 31–32)

- "The hidden curriculum ... (is) the tacit teaching to students of norms, values, and dispositions that goes on simply by their living in and coping with the institutional expectations and routines of schools day in and day out for a number of years." (Apple, 1990, p. 14)

- "Learning, we are coming to understand, is not simply a matter of motivation, repetition, presentation, stimulation, conditioning, and the like, although, of course, all of these things are part of the problem. Learning, we are coming to understand, is a problem of a total personality. It is a problem of an individual's *personal discovery of meaning*." (Combs, 1959, p. 9)

- "Abandon the notion of subject-matter as something fixed and ready-made in itself, outside the child's experience; cease thinking of the child's experience as also something hard and fast; see it as something fluent, embryonic, vital; and we realize that the child and the curriculum are simply two limits which define a single process. Just as two points define a straight line, so the present standpoint of the child and the facts and truths of studies define instruction. It is continuous reconstruction, moving from the child's present experience out into that represented by the organized bodies of truth that we call studies." (Dewey, 1902, p. 11)

- "The great books, read and discussed with an eye out for the basic truths and the equally basic errors or mistakes to be found in them, should be a part of everyone's general, liberal, and humanistic education. This program should begin with what might be called "junior great books" in the early grades, continued throughout basic schooling with more and more difficult books, and be pursued on an even higher level in college. It would still be everyone's obligation to read many of these books again in the course of adult learning, for the greatest among them cannot ever be plumbed to their full depths. They are inexhaustibly rereadable for pleasure and profit." (Adler, 1988, pp. xxx–xxxi)

- "The *Standards* are <u>not</u> a curriculum. They <u>are</u> a clear set of shared goals and expectations for what knowledge and skills will help our students succeed. Local teachers, principals, superintendents and others will decide *how* the standards are to be met. Teachers will continue to devise lesson plans and tailor instruction to the individual needs of the students in their classrooms. (From "Myths v. Facts About the Common Core Standards," *www.corestandards.org*)

- "The authors of standards note that a set of standards, like a content outline, is not a curriculum. Standards, however, are also more than a content outline and different from a scope and sequence. Standards often describe what students should be able to do, and in some cases, describe processes towards achieving the learning outcomes. Unlike scope and sequence, however, standards do not prescribe specific teaching activities." (Posner, 2004, p. 6)

The curriculum field is filled with taxonomies, attempts at categorizing positions, giving form to the field and its ideas. Your definitions for curriculum, as well as those above, may fall into one or more of these categories. In order to more closely examine your personal philosophies as they are related to curriculum, I invite you to complete the following Q-Sort exercise. A Q-Sort is a forced-choice paper/pencil instrument that helps people prioritize their ideas (Anastasi, 1976). Understanding your views about curriculum can help you understand their implications for how you identify the purposes of teaching and learning, how you conceive of knowledge, how you think of the role and function of the teacher, and how you view the relative place and nature of content in the curriculum (Poetter & Badiali, 2001).

Personal Curriculum Q-Sort

Below you will find 20 statements that characterize the public system of education. These statements are arranged in four categories: they address (1) the aims of education; (2) the nature of knowledge; (3) the role of the teacher; and (4) the purpose of the curriculum. These are foundational considerations for curriculum. Your task is to prioritize these statements by numbering them 1 to 5 in each category. Assign the number 5 to the statement you believe best represents your beliefs, 4 to the statement you believe represents your beliefs next best, and so on until you have numbered all five statements in each section. At the end of the Q-Sort exercise there is a scoring rubric.

Aims of Education
A.____ To improve and reconstruct society; education for change.

B.____ To promote democratic, social living; to foster creative self-learning.

C.____ To educate the rational person; to cultivate the intellect through transmitting worthwhile knowledge that has been gathered, organized, and systematized.

D.____ To provide for the construction of active citizens; to nourish civic literacy, citizen participation, and political responsibility.

E.____ To promote the intellectual growth of the individual; to educate the competent person for the benefit of humanity.

Nature of Knowledge
A.____ Focus on skills and subjects needed to identify and ameliorate problems of society; active concern with contemporary and future society.

B.____ Focus on past and permanent studies; mastery of facts and universal truths.

C.____ Focus on reconstructing a visionary language and public philosophy that puts equality, liberty, and human life at the center of the notions of democracy and citizenship.

D. ____ Focus on growth and development; a living-learning process; active and relevant learning.

E. ____ Focus on essential skills and academic subjects; mastery of concepts and principals of subject matter.

Role of the Teacher

A. ____ Teachers are critical intellectuals who create democratic sites for social transformation. They empower students to question how knowledge is produced and distributed.

B. ____ Teachers serve as change agents for reform; they help students become aware of problems confronting humanity.

C. ____ Teachers should help students think rationally; teach based on Socratic method, oral exposition, relaying explicit traditional values.

D. ____ Teachers are guides for problem solving and scientific inquiry.

E. ____ Teachers should act as authority figures who have expertise in subject areas.

Curriculum Purposes

A. ____ Curriculum centers on classical subjects and literary analysis. It is constant.

B. ____ Curriculum centers on social critique and social change dedicated to self and social-empowerment.

C. ____ Curriculum centers around essential skills in the three Rs (readin', 'ritin', 'rithmetic) and major content areas (English, science, math, history, foreign language).

D. ____ Curriculum centers on examining social, economic, and political problems, from present/future, national/international perspectives.

E. ____ Curriculum centers on student interests; involves the application of human problems; subject matter is interdisciplinary.

(Adapted from Badiali, 2000)

Scoring Guide for Curriculum Philosophy Q-Sort

When you have completed the Q-Sort exercise, go back and look at each category. Place the number that you assigned to each statement in the space provided in the rubric below. Add the columns to determine the educational/ curricular philosophy with which you most agree. Grouped together, these statements represent major tenets of five educational/curricular philosophies.

	Perennialism	Essentialism	Progressivism	Social Reconstruc-tionsim	Critical Theory
AIMS	C	E	B	A	D
KNOW	B	E	D	A	C
ROLE	C	E	D	B	A
CURR	A	C	E	D	B
Totals					

The taxonomy on the next two pages is adapted from Ornstein & Hunkins (1993), as found in Ornstein & Behar-Horenstein (1999, p. 16). Keep in mind that taxonomies are attempts at categorizing. While helpful, they can also be used to stereotype. In the end, they cannot fully represent the richness of individual's positions or actions. However, they will give some insight and clarity to the categories used in the above rubric.

● REFLECTION

Where did you land on the above Q-Sort chart? What does your position on the chart imply? Does this extension of your platform reveal any surprises?

Curriculum Categories (adapted from Ornstein & Behar-Horenstein, 1999)

	Philosophical Base	Instructional Objective	Knowledge	Role of Teacher	Curriculum Focus	Related Curriculum Trends
Perennialism	Realism	To educate the rational person; to cultivate the intellect	Focus on past and permanent studies; mastery of facts and timeless knowledge	Teacher helps students think rationally; based on the Socratic method and oral exposition; explicit teaching of traditional values	Classical subject; literary analysis; constant curriculum	Great books Paideia proposal (Hutchins, Adler)
Essentialism	Idealism; Realism	To promote the intellectual growth of the individual; to educate the competent person	Essential skills and academic subjects; mastery of concepts and principles of subject matter	Teacher is authority in his or her field; explicit teaching of traditional values	Essential skills (the three Rs) and essential subjects (Eng, math, science, history, foreign language)	Back to basics; excellence in education (Bagley, Bestor, Bennett)
Progressivism	Pragmatism	To promote democratic, social living	Knowledge lends to growth and development; a living-learning process; focus on active and interesting learning	Teacher is a guide for problem solving and scientific inquiry	Based on students' interests; involves the application of human problems and affairs; inter-disciplinary subject matter; activities and projects	Relevant curriculum; humanistic education; alternative and free schooling (Dewey, Beane)

(continued on next page)

(continued from previous page)

	Philosophical Base	Instructional Objective	Knowledge	Role of Teacher	Curriculum Focus	Related Curriculum Trends
Social Reconstructionism	Pragmatism	To improve and reconstruct society; education for change and social reform	Skills and subjects needed to identify and ameliorate problems of society; learning is active, concerned with contemporary and future society	Teacher serves as an agent of change and reform; acts as a project director and research leader; helps students become aware of problems confronting humanity	Emphasis on social sciences and social research; examining social, economic, and political problems; focus on present and future trends	Equality of education; cultural pluralism; international education; futurism (Counts, Grant, & Sleeter)
Critical Theory	Marxism	To challenge and deconstruct society, the status quo, powerful oppressors; to teach citizens to act politically for social justice	Focus on how the world works to privilege some and not others; awareness of race, class, gender, sexuality, and (dis)ability politics	Teacher acts with conscience and resolve as a social agent of change in the world with students	Teacher opens up societal norms to criticism and action	Some forms of service learning; socially active, alternative education programs (Freire, Apple, Giroux)

Reflection: *Curriculum Q-Sort*

I took the Personal Curriculum Q-sort. Prior to taking this quiz, I felt very conflicted on what my views on a good curriculum were. I felt there were many aspects of curriculum that were important, and I found it very hard to organize my thoughts on what really was more beneficial to the student. After taking this Q-sort, I have a much better understanding of my personal views on curriculum.

This Q-sort showed me that I believe in a progressive curriculum as well as a social reconstructive curriculum. I scored highest in these categories, tying at 17 points each. I feel that these two ideals overlap each other in many ways. Due to the tie, I decided to create my own curriculum view out of the two that I best related to. I decided to call it Progressive Social Reconstructionism.

I think that the philosophical base for my new category will be Pragmatism because this is what both of my choices reflect. Before this Q-sort I had no idea what Pragmatism was; after further research I have determined that it is a view that mainly states that education should be about life and growth. My instructional objective for progressive social reconstructionism states that the goal of classroom life is to promote democratic and social living while coincidently improving and reconstructing society. I believe that knowledge is a living and learning process and that knowledge should focus on subjects that are needed to identify and fix problems of society. The role of the teacher is to guide the students in a direction to promote problem solving and help make students aware of problems in human society. The curriculum should be based on students' interests. It should also focus on human problems, as well as focus on present and future trends. This curriculum should be relevant to the students, focus on equality of education and futurism.

I think I benefited by having two categories tie in my Q-sort because it made me really examine which parts of each category were most important to me as well as how I could use both of these big ideas to create the best possible curriculum and school ideals and focus as a teacher.

—Sammi Kushen, preservice teacher

Posner (2004) names five concurrent curricula that take us several steps forward beyond the philosophical taxonomy on the previous pages. His categories represent aspects of curriculum in educational settings such as schools. They reveal concepts that will allow us to discuss school-based curriculum on deeper, philosophical, and contextual bases.

- *Official Curriculum*: The curriculum described in formal documents
- *Operational Curriculum*: The curriculum embodied in actual teaching practices
- *Hidden Curriculum*: Institutional norms not openly acknowledged but acting powerfully in schools and society
- *Null Curriculum*: The subject matters not taught
- *Extra Curriculum*: The planned experiences outside the formal curriculum

(Adapted from Posner, 2004, pp. 12–14)

At some times and in some places the curriculum is written down in a "formal" document, and is therefore "explicit." (Goodlad, 1979; Eisner, 1994). The principal or the teachers in your school might be able to point to the curriculum, even pick it up from their desks or pull it down from a shelf, and they might even use it on a daily basis as they plan for teaching. When they use it by teaching it in the classroom, the curriculum becomes operational. At other times and places, no one in the school will be able to point to any curriculum documents because either they do not exist or they have never been used and cannot be found. What you need to know is that from state to state, from community to community (even within the same state), school department to school department, grade level to grade level, and teacher to teacher, there is a tremendous variability in how formal, written curricula look and are used.

School and community cultural norms have a great deal to do with this variability. In some places, the predisposition to control what teachers do results in a strictly mandated, tightly written curriculum, usually held in place by administrators who might even require written lesson plans from teachers for review on a daily or weekly basis. In other places, administrators and teacher leaders pay little or no attention to the formal curricula teachers use, expecting teachers themselves to create an interesting and exciting curriculum for students on a daily basis.

There is no question that textbooks have a great impact on the curriculum. Many teachers assume that the textbook *is* the curriculum, even to the point of thinking of textbook selection as their primary form of curriculum work. Large states like Texas and California have a powerful hand to play in selecting textbooks. They are such big markets that their selection procedures affect the decisions book publishers make about what gets in and what gets left out of books. Often these decisions are based on political, economic, and cultural positions and trends. Today one can order a textbook set and receive pre-packaged from the publishing company daily lesson plans, hand-outs, worksheets, tests, overhead transparencies, CDs, and website materials with even more supplementary items for the classroom. Who knows what the future will hold in terms of commercial curriculum packages. I wonder, "What is left for the teacher to do?" Sadly, nothing, for many teachers today, except to pick and choose among the materials and organize them for daily use. Worse are settings in which teachers are de-skilled even further, forced to read a script in the place of actually teaching.

Some teachers defend pre-packaged materials like textbooks and their use because they were created by "experts" and therefore must be "good." They also contend that "pre-packaged" or "canned" materials free teachers' time for other matters more essential to teaching besides curriculum making. But one teacher, a good friend and colleague in the field, tells about being cheated by an early lack of background and understanding about curriculum. He recalls an assignment made by his principal to write a curriculum for the course in economics he taught in his first year of teaching. Desperate, lacking in understanding of the deeper questions and issues of the curriculum, and running out of time on his assignment from the principal, he copied the table of contents from the textbook he was using on a notepad in pencil and turned it into the principal. She liked the "new" curriculum, and approved it as the official curriculum of the course for the department. He remained mired in a textbook-driven, lecture-based class, feeling as though something was missing, but not knowing how to solve the problem.

What a tragedy, considering how crucial curriculum planning is for the professional life of a teacher. To just hand over the creation of curriculum and materials for learning makes the curriculum less practical and no doubt less useful to students and teachers. This position distances teachers from a position that supports inquiry as a norm for teacher leaders and stunts their study of subject matter. With so many wonderful primary sources to be found in libraries and on the Internet, it seems extremely unprofessional to give the primary responsibility for creating curriculum away to outsiders who write textbooks. The practical reality is that canned curricula cannot address the particular, cultural norms of students in a community. They are created so far from the scene that they cannot possibly be relevant or connected. The political reality is that teachers need the time and the space to work on curriculum, and they need to learn what some of the initial questions and concerns about curriculum should be. And they have to start from the position that what they do create will generally be approved and allowed to be taught. This is not always a "given" today.

For starters, the push by states to create expensive, high-stakes achievement testing programs has caused school districts, boards, administrators, and teachers to focus their curriculum efforts on creating curricula that force teachers to "teach to the test." It is no secret that most curriculum documents made for and created by school districts and teachers are becoming more tightly controlled by legislative, state-controlled bodies, perhaps if not directly through "model courses of study" that states provide districts and on which districts might model their own curriculum for state approval, then indirectly by the content (subject specific) and nature (usually multiple choice) of the tests and lists of standards handed down by the states and other groups. And these tests are designed to measure "achievement levels" and students' mastery of the "basics," typically, so our curricula for use in public school classrooms are being geared down in this direction. Of course, this does not fit with the initial call in this book for creating classroom communities where high expectations are a norm and where inquiry takes place. Nor does the movement fit with the insights of others who call for more use of primary sources as classroom texts (whole language advocates in language arts, for instance) or more problem-solving approaches (put forward in math, for instance, by constructivists in the National Council of Teachers of Math [NCTM] and their myriad and comprehensive math curriculum materials and documents).

With regard to the tests and the curricula that often develop in school districts in reaction to the tests, I generally disagree that they help to enhance the learning and the academic achievement of students. One so-called "objective" measure like a multiple-choice test with a limited writing sample cannot tell us enough about a child's academic ability or achievement upon which to base life-changing decisions. This doesn't mean that the tests are not happening; they are. It's just that the way they are being used is wrong. The tests should be used for diagnostic purposes and not for high-stakes reporting purposes, not used as a basis for decisions on student movement from grade to grade or for graduation, not used as direct links to measures of teacher performance, etc. And even though laws may mandate certain actions in these areas, that doesn't make them educationally defensible.

My disagreement with the testing approaches proliferating through the nation doesn't mean they don't exist and that you won't have to attend to them as a teacher leader. But what's at stake for teacher leaders are issues and practical realities of everyday teaching related to how they view the educational value of the tests, how these tests have an impact on the day-to-day learning lives of children in schools through adjustments to curriculum and teaching, and how the tests can be effectively appropriated into the existing curriculum without impoverishing it. Also, if your position warrants it, how can the tests be sufficiently resisted and perhaps turned back politically as a viable option that communities will not accept any longer? Parent groups all over the country are lobbying legislators to ease or disband their allegiance to these tests and their use and misuse. Perhaps teachers will also join in the call for more effective and humane assessment of student achievement. (Visit the Fairtest organization website for issues related to testing at *http://www. fairtest.org.* Also, for another point of view regarding the positive aspects of standardized testing, visit your state department of education website, or the State of Ohio's at *http://www.ode.state.oh.us.* Or look at a wide array of resistance articles at *http://www.rethinkingschools.org.*)

Teacher leaders have several important decisions to make with regard to curriculum. To what extent will they take control over the creation of curriculum in their classrooms and schools? How will teacher leaders work with administrators to meet the political realities of achieving high achievement test scores that haunt districts? How will they retain a professional autonomy that gives them more control over the local curriculum? And what of students and their parents and communities? What role should these constituencies play in curriculum making? Some curriculum theorists posit that to be truly educational and not coercive and indoctrinaire in schools, planning for classroom experiences must include at least the input of students, even so far as asking them first, "What are your concerns? What would you like to study?" (Beane, 1998). One of the most pressing questions for beginners becomes, "If everyone seems to want to do all of this curriculum work for me by creating the philosophy, the goals, the activities, and the assessment tools for me, why should I struggle to do it myself?"

A Reflection on Common Core: Initiatives and Comparative Education
Our reading on the Finnish education system was super intriguing to me because I have never learned that much about Common Core Standards and how they came into development, what the goals behind them were, etc. I moved between states several times as a child and so the first thing I ever heard about Common Core was that it was good because students moving between states would have learned the same things and would not be behind or ahead of the school they moved into. When Common Core was first introduced, I remember that my teachers absolutely hated it because it meant they would have to change some of the concepts they were teaching, and they would have to have more standardized testing for their students.

Over time the dialogue around Common Core changed, and I heard it being talked about in a more positive light. However, through all of this, I never knew that the intention of introducing a national set of standards was to improve the economy. This idea is questionable considering the countries studied by the authors of the article we were reading—where high economic growth correlated with high education levels—most often had a population of fewer people than a single U.S. state. I appreciated that the reading brought in the example of Finland, because I took a comparative education course while I was studying abroad that focused on comparing the American education system to the Finnish one. I actually had the opportunity to observe three different schools in Finland on a study tour for this course. While they do have a national set of academic standards, there are also numerous other things that make a Finnish education so much better than an American one.

In Finland, the teaching profession is one of the most highly regarded; students are not tracked; students are allowed an enormous amount of independence from an early age; students get several breaks (recesses, if you will) throughout the day all the way through high school; students are not discouraged from going into vocational professions; students loop with the same teacher for three or four years; and the list goes on. Making the claim that having nation-wide standards are "working" for Finland is a disservice to all of the other things they are doing to make their education system and their economy as successful as they are.

—Grace Olsson, preservice teacher

The curriculum is much deeper and pervasive and important than what gets written down in curriculum documents, syllabi, and textbooks. Teachers and schools teach other things that are part of the curriculum of schooling that are "implicit" as opposed to "explicit," meaning that they never get written down, but they are nonetheless taught, and perhaps take much of our energy and focus as teachers. Many teachers today, for instance, find themselves teaching lessons in organizational skills and personal responsibility to students. Teachers, in fact, have always taught these lessons. These things usually are not written down in the curriculum, and they do not appear as content on the state test, but society tends to value them and schools teach them to students. Some teachers are more successful than others in getting students to learn or comply with the curriculum content that is implicit (and explicit for that matter), but these focuses constitute a part of the curriculum that is real, substantial, and important. And much that is positive, and that reflects shared cultural values (like teamwork, and hard work, and timeliness, and cooperation, etc.), is taught through the implicit curricula of schools (Eisner, 1994).

But some negative things abound there as well, and these things are often referred to as the "hidden curriculum" of schools, things that are implicit in what we do as teachers in the curriculum, or perhaps things we do as a matter of course that we might not do if we examined the assumptions behind the activities more carefully. Things that we do might be so deeply imbedded in who we are or claim to be, that we do not even really know we do them or that they could cause potential damage to children. For instance, the focus on competition in our schools, which pervades so much of what teachers do today, sets students up to compete for extrinsic rewards, and grades, and to get into the "higher ability level groups." We cannot know the depth of damage caused by creating winners and losers in almost everything we do in schools from the earliest ages (Kohn, 1994; Eisner, 1994). And what of our propensity to socialize students into the notion of "school as work" so early in their learning lives, to the point that the kindergarten, a place ostensibly for students to "learn through play," has been appropriated as a pre-first grade in which academic learning and achievement are paramount (Apple, 1979)?

So the beginning teacher leader who is confronted with challenges by the curriculum must ask several initial questions before jumping in:

- Can the formal, written curriculum for this school or for this grade level or for this subject area be found? If so, what seems to be the general content and nature of the curriculum for students in the school? If the curriculum cannot be found, why not (speculate and/or inquire)?
- To what extent (if any) is there any agreement on issues and practices related to the curriculum in the school among teachers, administrators, students, and the community?
- What degree of autonomy do teachers have to create the curriculum? How are textbooks and/or other materials for learning used?
- As you observe teaching and teach during your field experiences, what things are taught that are not written down in the curriculum?

Some Foundational Concepts for Thinking About Curriculum

As you begin exploring curriculum issues, I would like you to keep several things in mind. First, though I don't wish to treat issues of pedagogy or teaching methods in this book or course in great detail, I understand that a common question among beginning teachers is "What is the relationship between a certain set of teaching methods and the curriculum?" Do they have an impact on each other? If so, how?

I believe that teaching methods and curriculum are closely related. Of course, you can teach certain content in the curriculum in a multitude of ways, perhaps effectively in each way as well. But it seems that certain teaching methods and certain curriculum call for combinations that fit together. For instance, say you decide to base your curriculum and teaching approach on Gardner's theory of multiple intelligences, which posits that each of us has all eight of these intelligences to some degree, some more than others. These intelligences are:

1. linguistic: to think in words and to use language to express and appreciate complex meanings
2. logical-mathematical: to calculate, quantify, conserve propositions and hypotheses, and carry out complex mathematical operations

3. spatial: to think three-dimensionally; to perceive external and internal imagery; to recreate, transform, or modify images; to navigate oneself and objects through space; and to produce or decode graphic information

4. bodily-kinesthetic: to manipulate objects and fine-tune physical skills

5. musical: to be sensitive to pitch, melody, rhythm, and tone

6. interpersonal: to understand and interact effectively with others

7. intrapersonal: to construct an accurate perception of oneself and to use such knowledge in planning and directing one's life

8. naturalistic: to have well-developed awareness and sensitivity to the environment and to operate effectively in various natural habitats

(From Campbell, 1996, and Lucas, 2000)

You begin with the idea that all students have intelligences that can be developed with purposeful attention in the classroom. As a result, you probably would not spend all of your time designing curriculum that only has students working on rote computations in a whole group setting in mathematics. Instead, you would most likely be thinking about shaping the teaching methods and the curriculum content together to address students with kinesthetic or intrapersonal intelligence strengths for math as well. Perhaps the students would construct human number lines (kinesthetic) and write their mathematical thoughts in a dialogue journal (intrapersonal).

In the same scenario, in order to introduce students to the art of painting, you probably would go beyond the kinesthetic (the physical act of painting), though teaching the kinesthetic might be a very important part of your methods and content. In conjunction, you might ask "What about the works of great painters?" What could be written by students in an essay designed to persuade other class members to attend a Monet exhibit on their own time outside of class? A writing activity like this one would focus on verbal intelligence as well as the kinesthetic art of painting.

Second, what of all this talk of aims, goals, and objectives in the curriculum? Two perspectives have long dominated the curriculum field: the **behavioral perspective** and the **experiential perspective.** (These categories are not ironclad and are used here for descriptive purposes. A more detailed discussion of theoretical perspectives on curriculum can be found in Posner, 1995; Eisner, 1994; and Tanner & Tanner, 1975, among others). I look at the ideas of aims, goals, and objectives through the lenses of these two theoretical perspectives, the behavioral and the experiential.

I use Posner's discussion of the terms "aim," "goal," and "objective," as well as Eisner's understanding of "behavioral objective," "problem-solving objective," and "expressive outcomes," to frame the discussion. Neither one of these thinkers is "right" about this area of curriculum inquiry and there is little agreement among people with regard to the importance and definition of terms, but I think their ideas offer reasonable starting points.

Levels of Educational Purposes

Societal Goals   What citizens or policy makers want their country's political, economic, social, and educational institutions to accomplish.

Administrative Goals   What leaders of organizations want to accomplish that allows for the maintenance and improvement of the organization.

Educational Aims   What citizens or policy makers want society's educational institutions to accomplish; generally long-term and the result of many influences, only one of which is the school.

Educational Goals   What citizens or policy makers want formal educational institutions—i.e., schools and colleges—to accomplish expressed in terms of characteristics of people who have been well educated.

Learning Objectives   Whatever people are intended to learn as a consequence of being students in educational institutions. (Adapted from Posner, 1995, p. 80)

Eisner's Categories of Objectives/Outcomes

Behavioral Objectives   The specific goals that one hopes to achieve by formulating objectives with precision and clarity. Useful objectives are stated in behavioral or performance terms that describe a change in desired student behavior in relation to specific subject matter. A sound objective in behavioral terms for a social studies lesson might read something like "the student will be able to identify (behavior) the major causes of the Westward movement in the United States during the period 1840–1870 (subject matter)" (Eisner, 1984, p. 110).

Problem-Solving Objectives   The students formulate or are given a problem to solve:

say, to find out how deterrents to smoking might be made more effective, or how to design a paper structure that will hold two bricks sixteen inches above a table, or how the variety and quality of food served in the school cafeteria could be increased within the existing budget. In each of these examples, the problem is posed and the criteria that need to be achieved to resolve the problem are fairly clear. But the forms of its solution are virtually infinite ... The point is that the shapes of the solutions, the forms they take, are highly variable ... In such situations the potential answers are not known beforehand. What is known is the problem; what constitute appropriate solutions remains to be seen after the work has been done. (pp. 117–118)

Expressive Outcomes   Are "the consequences of curriculum activities that are intentionally planned to provide a fertile field for personal purposing and experience ... (I)t is perfectly appropriate for teachers and others involved in curriculum development to plan activities that have no explicit or precise objectives ... (T)here must be room in school for activities that promise to be fruitful, even though the teacher might no be able to say what specifically the students will learn or experience. Parents do this all the time. The trip to the zoo, weekends spent camping in the woods, the bicycle ride after dinner: no specific objectives or problems are posed prior to setting out on such activities, yet we feel that they will be enjoyable and that some 'good' will come from them" (pp. 120–121).

Eisner's Point: "Purposes need not precede activities; they can be formulated in the process of action itself" (p. 121).

The behavioral perspective suggests that the function of the curriculum is to set aims, goals, and objectives clearly, from the start, so that the paths for teaching and learning for teachers and students are laid out from beginning to end. Learning, from the behavioral perspective, lies in the change in behavior of the learner.

What you will find in the field is that most school curriculums on paper and in use align with behaviorism. The purpose of most school curriculums in these behavioral settings is to deliver a course or program of study through instruction and then to measure through some "reliable" format the achievement of learning by the students, usually through a paper and pencil test. The teaching and assessment methods employed resemble those that many of us experienced in our seats at school during our apprenticeships of observation: lots of listening to teacher talk, working with texts, performing drills, filling out worksheets, and taking tests for grades at the end of a lesson or unit. The focus of teaching and learning is the content, the material, the knowledge. Some might also refer to this approach, in general, as "traditional."

Those who conceive of teaching and learning and curriculum from an experiential perspective see and do many things in classrooms with students differently. Sometimes, teachers and learners discover the important points along the way; they are not laid out ahead of time. The aims, goals, and objectives of a learning experience emerge as students work to make sense of things they encounter in the world through "real-life" experiences and activities. As opposed to just working out of a book or listening to teachers talk, students search to discover personal meaning by constructing new realities and new knowledge through experience as they are engaged in activities (Combs, 1959). The focus is the learner, and the environments where this type of teaching and learning take place are sometimes referred to as "student-centered" or "progressive."

Sometimes students work on problems together in these settings, coming up with solutions through mutual efforts. Problem-solving objectives become the centerpiece of the curriculum, and students use a wide range of knowledge and approaches to encounter a problem. Some school curriculums focus on problem-solving objectives, relying on the natural instinct and curiosity of children to make their way through interesting problems that test their wit, will, and knowledge; students who engage in these activities, the theory goes, generate multiple, viable solutions and develop the abilities to solve a wide range of problems as they learn along the way the content that usually gets imbedded in more traditional lecture notes and quizzes. (They may even learn more!) Content is discovered along the way, as students and teachers together "generate" materials through primary sources that inform students' learning. Students become co-inquirers, learners in the most complete sense.

Eisner calls the engagement in meaningful activities planned by students and teachers "expressive" outcomes; these outcomes emerge when students are engaged in interesting materials and situations, purposefully, though they do not have a scripted agenda. For instance, a trip to the zoo usually does not follow a detailed itinerary, except for arrival and departure times. But a trip to the zoo is deeply educational and filled with learning; however, the focus is on the experience of the zoo, on the wonder, curiosity, questions, and discovery that animals and our own lives together in that same place cause. Teachers usually do not pass out worksheets for students to fill out at the zoo on "Carnivores"; shame on them if they do! I expound on the possibilities of exploring the metaphor of a field trip to the zoo in Chapter 11, "The Zoo Trip."

Third, consider our deeply held and blindly accepting allegiances to "subject matter" in school curriculum. Companies have parsed out the content for learning so that it fits nicely in curriculum packages for the language arts, for mathematics, for social studies, for science, etc. Certain contents are valued over others, both in terms of time and our focus. Math gets more time than art. Reading gets more time than music.

REFLECTION

What values lead us to make curriculum decisions about what does and does not get taught? What do these decisions say about us? What gets left out of the curriculum (what Eisner calls the "null" curriculum) when we make these decisions?

Teachers send students around the school each day, even during the early grades, to learn from subject matter specialists for short periods at a time; typically, the content is disjointed and unrelated from class to class or subject to subject during the day. Teachers expect children to make grand sense-making leaps between and among the disciplines that adults themselves cannot routinely make.

What about the idea of curriculum "integration"? (See Beane, 1998.) "Curriculum integration" is not a new idea, around at least for the better part of the 20th century. The point is that what is worth knowing in the world does not always fit nicely into the box of a discipline or a subject. And in the world, most problems or things of interest are perceived and interpreted from a number of different knowledge bases anyway. If we truly wish to educate our children well, we will help them integrate knowledge that is at least of three types: personal, social, and technical (Beane, 1998).

Fourth, and related to the major issue of cultural diversity discussed earlier, is the consideration of our deeply held cultural biases in America and our overwhelming resistance to the issues and the content of multiculturalism in the school curriculum. The dominant cultures in America—those being the white, male, upper middle class, straight, capitalist, Christian, and able cultures in America—have a lot to do with what gets accepted as true, legitimate, and teachable knowledge in American public schools today. This should seem problematic to you, at least to some degree, since most teachers are women and so many students are of minority status.

And you may also feel a sense of entitlement, no doubt, though you may not have ever asked for it since you get it by virtue of your identification with the dominant groups listed above, to have your view of the world privileged in school. Does anyone reading this text remember any lessons on early American colonization in elementary school that focused equally as much on the implications of the systematic extermination of Native Americans by European settlers as on the "patriotic" images of Plymouth Rock and the "generosity" of the early pilgrims at the first Thanksgiving? (Loewen, 2007). While I understand and value the purpose of a common, unifying narrative that makes us all participants in the American story as citizens of a democracy (Postman, 1995), are the sugar-coated stories of Plymouth Rock and the first Thanksgiving the only stories worth telling and knowing in school? The point is that power—political, economic, and cultural—plays a big part during the process of deciding what does or does not get included in the curriculum, or deciding who gets to decide what gets into it in the first place. These are all curriculum questions, answers to which teacher leaders carefully attend (as well as to even deeper questions).

The key to teaching a curriculum that is multicultural is to recognize the limitations of using added material to the already existing curriculum that we might think represents diversity or is multicultural. To simply engage in putting on cultural food day or reading poems by African-American writers during Black History Month may be steps in the right direction. But perhaps these activities push the good intentions of representing multiple perspectives of culture, society, and knowledge further to the margins. Why don't we have African-American, Asian, Latino, and Native American writers and scientists and their work represented in our textbooks and curriculum materials we create for classroom use? Why do we continue to treat civil rights leaders such as Rev. Dr. Martin Luther King, Rosa Parks, and Malcolm X, for instance, as mere icons in the curriculum without looking at the deep, long-term sacrifices and commitments by them and by individuals and by whole segments of society for justice, civil rights, and change? (See Banks, 1994.) What would happen if we moved in these directions? What would the curriculum look like? How would our teaching evolve?

Reflection: *More than Just Standards*

Curriculum. When I first heard this word in my school career I immediately pictured standards and a list of what teachers were supposed to teach. Curriculum is this, in a sense, yet so much more.

One of my professors asked us the other day, "What knowledge and experiences are most worthwhile?" It took me a moment to realize that we were talking about curriculum. This word and concept, which once deterred me, suddenly intrigued. She framed curriculum in a light I had previously not been aware of. She explained further that curriculum constantly changes depending on who you are and your surroundings. "Curriculum is not static, set in stone, or irreversible, even if it is put to paper with ink" (Poetter, this chapter) supports her claim that curriculum is constantly changing and never stagnant.

The most important take away I had from that chapter was the fact that it is up to the teacher to take the curriculum and make it impactful for the students and serve their best interests. "When push comes to shove, no matter what the curriculum says or looks like, teachers translate it, shape it and adapt it for classroom use, alone or in groups, perhaps even into forms that are unrecognizable from the original curriculum" (Poetter, this chapter).

Perhaps I never thought of curriculum as a guideline for teachers to "translate, shape and adapt" because my classroom teachers and ones I have observed did not mold the curriculum to best fit the students. Teaching the standards is one thing, but there is a way to do that while still making the curriculum relevant and meaningful to the students. I always believed that education is about the students, so why should the curriculum be any different, considering it is at the heart of the education system?

—Lianna McDonald, preservice teacher

10
CURRICULUM
DELIBERATION
AND TEACHER
LEADERSHIP

Deliberation is a process of reasoning about practical problems. It is solution oriented, that is, toward deciding on a course of action. A deliberative approach is a decision-making process in which people, individually or in groups, conceive a problem, create and weigh likely alternative solutions to it, envision the probable results of each alternative, and select or develop the best course of action. (McCutcheon, 1995, p. 4)

As you begin teaching in school settings, you will encounter the challenges of (1) creating curriculum on your own for daily teaching, or solo deliberation; and (2) working in small groups to create curriculum for a grade level or a subject area or some other organizational unit in the school, or group deliberation. Gail McCutcheon (1995) writes eloquently about how teachers do curriculum work "solo" and in "groups" through deliberation, listing nine characteristics of deliberation:

Curriculum deliberators, in both solo and group settings:

1. Consider and weigh possible, alternative solutions, and actions
2. Envision potential actions and outcomes of each
3. Consider equally means and ends, facts and values
4. Act with time constraints
5. Consider moral dimensions, attending to values, beliefs, and norms
6. Consider the social elements of teaching, learning, and curriculum decisions

7. Understand the simultaneity of the deliberation process, that is, many things vie simultaneously for the attention of the deliberators as they think and speak, creating a less than linear process
8. Interact with the interests of those involved
9. Interact with the conflicts created by deliberation (p. 5)

In terms of solo deliberation,

> … each teacher develops an idiosyncratic set of concepts, beliefs, and images about what to teach, how students learn, how to treat the curriculum guidelines, how to treat other adults, how to motivate students, and how to evaluate them. As a result, teachers transform curriculum policies and materials to such a degree that it is more appropriate to think of them as curriculum developers than as mere implementers. (McCutcheon, 1995, p. 34)

Teachers, on an individual and daily basis, test their practical theories of action against the questions, issues, problems, and possibilities of the day and create curriculum responses that are effective and productive. When they meet to do the work of group deliberation with others, they bring their individual experiences and practical theories of action to the table.

> Group deliberation is a process of making sense as the group seeks agreement, which is the foundation of the social construction of knowledge. During curriculum deliberation a group develops a set of agreed-upon (tacitly or overtly) interrelated ideas, values, and norms. The group focuses on beliefs and values about the content of schooling—what should be contained in the curriculum, its sequence, and organization. This process brings to the surface individual competing normative interests. Conflict among these interests ensues inevitably, tying the group together as it examines alternatives closely. (p. 147)

Most human beings enjoy and look forward to social interactions with peers on many levels. Beyond the personal interactions they have with colleagues and students each day, the professional interactions they have with peers often do not meet their expectations, especially when disagreements turn into socially inappropriate actions fueled by anger, for instance. Some teachers turn away from group interactions as result, considering the costs of participating to be too high. They sometimes ask, "Why should I take the risks associated with deliberating with others when the group won't do what I want to do anyway or even listen to me in the first place?" They wonder about spending time on deliberation when nothing ever seems to get resolved.

What teachers may be voicing from this perspective is the frustration they feel from negative group interactions they have had in the past in which the characteristics of deliberation were not honored or even known by the participants. Perhaps they feel as though their efforts led to results that are not entirely related to them and their concerns.

In response, teacher leaders must carefully lay the groundwork for deliberation, both solo and group, and essentially overcome the failings of group work they have experienced in the past. Following are several things teacher leaders can do to create productive contexts for deliberation.

First, teachers must set aside and use time for planning by themselves; that is solo deliberation. Effective teaching and learning require it, and time for it should be pursued as a professional norm for teachers in the school setting. Time does not always exist for planning in the crush of the day-to-day routine of schooling, and this can become difficult for teachers, who have to give up more and more of their own time after school hours to do the job well.

Second, time must be spent when groups first begin meeting, and perhaps even periodically throughout their life together, to familiarize the members with individuals' perspectives, interests, beliefs, values, and lives. It is crucial to take stock of where people stand, and to create norms, rules, and standards for the group and its proceedings forward with curriculum work. This step is enhanced when the group engages in socializing, perhaps meeting to talk about things other than the task at hand, and perhaps sharing food or entertainment together. Effective teams in schools allow for the establishment of personal time and space, as well as the sharing of the self in community. They are held in balance by norms created by the faculty and administration in the school. Their work together, which fosters both individual and group development, constitutes an opportunity to build community in the school.

Third, group members must agree *not* to run from or avoid conflict and conversely to construct conflict positively. So often conflict is viewed as completely negative. McCutcheon's view, however, supported by other theoretical perspectives, is that conflict leads to deeper, more meticulous consideration of alternatives. Groups often jump to conclusions and quick solutions. Groups make short work of very complicated tasks in order to avoid conflict, and look back with regret when the decisions do not seem to work out in practice in the long run. Working through conflict helps the group carefully consider alternatives; this position stands to benefit teachers and students, who can learn to trust that professionals can work through conflict and disagreement toward consensus.

It's not surprising that people avoid conflict. Teacher leaders must be aware of ways that people aspire and conspire to avoid conflict. McCutcheon reports Peck's (1987) work in this area, listing six common conflict-avoidance techniques: (1) scapegoating; (2) resorting to the authority of the organization; (3) building dependency on the leader; (4) ignoring conflict; (5) fighting; and (6) forming coalitions.

Also, and more complex, in order to counter the reflex to flee, groups need to build norms by understanding several important commitments (Smith & Berg, 1987). First, the group needs to build a safe emotional environment of trust in which even controversial statements can be made. Second, group members must simultaneously build personal knowledge of each other while they build social knowledge in the group, since persons and the group are simultaneously creating each other. Third, members must be aware that careful, active, reflective listening is key to building individual and group authority and voice.

Working in groups on problems and issues of teaching and learning is immensely satisfying. The opportunities to share ideas with peers, address immediate problems, and build relationships with students and teachers around issues of teaching and learning allow for and constitute tremendous opportunities for growth in the school setting. Also this process allows teachers to own the processes and the outcomes for school change, from dealing with individual students to changing important school structures in order to improve the learning process for the wider group. When all is said and done, two heads are better than one, and usually five heads are better than two. Teachers who work together effectively grow exponentially as professional colleagues and serve their students better as teachers.

It is also important to remember that attending to and pushing toward these aspects of group life might make the curriculum deliberation process longer and might even make the group seem disorganized. As a group forms, it creates a subtext (or group agreements about its work and life) and a text (or the curriculum itself). So curriculum work is hardly linear or organized, and it is typically complex, difficult, and contentious. However, there may be no other more rewarding aspect of teaching than engaging in a cycle of curriculum deliberations from problem posing to piloting a new curriculum in the classroom. Typically, coherence and understanding emerge from the process.

And last, for now, group members must agree not to "satisfice." Satisficing is settling, fulfilling the contractual agreement of the group's charge to the letter, barely investing the personal or the social perspectives in the process, examining few alternatives, and coming up with an efficient, seemingly reasonable and rational response to the problem. The problem with "satisficing" is that conventional wisdom isn't called for in all situations and that more thought and effort are required for most curriculum decisions, especially those that have an impact on teachers, students, and society. Teacher leaders bear a moral obligation to inquire and to deliberate into important matters, not to "get by" and "get home early." (McCutcheon credits Simon, 1976, with the term "satisfice." Read her treatment of curriculum deliberation in her book for further understanding, especially Chapter 5, "Developing the Curriculum: Solo and Group Deliberation.")

Deliberating on Curriculum: A Scenario

When I teach a course for undergraduate students on teacher leadership using this book, students engage in a more lengthy than usual group project (about three to four weeks) meant to immerse them in the experience of curriculum deliberation and the attending issues of leadership that accompany working in a small group, building a team, and creating a curriculum together. It is important to help students engage in the project by laying out some early guidelines. I focus most of our attention as teachers on the process of working as a group. I ask students to continuously reflect on the nature of the group as it forms and takes shape, to attend to specific means for creating a highly functioning group environment, and to address thoroughly points of conflict that emerge in the process.

Following is an example of a scenario that might be presented to preservice teachers, for which they would create a curriculum response together, usually in the form of a formal, explicit curriculum document. I always present some guidelines that help the groups function along the way as well.

Curriculum Deliberation Scenario

A small team of teachers has been charged by the Leeway School District to develop a model, integrated curriculum. As a member of the team, you are to deliberate with your colleagues in order to develop a prospective curriculum model to share with teachers for adoption consideration (each team receives a demographic sketch of Leeway that is different).

Some Background Details   The integrated course is for seventh grade students. The school has decided that the core subject areas (social studies, math, language arts, and science, with supporting teachers in the arts and special education) will meet in interdisciplinary blocks that are team-taught. The school hopes that the new curriculum will be interesting, substantive, hands-on and will engage students in higher order thinking skills and tasks, reflect the district's commitments to diversity and multiculturalism, and provide opportunities for students to show knowledge in use. Your team is to develop a curriculum design for the integrated course block that meets throughout the year; you have the freedom to explore creative options for the course, though you must pay particular attention to the following parts for presenting your proposal to colleagues for review and critique (the curriculum document must be at least eight pages, double-spaced/typed, including the reflective statement):

1.   *Deliberate on and develop a curriculum rationale for the course* (two pages, minimum): "A course rationale is a statement that makes explicit the values and educational goals underlying the course … The values and assumptions underlying the rationale concern the role of the individual in society, the societal role of education, the nature and purposes of society and human beings, the relation of the future to the present, the question of what knowledge is most useful, and the purpose for which it should be useful" (from Posner & Rudnitsky, *Course Design: A Guide to Curriculum Development for Teachers*, p. 42).

2.   *Deliberate on and develop a course description* (two pages, minimum): The course description will tell how the course is to be organized, and in general, what it will contain. The typical course description might include an explanation of the thematic focus of the course. It will show how students are to be involved in the curriculum process and how the school views student learning. It might include a list of questions to be answered by the course and students. It might include the underlying framework for organizing material, such as a focus on a particular theory for learning or on a particular aspect of human development, for example. It might include a general description of units to be included, along with suggested examples of learning outcomes, goals, or objectives, in general. It might show how disciplines are to be connected together, etc.

3. *Deliberate on and develop a conceptual map for the course* (one page): The conceptual map shows the course description in a graphic form.

4. *Deliberate on and develop a sample unit or lesson outline* (one page): Show how the broader planning for the course is connected to the possibilities for specific classroom practice.

5. *Deliberate on and develop a means for assessing student performance in the course* (one page): How would you approach assessment of students in the course, in general?

6. *Reflect on the deliberation process* (one page, each person contributes one page): What conflicts did the group experience and how did it work through them? What was your contribution to the project? What did you learn?

Along the way, students find it helpful to consider the following guidelines for building their group into a functioning deliberative team:

- Spend some time clarifying together what you think the purpose of the project is. Connect the course ideas with what this project might enable you to see, practice, and experience as a teacher leader.
- Spend some early time just meeting as a group and talking about things other than the project. Remember, you are building a curriculum *and* a team together. You must attend to both.
- Brainstorm some ideas about what the "central theme" or "organizing center" (see Beane, 1998) for the developed course could be. Tap into your experiences as a teacher and learner and also transcend them by considering what the possibilities for this developed course might be. Instead of reproducing an idea from your past, think about what might happen with a future group of students and classes. Also remember that brainstorming requires risk-taking, the suspension of the usual "rules" for making sense of things. This means that forms of thinking might tap the possibilities beyond the logical-rational. This doesn't mean that we engage in socially inappropriate behaviors that jeopardize our relationships with others. Even in Leeway District, there are social and professional boundaries. Be aware of them as you set them together.

As you are considering ideas, you will confront opposing views among your colleagues. The worst groups shut down; people don't get their way or are offended that others don't think exactly like they do, and the group becomes dysfunctional. The group might be prone to "satisficing" by meeting the project's minimum expectations. Guard against this at all costs. Instead, keep in mind that successful curriculum deliberations mean that conflicts will be met head on, and groups will use the energy of conflict for moving toward the best decision about the curriculum given a number of possible ideas/alternative solutions.

As you begin to get some of your ideas on paper and agree on some things, the group should build on these successes by agreeing on how the rest of the project should look. Some time in every meeting should be spent discussing ideas and possibilities. Some time should be spent completing processes that will yield the final product. No group will have enough time. Groups never do have the time they need, but they get their work accomplished because they have time constraints. This is a fact of the real world, and you will experience it during this project. This means you have to make reasoned decisions about what you can and can't do and what the placeholders you choose will look like. For example, you can't develop all of the units or lessons that you'd like to include. Developing lessons and units isn't a focus of this course, though providing an example constitutes an important aspect of curriculum development. So you should try to provide as much descriptive detail as possible about what you "intend" to do in this area, a placeholder that takes the place of a more elaborate, definitive example or plan that might follow.

At some point, you will not require coaching about what to do any longer. You'll be making your own decisions (i.e., exercising teacher leadership!).

And at some point, you may become frustrated with the process or with a group member(s). Do not come to the course instructor (unless conditions are abhorrent). Use what you have learned in the course to deal with the issues at hand as individuals and as a team. All through the project, think of exercising leadership and acting professionally.

The scenario and process outlined above is one approach to doing a deliberative curriculum project, and I've seen other approaches work well, too. Instructors might challenge you to consider an aspect of your field experiences in schools that you think should be addressed actively. For instance, say there are "knowledge gaps" that you see playing out in social studies classes in the local middle school, in particular that students seem to show little "map" literacy in the classes you've worked in. Perhaps you and colleagues can design a way to bring students up to speed in this area and design a curriculum to address it and actually have a chance to pilot it briefly during student teaching.

Say, for example, there are "hidden norms" in the high school you attended and have been working in that set up hostile conditions for gay and lesbian students. Your team could design a way to crack the school's code of silence on human sexuality issues and address fundamental needs of students struggling with making their way through school given the massive identity and social constraints that still loom for all.

Or perhaps there are new uses for social media that enhance learning that you would like to offer as an in-service professional development opportunity to practicing teachers who are open to the idea. You could design the curriculum for engaging them in next steps in this area. In reality, since the curriculum field is practically boundless, the possibilities for the type of deliberative curriculum project you could do are boundless as well. The most important thing to do is to get started, and practice.

Over the years, I've seen some amazing curriculum products come out of group projects for the course. Many times students will include material from the project in their portfolios, archiving them online and showing potential employers the extent to which they understand curriculum and its place in teaching and leadership. Some have said that their curriculum projects have come up in interviews with administrators or panels for new positions, and that they have impressed the interviewers with insights and ideas about curriculum and teaching. It's no secret that schools are looking for teachers who can make a contribution to the intellectual life of the school right away, having a positive impact on teachers and students simultaneously. As the last of the baby boomers leave their positions and retire, the next decades present great opportunities for beginning teachers, who must be conversant and practiced in curriculum work, teaching, and leadership. On your way to a career in teaching, paying attention to matters that are curricular, focusing on student learning, keeping the classroom lively and filled with intellectual stimulation, and helping students find a strong balance between knowledge and citizenship will define aspects of leadership for you in schools.

I have often believed in and seen in action the connections between curriculum work and democracy. In part, democracy is a form of "associated living," as Dewey called it, that deep set of social relations that leads us to a more democratic way of existing together in communities:

> Broadly speaking, Dewey believed that all human beings should have the conditions to develop to their fullest potential. In order for that to happen, they must be in society with other humans because humans are social beings by nature. Dewey also argued that the greater the diversity of the social setting, the more opportunity for people to develop their intellectual and moral being. Hence, the more social associations a student has, the more opportunity he or she has to develop his or her intellect and humanity. (Rotuno-Johnson, 2010, p. 170)

Therefore, the opportunities that we take and that we give for social growth, fueled by intellectual and academic stimulation, drive the development of democracy in our schools and in society. We need teachers who understand the critical role they play in helping students become citizens who are clear about their responsibilities, feel connected to and protective of the greater good, and value others and their differences. My particular perspective is that leadership in curriculum is one way to have a tremendous impact on the development of citizens and democracy. At root it's all about deliberation, practicing the art of communication and building relationships to support living conditions that are beneficial to all and that lead to justice, freedom, order, and meaning. I extend my argument for concentrating on curriculum leadership as an important form of teacher leadership in the next two chapters; in narrative form, the following chapters frame my own personal understanding of curriculum and teacher leadership and the challenges that face all of us as we venture deep into this century in public schools.

Concluding this chapter are examples of several student-generated curriculum projects. They follow the general form of attacking an educational issue or a problem, providing a rationale for the curriculum intervention, describing what the curriculum will look like, and explaining how it will be assessed.

Student Curriculum Projects

Read the following curriculum documents and then reflect on them using the following prompts.

> ## REFLECTION
>
> How do these curricula reflect the commitments of their authors? Do they address significant issues in schooling today? Could they be implemented effectively? What barriers would exist? How could these curricula be adapted for use in your setting?

Curriculum Project:
Engaging and Embracing Your Community

—Cody Dye, Quentin Russell, Allyson Klovekorn, Erin Worrell

Mission Statement The mission of our curriculum is to create a community within the walls of the school by connecting with the community outside of the school; engaging/embracing the wider community is the end goal.

Abstract This curriculum project focuses on fostering a sense of community within the school walls via engagement through service learning in the community. Students, faculty members, and community members are all free to interact and participate in this program that stresses a mutual benefit. The final objective of this curriculum is to show the importance of service to others and create a lasting impact among the students and their community.

Curriculum Rationale Fundamentally we believe in relation-centered pedagogy and organic learning experiences. We believe that learning comes most powerfully and most sincerely in relation to people. Harvard and Yale and many other universities are releasing so many good resources for learning online and for free, but simple access to information is not the goal of education. To simply give students access to knowledge could then be as easy as giving them all iPhones. This is all to say that our current education system is not only a resource for more information, but an environment in which learning is made most effective. The fundamental difference between going to class and just Googling information is the presence of teachers and peers. That is, relationships give education power.

Relationships allow students to receive personal guidance that is made more and more effective with growing trust. This requires a teacher who can give individual attention to each student. Peers can also learn together and group up in order to achieve growth that would normally be difficult or even impossible when alone (two heads are better than one).

This is directly connected with our curriculum because the Service Learning projects with which each student is involved are heavily influenced by both teacher guidance and peer support. It is certainly valuable to try to give to the community out of one's own resources and time, but without a community surrounding that giving, and giving of itself, the process defeats the very purpose of mutual benefit. At least part of the intent of education is to teach students how to be vibrant, productive citizens. So no matter whether the project that students pick for this curriculum is a local newspaper, a soup kitchen, a library, an environmental protection project, or anything else, the implicit push of this curriculum is that the content is important, but it is vital to the health of society to work together and that true progress does not come from purely the quality of ideas, but the quality of relationships. This project will be a great source for students to find teammates and mentors to help them pursue diverse goals.

Organic learning is also a crucial element to the community engagement project. Organic learning means that the knowledge and experience absorbed by the students is drawn from the life of people around the students, the life of the context and community in which those students find themselves, and that it is absorbed actively and intentionally by the students. Organic learning means that the knowledge gained will be active in the students' lives and constantly growing alongside the students as they act.

With the onset of the Information Age, it is becoming more and more important to boil information into its most fundamental components. The problem with systematizing information so heavily is that students are not computers; while a list of commands with no variation in format may be perfect for a computer to function, it is a terrible process and end goal for human beings. Perhaps even if we wanted to change that fact, as opposed to simply rejoicing in it, human beings are emotional creatures before they are logical ones. The implication here is that learning is fundamentally a contextualized process.

Further, this means that the community engagement project is a strong foundation for organic learning. Students are not memorizing lists of different aspects of their community or just reading about their community as if it is in outer space. The goal of the community engagement project is to send students outside of the school into the world-at-large in order to let them genuinely mesh themselves into the fabric of the world directly in front of them. Rather than making students memorize formulas for persuasive business letters or create a presentation on facts about the endangerment of species, we want students to actually write persuasive letters to businesses and research and test the environment in which they are living. The hope is that instead of filling heads with facts that will be forgotten in less than a semester, the project will give students a growing base of knowledge on how to interact with the world around them. They will use this experience and the subsequent skills they develop for the rest of their lives.

The reason it is so vital to the Community Engagement Project to be based on organic learning is because we want to teach students not just how to solve a specific problem, but how to confront a living issue and find a living solution. Just serving once a week for a little while at a community soup kitchen (or any other stand-in for a "community service project") completely misses the point of this project because when the student finishes a service shift, the learning stops and the benefits to other people stop. However, doing something like changing systems within the soup kitchen or interrogating community norms that promote subtly racist or sexist agendas in the distribution of food to the homeless would be a much more applicable project focus in this curriculum.

Curriculum Description   Our mission statement, or the purpose of our curriculum, is to create a community within the walls of the school by connecting with the community outside of the school. During their junior year of high school, students will be required to create and implement a project in the school's community. The project will last for one full academic year. One semester (two quarters) will be used to prepare for the project and one semester (two quarters) will be used to implement it.

During the fall semester the students will divide into small groups and brainstorm ideas about how to create a project that engages students into their school's community. The students will be a given a quarter to brainstorm their ideas with their group members. By the end of quarter one, they will submit their ideas to the teacher. Throughout the first quarter, students will have multiple opportunities to share their initial ideas with the teacher and make revisions or changes.

Once the teacher approves of their ideas then the students will create a poster board or tri-fold that explains their idea and how it can be applied to their community. The teacher or district will provide all of the necessary materials to create their presentations. In addition, the students will make their project idea presentations in the classroom. The purpose of having the students complete their group work during class time is to ensure that the teacher, who will facilitate collaboration and peer dialogue, supervises the students. Furthermore, it gives the students the opportunity to work together without trying to find time outside of class to complete the project.

The students will present their ideas at the annual community engagement fair, which will be held during the first week of the second quarter. This fair will take place at each high school in the district after school hours to allow the members of the community, who might be working during the day, to attend. Also, it gives them the opportunity to participate in the decision-making process of picking the "best" community engagement project. At the fair the students will discuss their presentations and have the chance to view other presentations. At the end of the event, the audience and students will decide together on the best project to be implemented by the entire class.

After the fair, the students will have the rest of the second quarter to concentrate on the project that was selected. During this time the class will adjust the project as necessary and be ready to implement it by the beginning of the third quarter. This process of refining the project will involve collaboration on a larger scale, which is vital for students to experience. The third and fourth quarters will then be used to fully implement their project into their community.

Each student will be assessed based on participation, completion, and applying their project to the community. The purpose of this project is to ensure that both parties (students and community) are mutually benefiting and learning from another. This course will be integrated into the curriculum, rather than simply an add-on. It will be a graduation requirement for all students.

When describing a "best" project, one must take into consideration the practicality and potential effectiveness of such a project. On one hand, the project that tackles the largest community issue or is on the grandest scale may not very well be feasible. However, a project that may be smaller in terms of impact might be the most sustainable and end up affecting the most people in a positive manner. This is one of the primary reasons the community will play a large role in determining the project of choice.

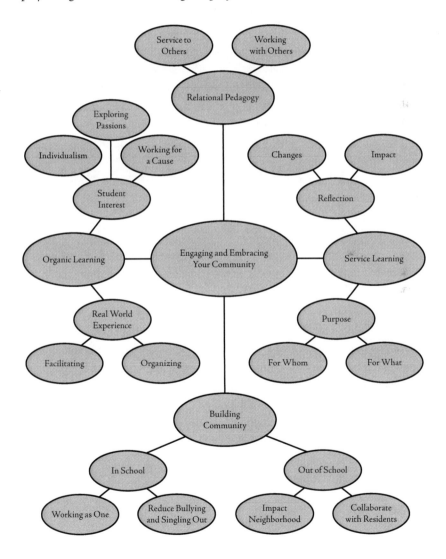

Graphic Depiction of the Curriculum

Example of How Core Ideas of the Curriculum Might Look in Practice
Shawn is a hardworking, engaged young man who, "Likes going to school, but hates homework." He does most of his work except for when he forgets to finish a math problem every now and again.

Most evenings or weekends, Shawn will spend time with his friends or family, but he also really enjoys playing piano. His family is very interested in the arts and often they all go to see the local orchestra or a jazz ensemble at a nearby club. Of course, Shawn regrets that he cannot make piano a greater part of his life, but school is focused on subjects like math and literature.

However, now that Shawn is a junior in his high school, in his new Community Engagement class, he is very excited to try to develop a project of his own in order to work on it throughout the year. His first thought is to work with piano in some way, but he is not sure how to work this into his project. He talks with his teacher, Mr. Smith:

"I don't know what project to suggest for the Community Engagement class."

"Is there anything you like to do in your free time that you could use to connect with your community on a deeper level?"

"Well, I play piano … But I don't know how to make that into a community project."

"That's actually a great idea! Do you ever go to piano performances?"

"Yeah, my family always goes to the orchestra and sometimes the local jazz club. I really like seeing different concerts. Do you think I could do something with the concerts? That's part of the community, right?"

"That's wonderful! That would work perfectly for this project; unfortunately, though, I don't know very much about the local music scene. You should use your research time to find out ways to engage in that further."

Shawn uses his first quarter to do research and compile information that will help him to find a project to choose.

"Mr. Smith, I found out online that the city concert hall is being torn down to make room for a highway extension within the next five years. A lot of people are really upset about it. Could I use my community engagement project to get involved with the concert hall?"

Shawn is excited to begin developing a plan for getting more people interested in the local concert hall. He plans on using social media to promote the concert hall and distribute a petition to as many people as he can in order to convince the city not to tear it down.

"This is pretty good," says Mr. Smith, "But how can we make it more of a multicultural project? How can we get more people to be able to use the concert hall for more activities?"

Shawn does more research on the city and finds out that while the concert hall is in jeopardy, the local jazz musicians rarely play at the concert hall, let alone many other performances of theatre or music that are intended to reach or represent a minority population. That is to say, the concert hall for some reason usually only plays the local symphony and the local theatre group, but rarely makes room for more diverse productions.

With the help of Mr. Smith, Shawn refines his petition and his goals so that the push is not only to save Concert Hall, but to improve it and draw more performances to the center.

When the students each submit their ideas for community engagement projects, there are many good ideas. One student proposed expanding the local library and holding more events there, as well as collecting more books. Another proposed adopting a relationship with an international school and creating intellectual and social interactions between schools and students. So the votes were close, and perhaps next year's students will get to try out many of these other ideas, but Shawn's Concert Hall effort ended up being the winner. The students drew together and wrote plans and goals for repurposing the concert hall.

Students began finding other bands and theatre troupes to perform a wide variety of shows and broaden the vision of the concert hall. Others helped to create blogs and connect with members of the community to get an active conversation moving in regard to the city's plan to tear down the building. Some students spoke with the local jazz musicians and managed to pull together a benefit concert for the city's local art scene in the concert hall. Even artists who painted or sculpted helped by displaying some of their art in the hall during the concert.

Not everyone in the community supported the effort; many citizens genuinely believed a highway would be better for the city.

In the end, the city would not decide to simply keep the concert hall, but allowed it to remain for the next few years until a different highway budget was discussed by the state. Perhaps the hall is safe, but perhaps not.

Shawn was a little discouraged at first because he wanted to create and participate in a more influential project.

"That's actually a really big deal, Shawn," Mr. Smith said, "You've all learned a lot about how your community functions and what matters to it and how to help make it better. The concert hall never would have hosted (and promise to continue hosting) such a wide variety of musical concerts without this project. The city isn't sure yet how it will react to the music scene here until the budget is changed again by the state, but communities are always changing and growing."

Shawn realizes he has learned a lot more about the structure of the world than he thought; he got so swept away with the project that he did not notice how much new information he had learned and the skills he had developed.

In his blog reflections, he is excited to see how quickly he began to develop; in his very first post, he seemed unsure and nervous about the project, but only a little while later recounts a blog post in which he and several of his classmates detail a meeting with an important local politician in order to see if it was possible to simply cancel the highway construction. The last post is simple, but profound: "I enjoy playing piano, but I'll bet a lot of other people play music, too. If we can keep music and other art in our community, people will be able to do things with their lives that they really love to do."

Curriculum Assessment   While the project is not focused around student assessment, there are numerous ways in which we will be evaluating students' individual work. During the first quarter, there will be checkpoints in which students have to submit initial research, ideas, and plans. For these assignments, there will be formative grades based on submission and participation; we want to ensure that students are doing work in class so they don't have to worry about anything outside of class. Also, this gives the teacher the opportunity to give students direct feedback on their actual ideas and nudge them in new directions, if necessary.

In the second quarter, the main grade will be for the poster project presented at the fair. Students will be evaluated on how clean and artistic it looks, if it flows logically, if they are able to answer questions posed by those passing by their project, etc. We want the students to utilize this opportunity to learn about designing effectively but also about presenting to audiences outside of the school walls. This will also give them the chance to take pride in their hard work and show the community all of their great ideas.

In the third and fourth quarters, when students are actually implementing the chosen project, we intend to make use of reflective writing. As students work in their community implementing their ideas, we want them to deeply reflect on their experiences, both good and bad. To do their reflections, we will use online blogs; we feel that using blogs allows for more creative writing vs. formal essays, thus engaging the students much more. Also, they will have the opportunity to comment on each other's blogs (all positive feedback or useful criticism, of course), building a stronger classroom environment in the process. For these reflections, small grades will be given for thoughtful reflection and comments, to ensure that students complete these assignments.

Curriculum Project:
From Seed to Community: Understanding the Complexity of Identity through Community Based Learning
—Annie Frazee, Nicole Geygan,
Lianna McDonald, and Rachel Murray

Rationale and Anchors
Purpose   For all students to know and understand their purpose and impact in the community.

Abstract   Our school is built on the idea that each child is a valuable member of the community. We use the metaphor of growth to describe each child's journey in school, and building upon Bronfenbrenner's Systems Theory, we recognize the child as the foundation that the classroom, school, and community are built upon. Students build on these concepts in their school experiences through an interactive community-based project.

Anchor 1: Bronfenbrenner's Ecological Systems Theory

We were inspired by Bronfenbrenner's Ecological Systems Theory when brainstorming ideas for supporting our curriculum. Bronfenbrenner's theory focuses on "how the inherent qualities of a child and his environment interact to influence how he will grow and develop" (Psychology Notes HQ, 2013). The theory is broken down into five different systems: the microsystem (pieces of the environment that directly affect the child); the mesosystem (connections between different microsystems); the exosystem (pieces of the environment that indirectly affect the child); the macrosystem (social and cultural values); and the chronosystem (cultural and world changes over time). The main idea to keep in mind is how all of these systems ultimately "interact with and influence each other in every aspect of the child's life," (Psychology Notes HQ, 2013).

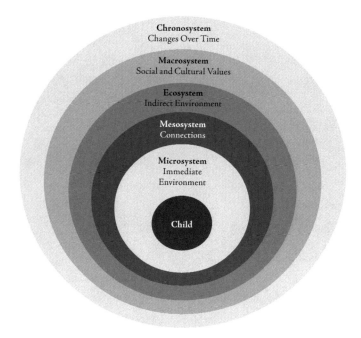

Anchor 2: The Child in the Garden and The Spiral Curriculum

Child in the Garden   Our model for the curriculum is inspired by this flower image that we created to bring our ideas into focus. The flower represents the growth of the child in different communities. The child is at the center of the plant, where the roots and the stem meet. The roots are the family because it often remains relatively consistent throughout the child's life and keeps them "rooted." The stem is the school, and the leaves are the classrooms. The child is only a part of one classroom, but the different classrooms make up the school. The flower is then the entire community. All of the communities work together and impact the child, and in turn, the child impacts each of the communities. The flower affects the roots, and the roots affect the flower. Everything is in a reciprocal relationship. The idea is that all people have their own flowers, but are involved in both the same and different communities. Everyone is a productive and important piece to the garden, interacting, experiencing, and thriving in their own right and as part of a community or multiple communities.

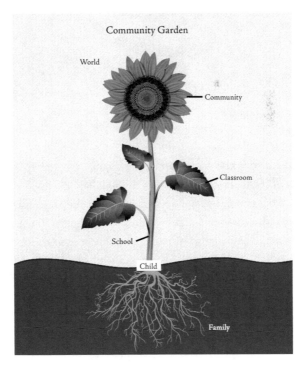

Child in the Garden

Spiral Curriculum   Spiral curriculums were theorized by Jerome Bruner. The key features of a spiral curriculum are "(1) The student revisits a topic, theme, or subject several times throughout their school career; (2) the complexity of the topic or theme increases with each revisit; and (3) new learning has a relationship with old learning and is put in context with the old information" (Johnston, 2012). We decided to structure our six themes in the format of a spiral curriculum to best communicate instruction to students. As a child grows and develops, his or her identity changes, causing certain themes to be more relevant than others. We hope by using a spiral curriculum, all children will be able to explore the different aspects of the community through their entire school experience.

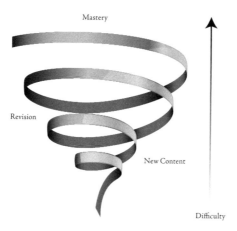

Anchor 3: Complexity of Identity, Cultural Wealth, and Teaching the Whole Child

Identity   We learned that the development of a child's identity is necessary to determine who they are as a person and where they fit in the world. Tatum (1997) argues: "The salience of particular aspects of our identify varies at different moments in our lives. The process of integrating the component parts of our self-definition is indeed a lifelong journey" (p. 43).

Complexity of Community and Cultural Wealth   We have learned that it is absolutely crucial to keep the "whole child" in context when educating, and this involves including their racial, cultural, and familial identities in the curriculum. Cooper, Nava, and Huh (2010) argue that "although there is a general acceptance that family involvement enhances student academic performance, Latino families are thought of as not having the social and cultural capital to be influential in this process" (p. 52). But all families, regardless of background, have rich, familial capital that enhances a child's life and can enhance school experience.

A key aspect of developing the ideas of community and cultural wealth is incorporating multicultural education throughout every aspect of the curriculum. The National Association for Multicultural Education defines multicultural education as "a philosophical concept built on the ideals of freedom, justice, equality, equity, and human dignity …. It affirms our need to prepare students for their responsibilities in an interdependent world. It recognizes the role schools can play in developing the attitudes and values necessary for a democratic society. It values cultural differences and affirms the pluralism that students, their communities, and teachers reflect" (The National Association for Multicultural Education, 2018).

John Dewey and the "Whole Child" The child is more than just a person inside a classroom; he or she has a life outside of the room as well. "Dewey maintained that education was for the whole child and must focus on the child's own experience and life in the contemporary world" (Samuel & Suh, 2012). Because of this, Samuel and Suh (2012) argue that "teachers need to nurture children's desires to learn and provide them with motivating experiences" (p. 187).

Description and Application

Application of Bronfenbrenner We were inspired by Bronfenbrenner's layers of community that surround the child throughout development and incorporated that into our six themes. Similar to Bronfenbrenner's concentric circles, we started with the child as the center and branched out to include the different communities and how they build on each other. Our curriculum is centered around the child's identity and how various outside forces and environments intersect to impact the child.

Application of the Child in the Garden We use the flower in the garden metaphor to represent the child's growth and development through the years. We recognize that the community is a garden where lots of people come and interact. Each student has a sense of identity within the community. Our goal is to ensure that every child has a place within the community. The overarching idea of our curriculum is to assure that each child has an understanding and appreciation for the role that they play in the community.

Application of the Spiral Curriculum   Our curriculum is explored by the student through six different themes. The student will explore the themes throughout every year; each theme is explored every year, but students go more in depth and there is a "focus theme" each year where the class will spend more time on a certain theme. However, progression through the themes is up to each class (students and teacher) on where their interest takes them and how long they wish to focus on each theme.

Application of Complexity of Identity   Our six themes that are addressed every year focus on students' identities and places in the world. Two of these themes focus on the student and their identity, two focus on the student as a member of their class and school, and the final two focus on their local community and the connected global community. It is much more difficult to serve others in the world without first knowing a bit about the self. Every year, the students will be diving a little deeper into each of the themes so they can discover more about themselves and the world they live in as they grow and mature.

Application of Community and Cultural Wealth   While our project goes beyond just Latino families as mentioned in the rationale quote by Cooper, Nava, and Huh (2010), we wanted our students to use the experiences they have in their families to develop their own identity and serve the communities that they live in through a hands on service project. Each class will be responsible for selecting a need in the community that they want to address and will work all year to develop a service project to address this need, using what they have learned about themselves and the world. Through this experience, they learn that they do indeed have social capital and worth, which is often lost in the typical curriculum implemented by most schools. We hope to get the families of our students involved as well so that they know that they also serve a central role in the education of their children. We realize that not all support from families looks the same due to jobs and other commitments, but any support is valuable and wanted. This is a key aspect of multicultural education: We want to keep children's cultures a central point in this curriculum.

Application of Teaching the Whole Child   If the children can't see themselves represented in the curriculum, they will not be motivated to work hard. What is the point of an education if students are not learning skills that offer real world applicability? Why should students care about what they are learning if they can't see their own culture represented in the past, present, and potential future? We believe that the schooling years are not just a time for students to learn these skills, but also an opportunity for them to make a positive change in the community right where they live. This is why we find it essential to have them working directly in the community as well as in the classroom because learning can and must occur in both environments. Working in these environments is necessary to the development and formation of a child to live in a world where he or she can act as a caring and aware adult.

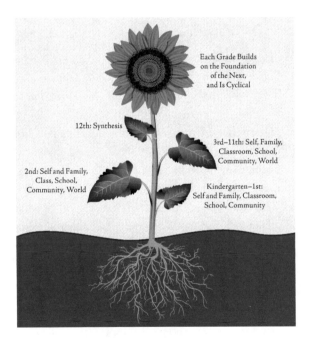

Sunflower Concept Map

Theme Plan

This is an example of pages you would find out of a "curriculum guide" for teachers explaining how to teach each theme. Each theme has multicultural education ideas interwoven throughout all aspects.

Theme 1: Me, Myself, and I
{This Is the Focus Theme for Grade 4}

Students will explore their own identity as a person and a learner through the lenses of diversity, values, and interests.

Process   Teachers can use resources such as interest inventories, surveys, multiple intelligences assessments, and when appropriate, personality assessments. Teachers will also focus on identities of the child and ensure that each child is represented in the classroom. The teacher will guide the students on their journey to self-discovery. Teachers will begin to discuss their community project.

Theme 2: My Family, My Heritage (3+)
[This Is a Sub-Genre of Theme 1 in Grades K–1 and Transitional in Grade 2; It Is Its Own Theme Beginning in Grade 3] {This Is the Focus Theme for Grade 3}

Students will develop their identity as a member of their family and heritage through the lenses of culture, diversity, and values.

Process   Students will conduct interviews, find primary and secondary sources, and do research on their family heritage. They will also discuss their role in the family and how that affects them (emotionally, mentally, and developmentally). They will also focus on family and cultural values.

Theme 3: Hand in Hand, Together We Can
{This Is the Focus Theme for Grades K–1}

Students will contemplate how their identity fits as a member of the classroom community through the lenses of diversity, shared values, and collaboration.

Process   Developing a classroom community will begin on day one with promoting democracy and making sure that every child feels valued. This theme is focused on how the children interact in the classroom. The child will also take what they have learned in the previous two themes to help them understand how they interact with others. The teacher promotes mindfulness and methods for the children to use when they feel angry, overwhelmed, or frustrated. Respect should be incorporated in the foundation of the classroom.

Theme 4: Our School, Our Heart
{This Is the Focus Theme for Grade 2}

Students will use what they have learned to develop their identity as an active member of their school community through diversity, social justice, and activism.

Process Students will take what they have learned in Theme 3 and transfer it to their larger school community. The school is run by the idea of mutual respect. It is the students' job to respect others, the school, their classroom, etc. Students are encouraged to advocate for others within the school walls. They are taught that they have a voice and that their voice is important.

Theme 5: Community Makes Unity
{This Is the Focus Theme for Grade 2}

Students will use their previous experiences as a catalyst for change of their community by exploring activism and advocacy, diversity, and social justice.

Brainstorming

- Option 1 If students show interest in a certain aspect of their community, go straight into choosing topics …
- Option 2 If students do not have a specific interest in a few aspects of their community, the teacher can present places that are in their community (show videos, pictures, fliers, articles, etc. of different places in their community, i.e., non-profits, assisted living, parks, animal shelters, soup kitchens, etc.).

Choosing a Topic The class will narrow the projects down into 3–4 options and have small groups research each project. Each group will give a mini-project proposal on their project. Students will then have a discussion about why and how they should do each project (or not!). The class will then reach a consensus, if possible, on their project.

Research and Problem Solving The class will research their project by contacting affiliated parties and seeing what problems exist. Students will then create an action plan to solve the problems that arose in the conversation. If multiple problems are proposed that are not connected, the class will then decide which problem to focus on (e.g., for the animal shelter, two connected problems would be that they need towels, and they need volunteers; these problems are connected and smaller, so they could both be done.

For the park, two non-connected problems would be that there is a great deal of litter, and the equipment is outdated or unsafe; these problems are not as connected and larger, so the class would need to pick one of these projects).

Outreach   The students will work in small groups to create different forms of outreach to the community to get their project off the ground. For example, a group could work on advertising either in print or digital and another group could work on outreach for volunteers and another group could work on political activism (for example, a petition). The goal of this step is to get the word out about the project and to include the community in their efforts to begin this project.

Implementation   The students and teacher will work together to find a few days where they can spend time at their project location. They will be working on implementing their project and leading as an example to the community. They will spend the day volunteering at their location and implementing their plan in the community.

Theme 6: Our Community Lends a Hand (2+)
[This Theme Is Focusing on the World and History in a Broader Sense and Is Introduced in Grade 2) {This Is the Focus Theme for Grade 5}
Students will gather knowledge of current and past events on a world-wide scale to discover how they can be a positive impact on the future through diversity, activism, and social justice.

Process   This theme begins with history. Students discover activism and advocacy throughout time. They then transition to the present. They begin to go beyond their local community and talk about how they can advocate for social change on a large scale. This will include study of current and former activists with a focus on peaceful conflict resolution and promoting social change.

Assessment of Student Progress
K–11   In K–11, the students will be working on smaller formative projects that chronicle what they've learned and what they've done that particular year in school with an overview of what they've done to satisfy each of the themes. Each theme will include a small project that shows what each student has accomplished in that area. Students will focus on their understanding of the content as well as how they have grown in their identity and community from their study of the theme. These formative projects can be done at the

teacher and student's discretion and will be developmentally appropriate (i.e., a mural, book, collage, paper, presentation). These will be saved in a portfolio that moves with the students through each year.

12th Grade   In the 12th year, students will generate a summative service project with an organization of their choosing that they will implement. Afterwards, they will take what they've learned and documented in their portfolio throughout their past 13 years to develop a final reflective capstone project presentation that showcases how they have grown. Their presentation will highlight their 12th-year project as well as offer an overview of what they've done throughout their 13-year journey and how they have grown into the person they are today.

They will present this project in an open or closed panel to a group. The students will have to invite at least three people to attend this presentation and assess their project. However, students have the option to make their presentation open to anyone (large setting) or to a select few people that they choose to invite. One of the people they invite has to be the primary teacher in the capstone project, the second person has to be someone in school or community administration, and the third person can be any former teacher. Beyond these, they can invite anyone else of their choosing connected to the project (parents, siblings, friends, other family members, etc.). Since this project is a requirement for graduation, the panelists will offer their feedback on this presentation, and this will be used to determine the student's final grade and their ability to graduate.

References for Curriculum Project

Aronson, B.A., & Poetter, T.S. (2018). *Teacher Leadership for Social Justice Building a Curriculum for Liberation.* Cognella Academic Publishing.

Johnston, H. (2012, February 29). The Spiral Curriculum. Research into Practice. Retrieved from https://eric.ed.gov/?id=ED538282.

Psychology Notes HQ. (2013, November 3). What is Bronfenbrenner's Ecological Systems Theory? Retrieved from https://www.psychology-noteshq.com/bronfenbrenner-ecological-theory/.

The National Association for Multicultural Education. (2018). Retrieved from https://www.nameorg.org/definitions_of_multicultural_e.php.

Special thanks to Pearl Whistler for helping with the "Sunflower Concept Map" on page 231.

11

THE ZOO TRIP:
OBJECTING TO
OBJECTIVES*

It's a beautiful day for a family trip to the zoo, and the arrival of a new baby elephant makes the prospect even more exciting. So why is Tim crying?

I've taught many graduate- and undergraduate-level courses in education for novice and veteran teachers over the years. Curriculum understanding and development are typically central aspects of these courses (Pinar et al., 2002; Zemelman, Daniels, & Hyde, 1998). I've often used Elliot Eisner's classic curriculum text *The Educational Imagination* (2001; previous editions in 1979, 1985, and 1994 have also been useful) to frame what I regard as a problem for the field and the practice of teaching in public schools: curricularists and teachers often believe that meaningful activities in school have to be scripted, planned to the nth degree, and assigned learning objectives and goals ahead of time, or they have no educational worth. Some behaviorists claim that no learning occurs if students' performance, as measured by the teacher, doesn't meet the exact specifications of the objective to be taught in the lesson (Mager, 1962). Many present-day "reformers" say that everything in the curriculum should be tied explicitly to "standards," "objectives," or "goals."

---

*Originally published as "The Zoo Trip: Objecting to Objectives," by Thomas S. Poetter, *Phi Delta Kappan*, Vol. 88, No. 4, December 2006: 319–323. Reprinted with permission of Phi Delta Kappa International, *www.pdkintl.org* <http://www.pdkintl.org>. All rights reserved.

It's just not enough for them and for those exercising surveillance over teachers and our classrooms if students find an experience meaningful and valuable in myriad ways or if an activity teaches without being tied to some set of learning outcomes or objectives. It's the classic question of whether ends have to come before means, or if means can precede undetermined ends in a meaningful way. Or maybe the bigger question is whether educational means are sometimes adequate educational ends in and of themselves. Perhaps some of our most educational experiences occur when we purposefully engage in them and then figure out after the fact just what it was that we gleaned from them. The gleaning can be done implicitly or explicitly with the teacher, on the student's own, or in a group. The point is that something was learned, and the learning may have been ineffable, deep, or profound—as when you hear your first beautiful aria at the opera or see a majestic home run hit out of a big league stadium.

Eisner calls these types of activities in our lives and in schools "expressive activities" or "expressive outcomes." They are things we do on purpose because something good and educational will come of doing them. Going to the movies, riding a bike, taking a walk, or making a field trip to the zoo are things human beings do for fun, for culture, for meaning, or for learning. There is an implicit understanding that, whatever the ends of the activity, they will be worthwhile and that the means experienced will be of value, no matter what. We know something good will happen in the midst of doing the activity; we just don't know ahead of time what it will be.

So, Eisner maintains, expressive outcomes are different from behavioral and problem-solving objectives. Behavioral objectives are time-worn educational ends that teachers typically learn how to write in preservice programs and then incorporate into their weekly planning, which they share with their principals every Monday morning. These objectives supposedly describe and predict what content and behaviors will be achieved from the interaction with certain materials, processes, and activities. Problem-solving objectives are more open than behavioral objectives and involve more student agency, but the ends are still tightly wound around particular problems and certain questions about them. The idea, in both behavioral and problem-solving circumstances, is to use the activity (means), whether teacher- or student-directed, to meet the stated, explicit goal (end).

Many times my students have been stumped during a discussion of these multiple ways to think about educational ends, especially if they've seen their own curriculum work as being centered on behavioral objectives for the better parts of their careers in teaching. They argue that they often set students to solving problems and allow them to discover how best to go about the work of reaching a stated end. I believe that they do this—and though it's good, it's certainly not nirvana. As we talk, many of my students see some value, on special occasions, in having their students engage in expressive activities. But how are they educational? What's wrong with always scripting the ends ahead of time, creating objectives that will guide the students' experience, helping students connect the learning they will be doing on the scene to broader and even more explicit objectives in their regular school curriculum? They ask, "Isn't this just good planning for instruction? Can't an expressive activity be even better if we turn it into a more tightly planned, more objective experience?"

In response, I tell the story of how my family takes its yearly zoo trip. Okay, I don't really go to the zoo this way. The story is told with a touch of irony, not always the best teaching tool, but it's effective in this case. I'm trying to show how ludicrous the students' hard and fast position is, carried to the extreme, just as we have carried it to the extreme in our classroom and school practices to date. In fact, the story is so hard-hitting that it once made a student cry; she walked in on the middle of the story without hearing my disclaimer at the beginning. I'm not so proud of that, though my oral interpretation skills must have been in peak form that day.

What follows is a dramatization—when I perform it, I act out the part of the driver and mimic the voices of the rest of the passengers. For effect, imagine that I am in front of a room full of students of teaching, pretending that I am driving a family of four to the zoo on a crisp, beautiful, and sunny Saturday morning.

The Zoo Trip

Overview   I take my seat at the wheel of our minivan. Every spring we go to the zoo as a family. We leave early in the morning so that we can get a free place to park on the street outside the $5 zoo lot. The car is packed with snacks and drinks for the ride and for the day on the zoo grounds; the goodies sit at the feet of my wife, Kate, on the passenger side. Our two sons, Jack, 8, and Tim, 6, sit in the back seats, all buckled in. I drive. They anticipate.

"Well, boys," I begin, as I look at them through the rearview mirror, adjusting my seating position for the 50-minute ride, "just for review, tell me again what it is that we agreed would be the focus of our glorious trip to the zoo today?"

"Daddy?" Tim pipes up immediately. "Before we start, I want you to know that we watched this one show last night on TV about the new baby eledrant at —"

"That's 'elephant,' Son. 'Elephant,' not 'eledrant,'" I emphasize.

"Right, a baby eledrant was —"

"No, 'elephant,' not 'eledrant.' Now say it right, after me. El-e-phant."

"Eledrant."

We go on like this for a few minutes. Frustrated, I finally say, "Just go on, Tim, forget it. You're in first grade and still messing up the pronunciation of easy words like that. Wow. Anyway, what were you saying about the baby eledrant, I mean, elephant?"

Tim takes my harsh critique in stride and continues, purposefully, "Well, we saw this part on the news, and it told about the new baby eledrant at the zoo. It was born just this past week, and they are going to have a special program today at 9:30 where they bring it out and show everyone and —"

"And?" I press.

"And I'd like to see him."

"And you'd like to see him? Well, that would be possible if today was about baby elephants, but today isn't about baby elephants." Turning my attention to Tim's older brother, I ask, "What is today about, Jack? Tell your little brother again."

"It's about carnivores, Dad. Carnivores!" He makes a growling, almost meat-eating-type noise, grinding the sounds in the back of his throat while answering. He'd just as soon gobble Tim up as put up with his nonsense.

That makes me beam. "Good, Son, it's the family's carnivore day at the zoo. Correct. We've been preparing for this trip for several weeks. Now, if it were about baby elephants, today we would be focusing on …?"

"Herbivores, of course," Jack answers with great confidence. "Everyone knows that elephants are herbivores, not carnivores. Herbivores, like elephants, eat plants and stuff, not meat." With a good bit of disdain for his younger sibling, he pounds this point home, looking directly at Tim.

"Right again!" I turn to Kate and ask, "Honey, would you please give Jack a cookie and a drink for his performance so far? Just outstanding. Good boy."

"Thanks, Dad."

"You're welcome, Son," I smile, while making eye contact with him in the rearview mirror. But I see Tim's hand in the air, patiently waiting to ask a question, knowing no cookie or punch will be forthcoming. He knows better than to ask for something like a snack at this point, considering how poorly he has done so far.

"Tim, what is it?"

"Well, Dad, I know that today is about carnivores, and that herbivores are not carnivores."

"Good, Tim, that's the smartest thing you've said so far today," I say, interrupting him.

"But I'd really like to see the baby eledrant. He's so cute, and just brand-new and everything."

Seething now, I pull the car over. "Now you listen to me, Tim." I wheel on him, scaring even Kate a bit. "You can try to derail this discussion all you want, but this isn't about you and what you want to do or see at the zoo. That's just selfish. I won't hear any more about it, do you hear me? Now just button it, and we'll get back to business. You got me?"

With a small tear welling, Tim whispers just loud enough for us to hear, "Okay, Dad, sorry."

"Fine." I pull the car back on the road. "Now—and there's nothing to cry about, by the way, young man. After all, we are going to the zoo today. Isn't that awesome?"

Now turning back to Kate, I ask, "Honey, do you have the warm-up worksheet I brought for the trip?"

"Yes, Dear, right here."

She fiddles around on the floor for the manila folder with the worksheets titled "Carnivores at the Zoo," finds them, and hands one each back to Tim and Jack along with pencils and clipboards.

"Now, these worksheets should help you prepare even more deeply for the zoo trip and especially for the special topic of carnivores. Get to it. We'll hear your preliminary answers in, oh, five minutes."

The boys both take up the work, quietly. They can both read well enough to handle the elementary questions with their own writing in response.

"Okay, Quiz Time!" I shout, after only about three minutes, because Tim's errant comments have made us lose some time.

"Let's hear it, Tim, come on, boy. Number 1 (I had the questions memorized). 'Name your favorite carnivore at the zoo.'"

"Eledrant," Tim answers, now defiant. He stares straight through me.

Trying not to draw too much attention to his defiant play, I respond, "No. Elephants are not carnivores. Jack?"

"Tigers!" Jack exclaims with an air of superiority. He senses that he has the upper hand for good now, as if he didn't have it already, and he circles for the kill. "And a whole bunch more, Dad, like lions and such, live at the zoo. I just love carnivores."

"Me, too, Son. Boy, have you come a long way in your work. Momma, give that boy another cookie!" Kate playfully throws back another cookie for Jack, which he snares in the air and pops into his mouth, lording it over Tim. I kind of like the challenge Jack lays down for Tim; competition is good for kids. "Number 2. Timmy, I know you can do it. Okay, 'What do carnivores eat?'"

Tim pauses for a moment, weighing his options, while feeling hungry and embarrassed and completely under the thumb of his big brother, a place he hates to be. "Dad, I'm going to say … eledrants."

"Hmm, interesting answer. But, no. Meat (or animal flesh) is the correct answer. In general, yes, I suppose elephants could be meat to some carnivores, but there are only a very limited number of carnivores that could actually eat an elephant. That's another treat, by default, to Jack. Good work, my boy."

Now Tim begins to cry onto his worksheet page, smudging up his answers. It's time to turn the worksheets in.

"Okay, that's enough. Let's have your completed worksheets so your mom can grade them and reward you, if applicable. Pass them up."

Kate takes them over the seat, marks the papers, comments briefly on the strength and weaknesses of their answers, then announces the totals: "Jack got 5 out of 5 correct. Great job. Tim got 0 right out of 5. Not so good. Smudgy, too."

She passes back another treat for Jack but then looks at Tim. With a motherly touch on his knee, she says, "Now, if you are going to pull this together, you are going to have to get with the program, Tim. This is for your own good—just put the elephants aside for now. Maybe we can come back some other time and see them."

He's not buying it one bit. "But the eledrant's a baby now, Mommy. He won't be a baby next time we come. I want to see him now. Why can't we go?" To his credit, the boy gets the words out while simultaneously bawling his eyes out; he does it without all the hiccupping and slobbering some kids can't control when they are upset. A tough customer, this one, and stubborn, too. Just the way I like them. They break harder, but boy, do they become good citizens: compliant, passive, upright.

I break in at this point, now approaching the final turn to the zoo. This is my territory, anyway. Sternly now, I drive home the main point of it all: "Why can't we go, Tim? Because when we come to the zoo, we come on purpose to see something in particular. We've seen the elephants before; remember last year we did the herbivore trip? Once an elephant, always an elephant.

Albeit a little smaller this time, and tugging at your heartstrings, though it's not like the elephant is named 'Tim' or something, right? But that's not the point, anyway. The point is that this trip is about something else, something worth learning. Something we planned. We aren't just wandering around the zoo at a leisurely pace, admiring the vegetation and the animals, playing and walking and laughing and looking. Maybe some other families like to do those things at the zoo. That's not what we do. We come here to learn stuff, important stuff you need to know. You need to know about carnivores, and we're here to teach you what you need to know. If you don't focus on it, you won't learn it. Got it?" I look back to see and hear the obligatory "Yes, Sir." Tim stares out the window, the tears drying on his face; he quickly whisks each one away with his shirt sleeve as they come.

"Good boy. Now, there's no treat for you until we're inside. You can catch up if you do a good job on your worksheet assignment inside the zoo. But there won't be any playing around and sneaking over to the elephant house. Got it?"

Jack perks up now, seeing the street signs for the zoo, "This is going to be great, Dad."

"Yes, Son." I smile at Kate, then back at Jack. "It's going to be great." It is great already. All three of us smile.

Tim just stares out the window. On a big billboard outside the zoo, the local news channel advertises its five o'clock series on the new baby elephant, with a big picture and a call to passersby, "Come see our new baby, Tim the Elephant. Fresh into the world and ready to go! Fresh, New Elephants— Fresh, New News. Channel 16."

Tim reads the words to himself and wonders—just like his friend on the other side of the zoo, the new one who carries the same name as he—if he might ever be released from his cage. Then in a last, fleeting attempt at some sense of connection, Tim shouts, "Hey, did you see that billboard? It had the baby eledrant on it! Right there!" He yells out, pointing to it, "And its name is Tim, too! Just like I saw it on TV!"

We all miss the sign, because those of us focused on the project at hand are busy looking for a free parking place on the street. Jack sees an open spot on the corner just ahead, brings it to our attention, and we race into it just ahead of another minivan. What a great kid, huh?

"Naw, Tim, we didn't see it. Who would name an elephant Tim, anyway? That's a little strange, isn't it? I mean, that's a bit diminutive even for a baby elephant. At any rate, out we go!" We have arrived. I turn the wheel to hug the curb on the steep incline of the street. Then I step out of the car and smell the clean zoo air. What a glorious day, indeed.

Learning to Let It Be

It's absolutely true that a young woman in my class cried during our discussion after I told the zoo trip story. At first, her reaction flabbergasted me. I was deeply concerned that I had upset her to this extent. Yes, I wanted to invoke certain feelings in the class, to make a point, but I didn't think things would get so charged. She had come in just after I started telling the story, sat down, and immediately looked appalled. She made it to the end, but apparently she was in distress the entire time. I didn't see it building to this degree and kept right on with the story, piling the details on. She was the first one to speak. "How could you do that to your son? What are you, some sort of monster? And how could all you guys laugh about it?" She said this to everyone in the room, her classmates. "That's horrible!"

I didn't know whether to laugh or cry myself. I tried to explain to her that I was telling a fictional story, trying to make the point that curriculum and teaching sometimes serve to kill student interest, debase the child, stymie natural curiosity. I don't take trips to the zoo like this, but many of us, especially in schools, objectify things that are as pure, as natural, and as expressive as we would expect a zoo trip to be. We needlessly turn such wonderful experiences—not meant as structured, organized learning activities—into labor. I was trying to show the impact that this tendency has on children like Tim—and also on those like Jack. The hyperbole in the story made people laugh; taking a zoo trip like this is absurd, and at the same time we nervously know that we are complicit. It has happened to us, and we could very easily make it happen to others; maybe we have already.

She never got over it, though; I still don't know that she even believed her classmates or me and our legitimate explanations. All tried to console her, assuring her that I was no monster, that it was just a story. None succeeded.

The fact of the matter is that this story traumatized her because she had played the part of Tim so often in school and perhaps in her own family—and needlessly so. Why does nearly everything we do in school have to be endlessly scripted, objectified, and stilted? And why do we have to put certain students, those who see a better, different way, through such misery?

Some things that we plan for students to engage in require that we simply let the students experience them. There's nothing wrong with debriefing afterward, during a discussion about the merits of the experience and about what students learned. But to script every move in advance and to specify every bit of knowledge that can and should be gleaned from expressive circumstances is to commit educational overkill. Of course, students learn no matter what we do as teachers. The question is, how will we find the right balance in this current climate and in the public school curriculum, in general, which don't support and often discourage anything that looks to be progressive, student-centered, and experience-oriented for experience's own sake?

I am constantly reminding teachers I know, and teach, and care for not to spoil the wonderful opportunities that emerge during the school year for inquiry and independent exploration. Don't take a completely scripted field trip to the zoo, for instance, I warn. Instead, take a more open, expressive approach to this and other activities, and let students have time and space to wonder and wander. There's just nothing wrong with it, and it will yield so much. In fact, if we're at all serious about cultivating true knowledge and intellect in school, we'll try harder to provide more such opportunities for our students even while the screws of the standardization and testing movements tighten the lid down on us and everything curricular. We'll try to make sure that we're not left, like Tim, looking out the window at billboards advertising our dashed hopes while we strike out into a stark, disadvantaged future filled with little more than requirements and nothing close to dreams.

School principals, curriculum specialists, and others can provide leadership in this regard. When the spring rolls around in states where the hazing of testing has ended, when teachers truly begin to teach and plan field trips, principals can tell the zoo trip story at a faculty meeting and then demand that no one in that room submit behavioral objectives for a month. At the very least, they shouldn't ruin the field trip by planning for the students to complete a worksheet at the zoo.

REFLECTION

What did you do on your last trip to the zoo? Was it an expressive trip, or one dominated by behavioral objectives? How can you work and play in your own classrooms to create a more expressive environment?

12

STEMMING THE TIDE: CALVIN'S HIGH-WATER MARK AND TEACHER RESISTANCE*

Many scholars have revealed the present-day school reform movement in the United States as a great sham (e.g., Bracey, 2009; Engel, 2009; McNeil, 2000; Pinar, 2012; Schniedewind & Sapon-Shevin, 2012; Tienken & Orlich, 2013). These scholars are among the many critics of what is being done to kill public schooling through (1) standardizing the curriculum; (2) teaching to high-stakes tests; (3) holding teachers "accountable" for conditions outside their control by using new evaluation schemes that tie student test scores to "merit"; and (4) punishing so-called "failing" schools by closing or outsourcing them to corporate interests.

The reformers, mainly politicians and wealthy pundits with their corporate backers, are quickly weakening public schools. Essentially, the reformers are stealing from the public the heart of democracy: thriving public schools. The public schools make up the only system able to provide large-scale educational opportunities for the development of a learned citizenry capable of pursuing a life of liberty and happiness.

---

*Originally published as "Stemming the Tide: Calvin's High-Water Mark and Teacher Resistance" by Thomas S. Poetter, *Kappa Delta Pi Record*, Vol. 49, No. 3, Jul.–Sept. 2013. Reprinted with permission of Kappa Delta Pi International Honor Society in Education, *http://www.kdp.org/publications/kdprecord/*. All rights reserved.

Standardized Schools

The practice of standardization seems to have been on a nonstop march through our schools since 2002. Herein lies the rub: not every student needs the same things! Classrooms should be rich places for intellectual activity, creativity, imagination, and wonder. Furthermore, choice, a critical aspect of a democratic life, has been almost completely removed from the classroom for both students and teachers. In many cases, teachers can't help but do what they're told to do, and often regress in their work, taking the path of least resistance to satisfy the boss and other powers that be. If test scores are going to be the one and only judge of educational worth, why jeopardize any stake you have in the enterprise? Teach to the test; students might score better, and all will be well. Right?

From Words to Actions

Early in the last decade, I was inspired to loosen myself from my perch, where I was merely railing against the machine from the ivory tower. I heard four magnates of the field of curriculum studies—John Goodlad, Maxine Greene, Eliot Eisner, and Madeline Grumet—answer the following question at a symposium during the 2001 annual meeting of the American Educational Research Association (AERA) in Seattle: "What would John Dewey have to say about the rise of high-stakes testing and the standardization of the curriculum?" Among many answers given and ideas shared, Goodlad reflected that Dewey "would be so disappointed that so many of us have done so little to stem the tide." So I did what scholars do and began to write. At the urging of my conscience, colleagues, and students, I wrote articles and books about the threat posed by these rampant cancers of standardization, surveillance, and high-stakes testing (Poetter, 2006, 2012).

By 2008 I faced a growing, personal disdain for the current state of things. Veteran teachers brought to my graduate classes endless stories of compromise and demise as they fought lesson-by-lesson and test-by-test against the powers that be. With their jobs on the line, these powers—mainly principals, curriculum directors, and superintendents—were similarly co-opted by the system and unable to take any sort of moral, educational stand. So they worked purposefully to keep passionate and capable teachers aligned with the scheduled scripts for instruction, which had been written by others for them to read in class. This is what teaching had become, the teachers said. But did it have to be that way?

Teaching with Autonomy

In response, as a university partner with an area school district, I was able to arrange a unique opportunity to teach a section of grade 9 English at the high school during Spring 2008. I wondered whether it was still possible to be creative in the current standardized environment. What I found was that teachers at the high school encouraged me to develop my own lessons, to teach and focus on what I thought the students needed and what I thought was best for them to be learning. The English department of the high school provided a curriculum outline filled with topics and themes and readings and such, but I merely found this helpful, not restrictive.

When push came to shove, and I had to enter my standards/goals for my lessons and course syllabus online, I simply cut and pasted the relevant standards for the ninth grade into that box as an experiment. As far as I know it never got checked, I never had to submit other formal lesson plans, and I was allowed to teach as I saw fit, based on what I knew and what I thought the students assigned to me knew and were interested in knowing. Literally, I was allowed to teach instead of being sentenced to follow someone else's script.

This experience confirmed a strong hunch I had at the start of that semester: In some places, especially in high schools where a significant margin of students commonly pass the standardized graduation tests, teachers, for the most part, can still teach without the omnipresent surveillance of the standards and hawking supervisors. In a few words, many high school teachers around the country, at least in 2008, still had at least some minimal flexibility and a range of autonomous decision-making ability within the system. That is, they could cover the standards without teaching explicitly to them, challenge students with appropriate methods without having to teach from a script, and worry mainly about engaging students, cultivating learning as the students grew in their knowledge, skills, and appreciation of the subject matter and the classroom community. This is teaching.

What a Difference Five Years Makes

Yet, as I am constantly learning from my teacher colleagues in public schools, movements to stamp out teaching thrive, while teachers scamper to maintain any level of academic freedom or control over the pedagogy and curriculum in use in their own classrooms. In fact, high school teachers who enjoyed freedom from the mandate of the high-stakes testing regime are now being chased, pursued, and finally hobbled by the standardization movement. Ultimately, the results are a not-so-subtle narrowing of the curriculum and the pedagogy of the classroom teacher.

In contrast to the freedom and professionalism I felt as a teacher returning to the high school classroom in 2008, my friend Calvin—a high school teacher in another area district—has seen teachers' academic freedom and his own ability to truly teach become severely challenged and tested by the powers that be.

Calvin is a 25-year veteran of high school social studies teaching, an award-winning, decorated classroom teacher. He is a person who has dedicated himself to the project of public education his entire career and has been especially committed to his students. He had spent the past ten years ducking for cover and dodging bullets, essentially ignoring the state standards because he basically covered all of them anyway. Instead, he was teaching his students, covering the curriculum without being chained to it, and helping students pass his course, graduate, and go on to have productive lives.

His former principal had told the master teachers in Calvin's school for many years: "The classroom, teaching, and curriculum are your territories, not mine. You do whatever you need to do to the get the academic and social jobs of teaching done. We hired you to teach, and you will teach well. I trust you." Calvin had lived by that mantra, enjoyed his work, and felt successful because his students were successful. Now the message was completely different.

His new principal communicated that Calvin, at the beginning of each semester, would have to submit for approval a final exam, aligned to the standards, and meeting certain "rigorous" criteria specified in a complex rubric. A certain percentage of students had to pass a certain percentage of the test items each semester, and these numbers would be used to calculate "merit" as well as to calculate a teacher evaluation score for him at the end of the academic year. He had protested, saying that creating a test would make him, by default, teach to the test, and he couldn't do it "ethically." That's not what professional teachers do, he argued. But the principal said that she didn't care about his ethics, that the end-of-semester exam was due on her desk by 4:00 p.m. Friday afternoon, and that there was no way around it. His hands were tied. The time had come for him to be a "team player."

"The irony of it all," Calvin said, "is that I am a team player. I have professional integrity. I serve the public, even when the public is wrong or school policy is wrong. While it is a professional commitment we all make contractually to follow the rules, it feels unprofessional to violate strong, time-tested educational principles that have been embedded in my teaching for so long. Personally, I don't think that is teaching, and that is what has been lost in this whole debate. The things we are being told to do don't enhance teaching and learning. They degrade them, don't improve things, demoralize teachers, and destroy public education."

Common Practice

Of course, what Calvin is experiencing has been happening to teachers all over the United States. In many aspects, teachers are subject to even more control with the inception of the Common Core State Standards and national standardized testing. More teachers than ever before are speaking from written scripts; juggling different classes with different students and different needs so they can be on the same page as their colleagues for every lesson; following strict curriculum pacing guides, lesson plans, and activity formats; giving pre-made formative assessments to every student in the same way at the same time; and scoring students with meaningless summative tests and quizzes, ad nauseam.

The truth is that secondary-level teachers have mostly been able to avoid this trap during the past ten years. I would contend that we are witnessing the destruction of one of the last frontiers of teaching; high school teaching is slipping away from us as the centralizing powers publish more confining standards, prepackaged materials, scripted assessments and lesson plans, pacing guides, and objectives at the secondary level. It's all part of a mad race to nowhere. The high waters of standardization and control are rising even further, and teachers are drowning as they lose autonomy, creativity, and connections with students. Teachers and students routinely feel a lack of passion and interest in what they are doing. Educators are losing sight of their own and their students' interests and concerns, of the power of intellectual curiosity, and of the importance of pursuing *meaning*.

The great public good of a comprehensive public education system that provides individualized, quality, equitable, and accessible education to every student is a distant dream, currently lost in a sea of standardized drivel, the primacy of arbitrary and contextual-less standards and tests, and a massive movement to privatize education through voucher programs and for-profit charter schools. Most creative teachers know that they are being standardized into extinction, and many feel absolutely powerless to stop it. At times, they take solace in what curricularist and teacher advocate Bill Schubert graciously called "the in-between places," small nooks and crannies of possibility between the mandated tests and lessons (personal communication).

But the fact of the matter is that, increasingly, the lessons and evaluations are scripted ahead of time by the corporate publishers and leave little room to maneuver, engage, or teach creatively. These tiny in-between places, although perhaps providing a momentary glimmer of legitimate educational experiences and real teaching, are fleeting and don't make for a satisfying professional career or a morally defensible approach to the enterprise of educating each student in our society. Now, even Calvin, model of mastering the art of the dodge, has been trapped. There seemingly is no way out.

Not Giving Up the Fight

To his credit, Calvin hasn't given up. He is a competitor. He tries to resist, working to maintain his commitment to students. He hopes for the tide to turn, perhaps politically. Maybe society will see its errors and stem the tide, delivering a turning that Goodlad and other educationists couldn't effect while the flood ensued. Maybe teachers will bring about change, by resisting and becoming more and more civilly disobedient. Maybe students and parents will opt out of the tests, saying enough is enough. Maybe a crusader will reclaim the high ground, topple the mandates, and put an end to the outside pressures that hurt schools. Maybe.

Glimmers of Resistance

As hobbled as Calvin is and as we all are by extension, dare we let public schooling, with all its inherent flaws, perils, and endless possibilities, be stolen from us without a fight? One thing I know is that Calvin is not really built for a big fight. He wants to be successful, to do the right thing, but at the same time he is conflicted. He has very little arsenal, beyond his own professional habits and excellent performance in the classroom, to resist, to fight for a semblance of integrity in his work day-to-day, to educate, to teach his students.

Although he struggles, hobbling along in his work to figure out the best path, others are taking up the good fight on other fronts, advancing his cause, and pushing for change on a regional and national stage. When they fight, these others, myself included, humbly fight for all the teachers, like Calvin, who want to be professional, teach with integrity, co-construct the curriculum with colleagues and students in their own setting, and be transformational agents for students in our most potential-filled and democratic of institutions, the public school classroom. And we fight for students, whose educational lives, curiosities, interests, concerns, and imaginations are being thwarted by a system as it is currently configured that cares nothing at all about them as individuals, only as a number.

As most teachers know, Chicago's Public School teachers struck last summer over many issues, but especially about the proposed changes to the teacher evaluation system that included student test scores as a prominent measure of teacher effectiveness—as if those scores said anything meaningful about teaching (Matthews, 2012). Their struggle has spawned other context-bound fights, like those being waged by teachers at Garfield High School in Seattle who refused to waste instructional time administering a faulty and time-consuming standardized test (Jones, 2013). In Portland, teachers will not participate in Race to the Top funding schemes that include faulty student test scores as a measure of effectiveness (Peterson, 2012). In that setting, students, parents, and families have shown their solidarity with teachers by opting out of the test (Ravitch, 2013).

In early April, citizen activists gathered for the second annual "Occupy the Department of Education" event in Washington, DC, sponsored by United Opt Out National (*www.unitedoptout.com*). The effort was meant to press a national conversation on the demoralization of teachers, the narrowing of the curriculum, and the corporatization and privatization of public education at such an alarming level and rate. This group encourages students, parents, and teachers to opt out of standardized testing by refusing to participate in it. Citizens also have been meeting to force the reclamation of the public agenda for school change through organizations like Save Our Schools, which has held large rallies in Washington, DC, and organizes teachers and citizens for resistance on a national level (*www.saveourschoolsmarch.org*).

Regionally, teacher activist groups are partnering with higher education and community organizations to form coalitions and to further the work of resisting and developing professional capacity to withstand change. I began the Teacher Resistance and Action Network ([TRAAN], *www.traan.weebly.com*) to heighten teacher's conception of and role in advocacy for public education, teaching, curriculum, and democracy in the Southwest Ohio region. The point of organizing is to bring into the open teacher experiences and concerns about the current reform agenda and to consider and exercise ways of resisting. If groups of us gather, think, and act, we can perhaps tip the scales, perhaps even stem the tide.

Final Thoughts

We are a more complete, productive, and effective democratic republic when the bells of freedom ring, overcoming the sights and sounds of tyranny like the ones barely audible and shuttered, but still glimpsed and heard far and wide, of students sitting quietly in desks in rows for hours at a time reading senseless test questions and filling in bubble sheets. We can do better, and we must. Calvin and his students, our schools and our society, deserve our best effort to stem the tide. In the end, perhaps, they deserve a revolution.

13
CRITICAL ISSUES FOR TEACHER LEADERS

Teacher leaders today and tomorrow will be required to have some knowledge concerning myriad crucial issues that face public education. The list and treatment of the issues presented here are not exhaustive of these issues, of course; you and your professors and teacher colleagues will have your own lists of critical issues for attention. And you will no doubt address the issues in your teacher education coursework as well as during field experiences. Beginning teachers will have to know about a lot more than these things to be able to contribute productively in their initial teaching settings, and a career in teaching involves the necessity of persistent inquiry. But the following sections of this chapter represent several crucial issues for students of teaching to consider and challenge at the beginning. You will be confronting these issues as you begin your earliest forays into the field.

1. **Your Rights and Responsibilities as a Teacher:** Read McCarthy, Cambron-McCabe, & Eckes (2013) chapter "Teachers' Substantive Constitutional Rights" in their *Public School Law: Teachers' and Students' Rights*, 7th edition, which I rely on here extensively for guidance.

2. **School Finance and the Classroom:** Look at websites listed below, each instructive for the current dilemmas facing states like Ohio, which has been determined in the past by its own supreme court to

be out of compliance with the state's constitution by not providing the funding necessary for a "thorough and efficient" system for educating each child in Ohio (see Coalition for Equity & Adequacy for School Funding, ***http://www.ohiocoalition.org,*** and Ohio Department of Education, ***www.ode.state.oh.us***).

3. **Approaching the Common Core Standards:** What are teachers in your field experiences, student teaching, or first job saying about the Common Core? How are they using the standards? What do you know about the standards, how they were founded what they mean for teaching, learning, and assessment?

4. **Human Difference and the Curriculum:** I want to leave the reader with a plea to become educated about difference and to find ways to nurture and celebrate difference in the classroom.

Your Rights and Responsibilities as a Teacher

The following section is an attempt to introduce you to several aspects of the legal issues surrounding teaching. This section is not exhaustive by any means, but it does serve to make you aware of several considerations beginning teachers should keep in mind.

Susan's Stand

Susan loved her new school. As a first year teacher, she had a room full of energetic, bright fifth graders who were full of the world and themselves. Their parents were very happy with her teaching, praising her commitment and excellent work in several commendation notes the principal had received from them. Despite the early fatigue associated with starting to teach from scratch, Susan felt strongly about her preparation to teach and her decision to devote her life to children and to learning. Gaining confidence everyday, the principal and the other teachers supported her with materials and coaching. During the winter break, she and her best friend from college, who was teaching in a nearby district, celebrated their early successes in teaching by having their eyebrows pierced. They had talked about it before, but decided while shopping at the mall that it was as good a time as any. They mutually agreed that the piercings were attractive, and they were glad they did it.

On the second day back from school after winter break, the principal asked Susan to stop by her office after school for a short chat. As they talked, Dr. Hastings mentioned Susan's eyebrow piercing and the ring in it and calmly pulled out the district's student conduct manual from her desk drawer, saying, "Susan, I'm sure you didn't know that it is a violation of district policy for students to have body piercings, besides earrings. I would appreciate it if you do not wear the eyebrow ring to school anymore after today." Susan responded, *without even a moment's pause, "I'm aware of the student policy against piercings, Dr. Hastings, but there is nothing in that handbook or the faculty policy handbook saying piercings are not allowed for teachers. I really like the eyebrow ring, and it doesn't seem to be upsetting the children. If it's all the same to you, I'd really like to keep it."*

REFLECTION

What do you think the principal will do or say next? What should Susan do? What would you have done or said in response to the principal's request if you were in Susan's position? How do you think this story might continue, and end?

An easy resolution to this case, like any good case, is not cut and dry and may even be impossible to determine or find. The case points to the rather complicated nature of this section of the chapter. Students of teaching and leadership often note the tension between (1) exercising their rights as citizens, and (2) leading responsibly as teachers. Exercising your rights is not always synonymous with leading, nor are the two acts always mutually exclusive. In this case, how is Susan's act of defiance an act of teacher leadership? How would you argue that complying with the principal's request would be an act of teacher leadership? Your answers depend on many things: your personal values and goals, the values and norms of the people and the culture surrounding you, as well as precedent and the law, among other considerations.

To add a further twist to the story, your answer depends almost solely on the context. While courts have generally been supportive of school system's positions on matters of personal appearance, the local twist is that in some districts Susan's appearance may be an issue and in others it may not be (McCarthy, Cambron-McCabe, & Eckes, 2013). I doubt, except in the most homogenous of contexts, that you and your peers' answers will be even remotely the same in response to this case. I wonder if you and your peers can come to some consensus on Susan's response or on how you perceive the school, as represented by Dr. Hastings, should react to the situation given Susan's initial reluctance to comply. Should the principal have said anything in the first place?

One of the realities beginning teacher leaders face is that as they begin a career of teaching and leading in schools, school districts almost invariably place them in a "probationary" teaching position for a probationary period. During the "probationary period," usually one to three years, depending on state law as well as the district's master contract with teachers, teachers can be nonrenewed without a statement of cause and may not get due process unless the reason for nonrenewal is not constitutionally permissible (for example, the denial of protected speech, McCarthy, Cambron-McCabe, & Eckes, 2013). This makes the position of beginning teachers rather tenuous and the power and control over their jobs by school boards and administrators seem ominous. Tenured teachers are always due full procedural protection if they are being dismissed for some cause. Probationary teachers are usually not granted full procedural protection.

This is the point of discussion at which many preservice teachers begin to panic with questions and worries. Knowing that each of your actions may be scrutinized sharply and that your actions, even if well-meaning though ill-informed, could result in the loss of your position can be unsettling. But keep in mind that this is the case for any profession. Keep in mind also that you will no doubt make mistakes of "commission" (as opposed to mistakes of "omission"), meaning that you were acting with the best of intentions and without malice when something went wrong. This does not constitute legal grounds for exonerating you, but in a plethora of common-sense situations, your intent may act to soften the situation.

Administrators and school boards understand that beginning and veteran teachers are going to make mistakes, and that in most situations a second chance is in order. You cannot know every law that has an impact on every possible situation that can occur in school; lawyers do not know case law for every situation. Lawyers rely on books of case law to help them interpret and argue for positions after the fact. You won't be able to consult law books the next time you have to make a split-second decision. This constant dilemma comes with the job, and you must be aware that this situation exists before going into your work. Instead of striving for some specific knowledge on these matters, beginning teachers should know some broader legal parameters that affect the profession, such as legal issues surrounding not only injury and student discipline and personal appearance but also the placement of students, curriculum, testing, and teaching methodology, church/state issues, and academic freedom, among others. Knowing that these broader categories exist will help you to ask questions of more experienced teachers and administrators when you are in the field.

This does not mean, of course, that you should just do what you please as a teacher because you cannot know the "right" or "legal" (they aren't necessarily the same thing!) course of action in most situations. In fact, you can learn some basic ideas related to the law and your responsibilities as a teacher leader that will help you build a set of practical theories of action for working day to day in the very complex milieu of schools.

What you should do in your own local scene is be aware of support systems for teachers who face disciplinary actions or other difficulties. Typically, the teacher union representatives in your school district will act as allies given trouble, as discussed in Chapter 8 here, "Teachers' Unions and Leadership." Your union representative will typically help you to the extent of assisting you in finding legal representation if a situation warrants such action. You should know who your union representatives are (if there is a union presence in your school), as well as members of the school administration who can help with issues related to your employment and practice. There is no reason, in a school community in which the school administration and the teaching faculty and staff act in good faith toward each other, that school administrators and teachers should treat each other as though their purposes and interests are diametrically opposed.

> Tort law offers civil rather than criminal remedies to individuals for harm caused by the unreasonable conduct of others. Generally, a tort is described as a civil wrong, independent of breach of contract, for which a court will provide relief in the form of damages. Tort cases primarily involve state law and are grounded in the fundamental premise that individuals are liable for the consequences of their conduct that result in injury to others. (McCarthy, Cambron-McCabe, & Eckes, 2013)

You should commit yourself to exercising what is known as "an appropriate standard of care" in your classroom as a teacher leader. It is possible for you, as the teacher, to be held liable for damages to students caused by your negligence or intentional gross misconduct in the classroom or extracurricular setting. What typically has to be proven in a case—such as when a student is injured in the classroom—is whether or not the teacher failed to use an appropriate standard of care in the situation. Did the teacher's actions precipitate the accident, or did the students' own negligence contribute to the accident? If a student slips in a puddle of water and breaks an arm while running in the classroom, to what extent did the teacher exercise an appropriate standard of care? Did she attempt to stop the student from running or attempt to remove the hazard? Did the student's gross misconduct itself lead to the accident? Answers to these questions would help a deliberative body such as a jury or judge to decide if a teacher were negligent in the classroom (Newman, 1998, p. 143).

> School tort actions can be grouped into two primary categories: negligence and intentional torts. Negligence is a breach of one's legal duty to protect others from unreasonable risks of harm. The failure to act or the commission of an improper act, which results in injury or loss to another person, can constitute negligence. To establish negligence, however, an injury must be avoidable by the exercise of reasonable care. Moreover, each of the following four elements must be present to support a successful claim: (1) the defendant had a duty to protect the plaintiff from unreasonable risks, (2) the duty was breached by the failure to exercise an appropriate standard of care, (3) there was a causal connection between the negligent conduct and the resulting injury ... and (4) an actual injury resulted ... Among the more common types of intentional torts are assault, battery, false imprisonment, infliction of mental distress, and defamation. (McCarthy, Cambron-McCabe, & Thomas, 2013)

Preventative measures may be prudent, of course, in an attempt to establish an overall appropriate standard of care in your work in the classroom and school. One basic consideration, as a rule, is to not leave your classroom and the students alone. Of course, an emergency situation may warrant your leaving students alone, but this should happen rarely. Perhaps you should periodically distribute and publish safety concerns and rules to your own students for your own classroom, especially with regard to potentially dangerous items and their use, such as scissors or gas burners. Creating norms for safety in procedures and student conduct establish a baseline of care. Your efforts to establish an appropriate standard of care throughout your teaching will help teach students the basics of safety in the classroom and help protect them as students and you as teacher.

Newman (1998) discusses several other crucial areas of consideration for the beginning teacher leader. The first area is the dismissal of tenured teachers. Already referred to above as a possibility, dismissal generally involves some aspect of the three "I's": incompetence, insubordination, and immorality. Incompetence refers to an inability to do the job one is under contract to do, and usually is determined in light of a detailed account of the teacher's shortcomings over time. Insubordination consists of willful violation of reasonable rules or the deliberate defiance of school officials (p. 140). Under certain circumstances, Susan's case of not complying with the principal's request to remove her eyebrow ring could be construed as grounds for dismissal based on insubordination. Perceptions and conceptions of immorality vary from community to community, but given the perceived interference with a teacher's effectiveness, so-called immoral acts may be deemed grounds for dismissal.

Other broad grounds for dismissal include "unprofessional conduct." Unprofessional conduct may seem like an extremely vague term, and it is. Newman states that given the moral importance of public education, teachers are typically held to extremely high standards. Actions hard to categorize as fitting one of the three I's may still be grounds for dismissal as unprofessional conduct.

It should go without saying (but I will say it as clearly as possible here) that there are several ways to get a ticket straight out of teaching, including engaging in sexual relations of any kind with students or using/dealing illegal drugs. You can do a routine Google search of these topics and find a myriad of awful stories about teachers abusing children and establishing inappropriate relationships and/or participating in illegal activities with them. Believe me, if you engage in these activities you will be found out. *Breaking Bad* may be compelling TV, but it's a fantasy. You will be caught and will leave a wake of personal and societal devastation as a result.

However, students of teaching often ask me questions about the limits of appropriate/inappropriate relationships with students. They remember friendships with teachers and long-lasting connections with adults in school that were life changing, inspiring, and wholesome. They worry these days with so much scrutiny and surveillance of teachers and their personal life that even innocent acts of kindness might be perceived to be immoral and/ or unprofessional.

My response is always that strong relationships with students and their families are things to strive for, but there is a certain level of care that a beginning teacher or any teacher needs to establish with students in this regard. For instance, teachers shouldn't have excessive contact with students outside of school, probably, except as a result of extracurricular activities. By this I mean that it may not be such a great idea to "friend" all of your students on Facebook or send them tweets and texts during all hours of the day and night. It is ill-advised to share most intimate facts of your life with or without family, as well as your weekend experiences outside of school, with students. Also, while some school districts push teachers to establish even stronger relationships with students through the use of technology, I would advise that teachers only use school-approved platforms for this type of activity unless completely necessary (like using Edmodo instead of Facebook) and group text lists only for logistical purposes, like gathering students for a sports practice on short notice or setting a time for students to meet the bus on a road trip with the debate team.

While it is unclear whether school officials can compel teachers to share their social media sites, it's mostly clear that school districts can request to see your social media sites and other digital activities in order to make a judgment about your job worthiness before or after the job-hiring process (Nelda Cambron-McCabe, Personal Communication). But there are, of course, legal limits to their requests in terms of access. The question is to what extent do you think that compromising photos and other items belong on your personal sites and in your computer, all of which may be accessed at some point by skillful hackers or the authorities? I would say that now is the time to monitor your own activities and make sure that your own professional "house" is in order, presentable, and free of compromising material, if any ever existed.

Another situation in which nonrenewal or dismissal occurs lies outside the teacher's control is when a district exercises a "Reduction In Force" action (or "Riffing," Newman, 1998, pp. 138–139). Riffing happens when school programs are cut due to finances, for instance, or a lack of student interest in a particular course of study. Most contracts call for the newest hires to be cut first in a riffing situation. In some case, teachers are called back after being let go.

Maria Flees: A Case Study

Maria, Tonya, and Jerome begin coming to Ms. Stanley's classroom at lunch time, nearly everyday, to eat and to talk. These are three of her best students. Each of them likes Ms. Stanley and her eighth grade science class, and they find a certain peacefulness in her room, away from the rush of the middle school cafeteria crowds. They don't sit with Ms. Stanley at her desk, though, leaving her to eat her salad and to catch up on paperwork. She doesn't mind them, and they don't mind her. One day after about two months of this daily lunch time routine, Ms. Stanley overheard a very animated conversation that ends with Maria addressing Jerome directly, "Jerome, I'm infected, and the baby probably is, too! What are you going to do?" Crying, Maria storms out of the room with Tonya right behind her. Stunned, Jerome sits quietly in his seat. After a few moments, he looks back at Ms. Stanley, almost pleadingly, and then rushes out after Maria and Tonya. Astonished, Ms. Stanley puts down her pencil and considers her next steps.

REFLECTION

Put yourself in Ms. Stanley's shoes, after just overhearing this conversation. What does she do next? Why? Write your response before reading ahead.

The case above should cause you to pause. The fact is that events like the ones depicted will happen to you as a teacher. There is no easy answer to the case, though there are probably several incorrect answers that you must avoid if you face a situation such as this one. The first incorrect answer is to do nothing, pretending as though the incident never happened. It did happen, and potentially dangerous health and emotional issues could be at hand. The teacher has a legal and moral responsibility to report what happened. Legally, a duty exists to care for students, which means teachers must report such information. Many states are "reporting" states, meaning that teachers are responsible for reporting cases of child abuse and neglect. Much of this ground came into stark relief with the Penn State case, which broke in 2011 and is still having ramifications in public discourse and action about and for children.

Second, let's take a look at one very common—though incorrect—response to "Maria Flees" in more detail. You cannot rush to the phone to call the students' parents or guardians to tell them about the conversation you just overheard. Instead, you should follow the reporting procedures established by your school, probably by reporting the information to the principal or school counselor. Plus, you really don't have enough information to make a judgment that would warrant calling next of kin. No matter your history with the students, or your comfort in making an initial judgment about what the situation is, or your most intuitive maternal or paternal instincts ("If someone knows something about my child, I would want to know it right away!"), you cannot make the call. You are not a counselor, lawyer, nurse, or doctor. Besides, you don't even know to what the students are referring. Do you? What if they are referring to a new computer and a virus that just killed their hard drive? You don't really know, either—if they do truly happen to be referring to a pregnancy and a health-threatening infection—whether or not they are actually telling the truth about either thing. Do you?

Now, let's assume that these very young students are referring to a human baby, perhaps a health-threatening infection, and their story is legitimate. Perhaps your first step is to find out what the story truly is. Asking the students to explain what is going on, in a timely manner (not two months later, or even a week, maybe not even a day!), and assuring them that you care to hear them out and help in any way, are appropriate places to start. The tricky part is making clear to the students that despite your commitment to confidence, you cannot legally promise confidentiality since courts do not recognize this right. This may cause them to shut down communications, but you have to be honest. If they shut down, you may have to report the little bit that you do know from the incident in hopes that the students receive the appropriate assistance. In many cases, students will still reveal their stories even if they know you will have to tell; they are, after all, in many cases such as this one perhaps, no doubt seeking help. After all, Maria could have chosen any number of other "private" places to tell Jerome, but she told him in front of Ms. Stanley.

As a teacher leader, you should know with whom it is appropriate to talk about such matters, you should document your role and action in such a situation, noting the details of the story, dates, and places, and you should keep a record of your notes on the matter in a safe, secure place. You should document facts, not judgments. You may be asked to write an official statement of your role in the event by a school administrator at some later date. Documentation is crucial in an event such as this one.

Several principles operate here. You should report the situation to the appropriate party regardless of whether or not you think the situation has been resolved. In cases having to do with student safety and well-being, physical and psychological, it is prudent, necessary, and in everyone's best interest for you to report. You should not try to handle the situation on your own. You are not educated for this work, though you may get caught up in the middle of it sometimes. Other professionals can be more supportive and effective. Your students are people, and they will encounter life-altering events, some of which you will be intimately involved. But you cannot go it alone.

The same holds true for all cases of abuse and neglect. Unfortunately, during your career you will see and hear about cases of verbal and physical abuse as well as neglect. Your students may confide to you information regarding abuse and neglect they are experiencing, in which case you must report. This is a mandatory action. Your suspicions of abuse or neglect warrant that you report suspected cases to the appropriate authorities. In some cases, teachers have been held liable for keeping quiet. You are protected when you report in good faith, even if you report incorrectly (Newman, 1998, p. 144). It is your moral and legal duty to report suspected cases of abuse and neglect. Consult your administrators or union representatives regarding the laws by which teachers in your district must abide, since laws vary across jurisdictions. Also, consult Newman (1998, p. 145) to review a preliminary list of student indicators to watch for with regard to abuse and neglect.

Finally, though this section of the chapter is not exhaustive of the issues regarding your rights and responsibilities as a teacher, I want to return to issues surrounding "expression." Susan's case of wanting to continue to wear her new eyebrow ring tests the limits of expression. It is a reality that school districts usually win these cases, either forcing parties to obey set standards or dismissing teachers from their jobs (Newman, 1998, p. 155). As citizens in schools, neither students nor teachers shed their freedoms of expression, but the courts have ruled that teachers do not have absolute freedoms of expression. In some cases, speech, symbols, actions, and other means of expression can be regulated by authorities.

One of the great opportunities that teaching presents to all is the opportunity to participate in acts of expression. As a teacher, you may become involved in challenging the "banned books list" in your district by teaching *The Adventures of Huckleberry Finn* or *Of Mice and Men* (two of the most frequently banned books), or in engaging in political activity, or in teaching about sexual orientation or about evolution, for instance. All of these areas pose problems and potential legal challenges. I'm not suggesting that you refrain from expression. You cannot teach without expressing yourself. I'm not saying that you should always be compliant with the status quo or the authorities' versions of what is appropriate or not to express. And I am not saying that you should constantly be disagreeing with everything the authorities say to do. But please keep in mind that your actions as a teacher carry risks and costs. Your conceptions of teaching and leadership will no doubt be challenged and formed by the experiences you have as a teacher testing these boundaries of expression with colleagues, students, and school communities as you determine just what your rights and responsibilities are as a teacher leader.

School Finance and the Classroom

Perhaps there is no more pervasive issue, across the experience of schooling and our lives, than finance. How we raise and spend money for schooling both have an impact on the classroom and each student and reflect back on who we are as human beings, educators, teacher leaders, and citizens. There is no doubt, like all the issues and positions raised so far in this book, that politics plays a major role in school finance and the public's attempts to make sense of it for themselves. School finance is an extremely complicated and complex area in the field of education. I'm not an "expert" in this field by any means, but I intend to share several positions so that you can become aware of the important issues and decisions at stake for you as a teacher leader.

In general, public schools receive public money from state and local taxes to pay for the costs of educating students. Schools need money to pay for supplies, teacher salaries, support staff salaries, learning materials, and building and maintaining facilities, among many other expenses. In round percentages, about 6 to 8% of all funding for schooling comes from the federal government. Most of this federal money comes to states, local districts, and schools in the form of Title I money, money appropriated to support and serve students in underserved settings, especially through academic remedial programs and school-wide reform programs. Other major funding amounts come through special grants to schools through the Department of Education. But as you can see from the low percentage figure, the federal government plays a minor role in school funding. The remaining 92 to 94% or so of funds needed to educate children in local settings comes from two primary sources: (1) state governments, through taxes appropriated for school funding; and (2) local governments, typically through taxes on residential and business properties.

Let's look at state funding for education in Ohio, for example, in order to show the difficult problems that so many states and locales face in this area. Just recently, in the early part of 2013, the state released a new budget for funding schools, but many school districts have been left to scramble to cover the deficits that the new, lower appropriations have caused for individual school districts. These state cuts cause districts to make cuts, often resulting in the shelving of teachers and programs. In some districts in Ohio, art and music and physical education have been cut. How can we have excellent 21st century public schools and cut essential programs?

Some citizens, politicians, and pundits (even some in the field of education) argue, conversely, that schools spend and waste too much money already, and that pouring more money into the public education system won't do any good anyway. But what we miss when taking this position is several facts and at least one moral consideration. Schools are faced with increasing costs, just like the rest of society's institutions, but we don't keep up with the costs associated with inflation and new technology. We have neglected buildings that are crumbling, while at the same time we barely have enough money in some districts, especially in poorer urban and rural districts, to pay teachers adequate salaries and provide adequate materials in the classroom. The gross neglect of the underserved and underprivileged in urban and rural areas by the public is well documented by several sources, including Jonathan Kozol's (1995) book *Savage Inequalities*, which highlights the stark, moving effects of under-funding in inner city schools. Also Bill Moyers' (1996) influential, widely viewed documentary *Children in America's Schools* focuses on Ohio's crumbling schools. It has been estimated that Ohio required $16 billion (in 1999) to repair and rebuild currently existing school structures that are inadequate for educating today's students. It is fair to add that some recent relief has been coming in terms of both federal and state expenditures for capital improvements in Ohio and around the country—and that despite current setbacks to public education funding in Ohio, it is hoped that funding levels can keep up at least with inflation through the next decade.

So the problems increase exponentially in both the discrepancy between what it costs to operate school on a daily basis and what it costs to keep up with maintenance of existing structures. And the gap between what those who "have" get and what those who "have not" don't get grows exponentially, too. The gap is so extremely evident when students of teaching walk into a suburban school for their first experience and see computers being used by students in nearly every classroom. Then they walk into an urban or rural school for their second field experience where it is difficult to find any computers even working anywhere in the school.

The bottom line may be that many of us, if we were parents of school-age children, would not stand for the poor conditions that exist in so many of Ohio's and the nation's public schools due to underfunding. In fact, many parents and guardians with financial means avoid the public schools their children would attend because of geography. Instead, they pay tuition (on top of the property taxes that they pay for some form of a public school education anyway) at parochial and independent, private schools or provide an education at home through home schooling. While there certainly is a place for these institutions in our society (both private education and home schooling, of course), the cost to the public school sector of citizens leaving the public school system behind is great both in terms of financial capital and human capital.

What recourse do those who have fewer resources in terms of wealth and time have to fight the inequities their children face? For them, there is little opportunity to flee. And as their schools face tighter and tighter budgets, the corporate takeover experts and the anti-government pundits gain ground in their fight to dismantle public schools and sell them off to private companies running private charter schools, as if they can deliver a better "product" with less expenditure. Often, parents trying to do the right thing put their children into new private charter schools making big promises, and then they don't deliver. Even the promised rise in test scores most often fails to materialize. The squeeze leaves many families and locales extremely compromised. We see this playing out across the country where massive public school closures are planned and being carried out in Philadelphia and Chicago, for instance. What will happen to all of the displaced students and their families? What will happen to the neighborhoods where schools that are being closed and the people who taught and worked there acted as the centerpiece of positive action and safety in the community? The consequences of these situations and the deterioration between the public and the public schools present a grave picture of where we are going.

At this moment, state legislators and the courts are locked in battles over whether it is constitutional for states to allocate public monies to help parents pay tuition to private schools, even outside of failing districts. Making a voucher available to any disenchanted citizen undermines, in my opinion, the entire enterprise of the state to provide a fair and equitable, "thorough and efficient" education to all students.

In Ohio in the early 1990s, 587 of the state's 611 school districts filed suit against the state, claiming that its school funding formula disadvantages children and school districts. The act of disadvantaging students breached the state's own constitution, which calls for the state to provide a "thorough and efficient" education for all citizens. This group of nearly 600 school districts continues to be represented by an organization called The Ohio Coalition for Equity & Adequacy of School Funding (*http://www. ohiocoalition.org*). Its executive director, William Phillis, works tirelessly with other citizens and educators in the state to pressure the state government to nurture, fund, and protect public education, teaching, teachers, students, and their families.

The lawsuit, known as the DeRolph case, is so named after a ninth grade student (in 1991), Nathan DeRolph, whose school experience was often cited as an example of the deleterious effects of underfunding on the quality of education services delivered. Now a college graduate, Nathan tells of the day he had to take a test sitting on the floor in Sheridan High School in the Northern Local School District, about 20 miles east of Columbus:

> There were about 30 kids and the classroom was probably big enough to have 20 max," he said. "People were sitting at the teacher's desk, on the floor—it was a nightmare ... (Associated Press, p. 7A, The Dayton Daily News, 5/12/2000)

In its initial and subsequent decisions, the Ohio Supreme Court ruled that the state was out of compliance with the state constitution and must come up with a plan to more equitably fund public education. It ruled that the state must address things such as the inequity and inadequacy of current funding formulas as well as the crumbling infrastructures of actual school buildings. So far, the Ohio state legislature has not responded adequately, according to the court, which has given the state legislators more time to comply with its ruling (Hershey & Wagner, 2000). As of this writing, the courts have subsequently thrown the issue back to the state legislature, which over the past decade has not adequately remedied the situation.

Around the country, states and local districts struggle with the demands of funding schools adequately. Schools with means continually ask voters to appropriate more money for operating expenses and building projects. The tax burden does get heavy for some property owners, and citizens in some locales have been forced to choose between the common good (including the benefits to their own and to neighbors' children's educational experiences) and their own personal financial well-being (keeping taxes from rising).

Some states and areas have attempted solutions with so-called "Robin Hood" laws, in which tax schemes apportion pools of tax money more equitably to poorer districts using moneys generated by richer districts (remember Robin Hood robbed the rich to give to the poor?). Widely unpopular, these solutions typically lead to dissatisfaction among almost all parties. But how can legislatures get closer to responses that truly deal with the spirit of the Ohio Supreme Court's ruling against the state itself, which basically says that the school funding formulas now in place rely too heavily on local property tax revenue? How can the state do its part more adequately? Where will the money for education come from to provide an equitable education if local property owners don't provide it? The money won't just appear. It must come from something and from somewhere, so someone will still have to pay. How can legislators find a solution to such a difficult problem when the political stakes of raising taxes are so high? Conversely, how long can our children and students wait? Nathan DeRolph waited more than a decade for a decision and is still waiting for action; he has already graduated from college, and the state still hasn't adequately addressed the initial problem of underfunding Ohio schools. The problem grows daily.

In New Hampshire, the legislature abolished the use of property taxes to fund schools (Bayles, 1999). As of this printing, New Hampshire is still attempting to figure out how it will adequately provide for each student's education after a series of lawsuits tried up to the supreme court level yielded no adequate plan for funding school adequately and equitably long-term, given that a major source of funding, local property taxes, was required to be replaced by another source of funding. New Hampshire has had a long and winding road toward a satisfactory resolution and is still looking for it, as is Ohio (see *http://schoolfunding.info*). These cases point to the role that the legislative and judicial branches have played in attempts to provide equitable funding. Courts and legislatures have acted swiftly and with clear mandates in the Ohio and New Hampshire situations, while allowing, of course, legislators to work out the details of adequate responses. The results have been extremely mixed, with many yielding unsatisfactory results for students and schools.

Courts in other locales like Kansas City, Missouri, have taken other more drastic actions, for example. The city's schools were inadequately funded and serving mostly students of color (more than 70%). The failing, decrepit school system had been left to wither from years of neglect and underfunding. In the 1990s, courts ordered tax and spending plans to provide nearly two billion dollars to rebuild, refurbish, and reform Kansas City's urban schools, which had been determined to be out of compliance with a long-standing desegregation order, and to integrate them adequately with a bold plan to entice white suburban students into new city magnet schools. The results of the plan are mixed. Some saw the spending as an adequate, justifiable, and moral step toward "leveling the playing field." Some cite the lack of tangible improvements in student achievement as evidence that throwing money at a problem does not solve it (see Gewertz, 2000, and her treatment of Kansas City's dilemma in "A Hard Lesson for Kansas City Schools," and more recent news about the closing of many of the city's schools due to budget woes and lower school enrollment in the city).

Schools must be funded adequately by citizens and state governments. Students deserve, because they are citizens and human beings, to receive an equitable and adequate education. As teachers, you need to have an adequate salary, and you have to have financial support for academic and other learning programs in order to do your job well. Adequate funding for an adequate education is guaranteed by most state's constitutions. Most states and school districts continue to have to rely on means for funding schooling that burden particular citizens through property taxes and create discrepancies among districts that constitute inequity and inadequacy for some, in this case poorer citizens who are often people of color. The jury is still out on the effects of funding on school achievement. Perhaps beyond the probable impacts of adequate and inadequate funding for education on student achievement lies the moral imperative for citizens to provide adequately for the education of all citizens.

REFLECTION

Imagine three ways in which a teacher leader can be active in the community with regard to the issue of school finance.

The Common Core Standards

I've never thought it honest or helpful to argue completely and utterly against standards. I don't have a particular beef with standards, since they are simply desired ends of educational activities. After all, I usually have desired ends in mind when I teach, even when I am simultaneously asking students what they would like to do and accomplish in the class (this should make sense to you after reading Chapters 9 and 10 on Curriculum).

But as Eisner so beautifully posits, "Ends need not precede means." Meaning, as professional teachers, we may expressively have something very valuable in mind for students to be doing (means) without knowing exactly what it is that will be accomplished (ends). Great learning and experience often take place in this space where the ends aren't so succinctly defined, or maybe not even known at all. Great education depends on context, experience, and the associative construction of social, intellectual, and personal meanings. This space is what gives Americans room to maneuver, to experiment, to dream, to fail, and to create. Standards, depending on what they are and who created them, can defeat this space, close it down, and make us merely designers of scripted means in order to reach pre-scripted ends.

In terms of leadership, I wonder to what degree students of teaching have actually questioned or challenged the Common Core Standards, or have just accepted them as a fait accompli. I wonder what would happen if teachers thought of themselves more as public intellectuals with something to say about what's being asked of them, especially if they think what is being asked lacks legitimacy.

I can be honest in saying that I often take exception to the standardization movement and the standards we now seem to be stuck with—the Common Core Standards. The exceptions I take lie in the complex give and take when searching for answers to two critical questions about standards: (1) Who decides (or decided) what the standards are? (2) What are the actual standards, and do they make sense and are they defensible? That is, are they good enough to base a teaching and learning program on for every citizen? Saying yes to that question is a tall order.

These two questions, for me, get at the deeper curriculum questions: How democratic is it to have no say over the ends of education, from curriculum standards, to curriculum materials and lesson plans, and ultimately to the assessments used to determine student progress or achievement?

Then what is left to teaching and curriculum planning when someone else besides the teachers, the students, schools, and the community has pre-scripted the entire enterprise?

That is to ask, ultimately, what input should and can teachers have with regard to the craft of teaching if the ends are scripted so tightly that the tests are already in place before any teaching and learning even happens?

I ask and answer some of these questions in Chapter 12, "Stemming the Tide," especially through the real-life story of my friend Calvin and his teaching journey. Of course, one line of inquiry is trying to determine what the standardization movement's own ends are, and why the underlying energy for them seems to be merely a negative critique of public education, schools, and teachers as "failing" and "inadequate."

And I want to add that you can visit and peruse several extremely convincing, very influential websites fighting the good fight against the over-standardization of teaching and the curriculum. New teachers need to ask, how can I be a part of the conversation regarding the issues challenging public education, while also teaching my students and my classes well? To this "end," take a look at:

- *http://dianeravitch.net/2012/07/17/ stephen-krashen-on-the-common-core-standards/*
- *http://susanohanian.org/core.php?id=314*
- *http://brianpjones.tumblr.com/BrianJones*
- *http://unitedoptout.com/flyers/architects-of-a-brave-new-world/*
- *http://www.substancenews.net/articles.php?page=3004*

(Morna McDermott referred these websites/blogs, personal communication.)

In my opinion, this journey should be a unifying one, one that helps solidify the beginning teacher's conception of the realities of public education with the development of the self as teacher. To me this should all be a part of the same project of professional development, but sometimes these two things in terms of (1) teacher professional development and activism and (2) professional development and teacher performance during the probationary period get tangled up and become conflicting, maybe even mutually exclusive, or are thought to be two sides of two very different coins, unrelated. My sincere hope is that beginning teacher leaders have an eye on the classroom and on the profession as well, and work across constituencies and issues to create a better profession and better professional practice for themselves. This can only be possible if teachers are aware of what's going on around them, and a lot is going on right now! Be aware ...

So what can beginning teachers do on Monday morning when confronted by the Common Core? I have several very practical recommendations for action:

First, I recommend that beginning teacher leaders educate themselves as completely as possible about what is required by their school districts at this time regarding implementation of the Common Core Standards, and how curriculum development and assessment are related both conceptually and practically to the Common Core.

Second, I recommend that beginning teacher leaders take the position that a rich, engaging curriculum, one not scripted by someone else and not tied to static, pre-packaged curriculum materials, poses a better option for teaching. Engaging colleagues in group curriculum development activities will strengthen both the classroom based and the school based program in all subject areas.

Third, I recommend that beginning teacher leaders push to maintain as much instructional time as possible, working as diligently as they can with coalitions of teachers and their unions to keep the incessant creep of over-assessing and over-testing of students at bay. The national model is the movement by Garfield High School teachers in Seattle, who successfully pushed back an illegitimate testing regime in the spring of 2013.

Fourth, I recommend that beginning teacher leaders begin the curriculum process by understanding students' prior knowledge of the subject at hand, and assuring that students are included in the planning process. Also, I recommend that as much as possible, teacher leaders seek to establish a legitimately multicultural and culturally responsive approach to the curriculum and to teaching, privileging strong primary and secondary resources and relying less on pre-packaged materials.

And fifth, I believe that starting with meaningful, engaging activities and projects taps the interests, concerns, and talents of students. Mapping backward from the experiences of educational activities to the standards, if necessary, will yield a more textured, nuanced, and meaningful curriculum for students. I also believe that students will score on tests as a result. This method of mapping backward is a part to whole approach, as opposed to the whole to part approach championed by McTighe and Wiggins (2004) as "backward design." They recommend starting with the standards. I recommend starting with students, materials, activities, and projects. You'll meet the standards if you engage students and the topics at hand.

Reflection on Schools

School today has a much more "quantity over quality" feel, as in we need to mass educate our population by whatever means necessary. The easiest way to do that is standardize what needs to be learned and test students, a lot, to show results to the country that we are educating all children. In this system you need to be incredibly self determined as a student to actually learn material, and to become educated. So much is thrown at students, it's hard to see how all the content relates, and why it is important. To gain this further knowledge, students need to push themselves to learn it, and not rely solely on the teachers taking the time to explain content in great detail.

It is fairly obvious that most students do not have this kind of determination, and I do not believe it is because they are lazy. I think its because they do not see the point in learning about Beowulf, structures of cell membranes, or geometric proofs. Students do not see why the curriculum is going to help their lives, and so they frankly do not try as much and get run over by the ridiculous number of standardized tests. So now students do not see the point of what they learn in schools and then take tests that tell them they are not smart. Big issue here.

Teachers want to give more time on each topic and relate the curriculum to students' lives. This more in-depth look—where the quality of learning is emphasized—would allow more students to grow and succeed. However, it is hard to report this kind of growth, and so testing will sadly be the best option, for the time being, to report this. "Learning" is done so quickly now, and tested so much, that many students will fail in this structure, fail to learn and fail to become educated. Change needs to be made to help our students really succeed in life and not just on paper.

—Brian Veil, preservice teacher

Human Difference and the Curriculum

I addressed difference in parts of the chapters in this book, particularly in Chapter 5 and in Chapters 9 and 10 on curriculum. But in an effort to communicate that difference should be a part of the entire curriculum and how we think about students, teaching, learning, the community, the school, and society, I want to say a few final words here about its importance.

The notion of difference doesn't just go to learning differences, which might cause a pedagogical or curricular shift in the classroom. Differentiation is an attempt in the classroom to modify lessons and student work to reflect the broad range of learning approaches that students bring to the classroom as well as to foster a diversity of approaches in teaching and the curriculum. It may seem ironic that differentiation—as important as it is to opening teachers up to thinking about multiple ways that students learn and the different ways that the classroom can be organized and content shared—is becoming a normative way of thinking about classroom teaching even as rote curriculum packages continue coming down the pike, generated to "serve" classrooms where student performance on pre-packaged tests, aligned to the Common Core Standards, and supposedly tied to high stakes, including not only student advancement from grade to grade, and graduation, but also to the evaluation of teacher performance and their salaries.

But one of the key issues related to difference that transcends the curriculum designed for the classroom is the curriculum of how we relate to each other in the school as human beings, different as we are in terms of cultural background, social class, race and ethnicity, and sexual identity. In this short section I want to raise just a few issues and a challenge or two for teachers in the 21st century. Most of the work in multicultural education and curriculum over the past several decades has attempted to be inclusive of multiple differences that manifest in people and communities. Typically, curriculum in schools, if it takes difference on at all, addresses race, ethnicity, gender, social class, and disability.

But we are finally making some headway as a society on one of the remaining areas of difference that is critical to human identity, liberation, and life: sexual identity. Just in my lifetime, since the Stonewall Riots of 1969 brought issues surrounding the gay community and its liberation to the forefront, there have been many markers of advancement, liberation, and setback for those who have fought for equality and just treatment with regard to sexual identity. It is encouraging that student groups supporting students who identify themselves as gay, lesbian, bisexual, transgender, queer/questioning, intersex, or ally/asexual (LGBTQIA) are flourishing and helping students to find their place in the world, especially on college campuses and in high schools (Schulman, *New York Times*, January 9, 2013 at ***http://www.nytimes. com/2013/01/10/fashion/generation-lgbtqia.html?pagewanted=all***). As of this writing, the most accepted designation by scholars and practitioners in the field is LGBTQ (Dennis Carlson, personal communication).

The movements by fledgling groups supporting student difference are also pulling teachers in as supporters, as advocates, as citizen activists for fair treatment, equity, and understanding in ways that teacher leaders have not typically been before. It's time we provided leadership and support in this area for students and their families, communities.

But teacher leaders, parents, citizens, and activists must remain vigilant and continue to educate themselves and others about tolerance and acceptance of sexual identity in terms of difference. We know that technology has ramped up the prospects for bullying in the past decade since the hate-crime murder of Matthew Shepard in 1998 in Laramie, Wyoming (***http://www. matthewshepard.org***). The recent case at Rutgers University involving the subsequent suicide of Tyler Clementi as an apparent result of compromising webcam footage and tweets and texts encouraging others to watch must inspire us to work as diligently as possible to educate and to protect. We can't be silent as teachers when students are hurting and need support. And we must do our best to educate all students, especially those who present as homophobic and angry about the sexual identity issues at hand that have an impact on all students.

My hope is that teacher leaders in the 21st century will become advocates for all students, and especially work to liberate themselves from static categorizations of people and in some cases their own values to truly value other human beings for who they are and who they are to become. To me, a truly inclusive curriculum, classroom, and school require openness. To me, they require acceptance. To me, they require diligent, purposeful pursuit of knowledge and understanding of others. No matter the grade level or subject area you teach in school, I hope that you will become a person who values difference and explores how it is that you can be supportive of students across a wide spectrum of issues and differences.

REFLECTION

What are you willing to do as a teacher leader to support student differences? How will you advocate for students who challenge your own values?

Reflection on Teacher Leadership: *Supporting Student Differences*

The first part of the reflective prompt above has two answers for me: an easy one and a difficult one. The easy answer is that I'm willing to go to great lengths to support my students and their well-being. But the difficult part to answering that question is actually identifying when a student needs help and what you as a teacher can do. I think that in a lot of cases, the student is more likely to avoid bringing his or her personal problems to the teacher. Whenever I was upset as a student, I avoided making my problems into someone else's problems; it's how children are sometimes socially programmed. I think that level of avoidance is still common in students today. So sometimes the question is not how you will help students, but how you will know when and how to help your students. As a teacher, it is your responsibility to be sensitive to the student's needs and their well-being, and to help when you can to the best of your ability.

As far as the question of how to advocate for students who don't share my values, I am not too sure of my answer. I strongly believe in the values I hold, but respecting the values of those who disagree with you is also important. In order to best do that, a good teacher should educate herself on the arguments on both sides of the issue, with an open mind. Try to understand why the student disagrees with you, and understand that even if you believe the student is wrong, his opinions deserve at least some level of respect. A teacher should also be able to respectfully engage with the student to better understand his values and weigh in with an opinion. All in all, the most important thing is that the student feels safe and comfortable expressing his opinion in the class, and he might even have the chance to expand his knowledge to the benefit of all.

—Melina Hazzard, preservice teacher

14
Continuing to Learn: Professional Development for You and Your School

This chapter brings the book to a close. However, I know that you know it is not the end, but only a beginning. I want to leave you with some ideas that have to do with your continuing development as a teacher leader. No, you won't be a master teacher the moment someone confers a college degree upon you and offers you a teaching position, but you can be a teacher leader right now and exercise teacher leadership your entire career on your way to becoming a master teacher. While you will have many essential skills and a good store of knowledge, becoming a master teacher will require that you seek out and take advantage of further opportunities to learn.

One of the joys of becoming a teacher is that opportunities to learn will continue all around you as you work. You will learn from your own day-to-day experiences with children. If you observe them closely, there is no doubt that your students will be your best teachers. You will learn from other teachers. Your colleagues will be an invaluable source of knowledge and ideas for you. Above all else, the people you teach with will understand and appreciate what you go through everyday. They can help you untangle the complex demands of teaching. You will also learn by continuing your formal studies of teaching and education.

For as much as I have understated the impact of your professors in the college classroom, it is a fact that there are brilliant and insightful teacher educators at the college level (I know because I work with some). You will also learn by developing a professional library of your own. More and more texts are being published about teacher leadership. And keeping up with the fields of teaching/pedagogy, curriculum, and your subject area(s) by reading at least selectively, if not widely, should keep you busy!

I feel very strongly that you should create a record of your professional growth experiences. Continue to write reflections about your practice and about problems and issues in education. What you write may actually surprise you. Keep an updated resume. Keep samples of your students' work and of selected exemplary units or lessons you create and teach. Develop a professional portfolio and keep it current. Keeping account of your professional growth will sustain you and provide direction for your continued learning.

Creating a Teaching Portfolio

Below I share the specifications for a beginning teaching portfolio that is a requirement for my class. A teaching portfolio is an excellent means for keeping track of your development and for communicating with others about your strong qualifications for a teaching position.

The teacher portfolio draft is an opportunity to do at least two things as a pre-professional teacher:

1. To showcase yourself as a prospective teacher, highlighting your strengths and experiences for potential employers; and
2. To create a place to put your best, beginning teaching/professional materials (treat it like your first professional teaching "filing cabinet" or "dossier")

You are free to create your portfolio web page however you see fit. I recommend free web creation/host sites like Weebly.com.

Below are the things that I think constitute an excellent portfolio draft for this course. You might not have some of these items yet, in which case you can create a placeholder in your website's navigational scheme. Some of the items can be gleaned from your study of teacher leadership. You might also use items from other courses and field experiences as you create your draft:

- **Resume**
- **Teaching Platform/Statement**
- **Personal Background (biography or autobiographical sketch)**
- **Description of Teaching Experiences (pictures or videos of you in action are great, too!)**

- Examples of Curriculum Development/Teaching (files of original materials created)
- Professional Development (memberships in professional organizations, conference attendance, presentations, etc.)
- Interactive Teaching Blog (links to Twitter, Tumblr, Facebook, Glogster, etc.)
- Contact Information

One of the most important aspects of your growth and learning will be the associations you make with the colleagues immediately surrounding you. However, you should make every effort to form wider alliances with colleagues throughout your region and around the country. You must be selective or this activity can be overwhelming, but there are numerous professional organizations for teachers where you will find great ideas from colleagues who are also teacher leaders. Organizations such as the National Council of Teachers of English (NCTE, *http://www.ncte.org*); the National Council of Teachers of Mathematics (NCTM, *http://www.nctm.org*); the National Council for the Social Studies (NCSS, *http://www.ncss.org*); the National Science Teachers Association (NSTA, *http://www.nsta.org*); the National Association for Special Education Teachers (NASET, *http://www.naset.org*); the National Art Education Association (NAEA, *http://www.arteducators.org*); the National Association for Music Education (MENC, *http://www.menc.org*); the National Education Association (NEA, *http://www.nea.org*); the American Federation of Teachers (AFT, *http://www.aft.org*); Kappa Delta Pi (*http://www.kdp.org*); the Association for Supervision and Curriculum Development (ASCD, *http://www.ascd.org*); and Phi Delta Kappa (*http://www.pdkintl.org*) are just a few of the many national organizations you may join as a teacher and educator. Each has a state affiliate. Many have student membership programs available. They may be contacted through their websites given here or found elsewhere online. One of the best things they offer is access to scholarly, practitioner-oriented journals with discussions of current trends and approaches in the field. Keep up to date!

Finally, you will continue to learn because you are in a setting in which you can discover deep meaning in the material you teach. Whatever your academic interest, teaching affords, actually demands, that you delve deeply into subject matter in order for you to help students make connections with concepts to their own lives. Teachers, as Goodlad puts it, have to learn things twice; once for their own understanding and a second time when they must invent ways to aid their learners' understanding as well.

There is a tradition in public education that acknowledges and encourages you to continue to develop in the profession. It is referred to by many names: staff development, professional development, in-service education, continuing education, etc. Unfortunately, the quality of professional development experiences in our fields varies greatly. Traditional "in-service days" are not well regarded as useful by most teachers for several reasons. They are often selected and organized by administrators without consulting with faculty. They often have more to do with what administrators want than with what staff members want, sometimes with little regard to what teachers need. They are almost always conducted with a "one size fits all" approach, which makes even the best programs irrelevant for many teachers.

The good news is that schools recognize their responsibility to help teachers develop professionally. Schools have a responsibility to support teachers' professional development because they want the very best teachers for the children in their care. The bad news is that most schools don't devote enough time or resources to create professional development programs of high quality. A glance at almost any school budget reveals that relatively few dollars are dedicated to the professional development of staff. Compared to other learning organizations where 10 to 20% of the budget is devoted to personnel development, schools invest less than 1% of their total budgets on professional development programs (Perelman, 1989).

Traditional in-service programs have a reputation for violating many of the principles of adult learning, especially disregarding the needs and wants of teachers. Over time, the effect of useless in-service programs creates a cynical mentality in a faculty that is difficult to break. Thankfully, better schools are beginning to see the folly in "one shot, commando raid" in-service programs and are moving to teacher-directed, collaborative activities that are thematic and have well-defined follow-up components and support.

Truly, no one ever sets out to create irrelevant and useless professional development programs. Planners simply suffer from a lack of resources or a lack of understanding about how to create meaningful, professional growth activities for teachers. Like other persistent traditions in education, the practice of professional development has to be examined closely, particularly by the very teachers it is designed to assist. This is an area where teacher leaders can make a real impact. I would like you to know something about how to help your school improve its approach to professional development. Please consider the following ideas carefully.

> ## REFLECTION
>
> What makes a powerful professional development experience? What are some of the driving questions to ask before planning such experiences? How can we address the current ineffectiveness of professional development programs in such a way as to change the connotation of "in-service" training and neutralize teacher's cynicism toward it?

In the 1980s the concept of professional or staff development received considerable attention. Dennis Sparks and Susan Louckes Horsley (1989) summarized the various kinds of staff development that emerged during the decade into five distinct types they called models. Their groundbreaking work had an influence on how staff development was regarded by practitioners. Their work can help to make you aware of the variety of ways in which you can grow professionally and help others to grow as well. Before introducing the models, I would like you to complete the following survey on professional development. Similar to the Q-Sort exercise on curriculum in Chapter 9, this exercise will help frame your positions and assumptions about professional development.

Surveying Your Assumptions About Professional Development

The following statements are meant to help you reflect on your personal assumptions about professional development. What makes this a little difficult is that you are asked to rank order the 20 belief statements below. Be patient. This is a forced choice format that you may find frustrating at first. One way to do this efficiently and accurately is to segment the 20 statements into categories "High," "Medium," or "Low" with regard to how closely the statements align with your beliefs. When you have completed the initial rating, go through and rank each statement 1 to 20, with 1 being most important and 20 being least important.

_____ A. Teachers are capable of self-initiated learning.

_____ B. Providing opportunities for analyzing their classroom performance is an important avenue for promoting teacher growth.

_____ C. Teachers learn most effectively when they have the need to know or a problem to solve.

_____ D. Research-based techniques and behaviors are worthy of replication in the classroom.

_____ E. Teachers are individuals who are inclined to formulate valid questions about their own teaching practice.

_____ F. Teachers are the best judges of their own learning needs.

_____ G. Teacher self-analysis and reflection can be enhanced by the observation of others.

_____ H. Teachers have the best understanding of the improvements needed in curriculum since they are the closest to it on a daily basis.

_____ I. Teachers can learn new behaviors that were not previously in their repertoire of teaching behaviors.

_____ J. A most effective avenue for staff development is cooperative study by groups of teachers themselves of problems that arise from their daily teaching practices.

_____ K. Teachers learn most effectively when they initiate and plan their own learning activities.

_____ L. Classroom observation and assessment benefit both the observer and the observed.

_____ M. Teachers grow professionally through their involvement in curriculum development and school improvement projects.

_____ N. Workshops conducted by experts are an excellent way to improve teacher performance.

_____ O. Teachers are inclined to search for objective data to answer important questions about their own teaching practice.

_____ P. Teachers are most motivated to learn when they select their own learning goals.

___ Q. Once teachers begin to see positive results from changing their classroom behavior, they will be motivated to improve even more.

___ R. Experience in school improvement projects provides teachers with guidance for recognizing problems and developing relevant solutions.

___ S. Experts can be very effective in showing groups of teachers how to adapt research-based teaching methods to the teacher's own classroom.

___ T. Teachers develop new understandings and change their behavior as they work in groups to study questions directly connected to their daily teaching practice.

Rank the assumptions below. One (1) would indicate most important and twenty (20) would indicate least important.

A._____ B. _____ C. _____ D._____ E. _____

F. _____ G._____ H. _____ I. _____ J. _____

K._____ L. _____ M._____ N. _____ O._____

P. _____ Q._____ R. _____ S. _____ T. _____

Scoring Directions

Follow the scoring directions below by placing the appropriate number on the blanks provided above:

- The letter above that you have identified as number 1 receives a score of 12.
- The two letters above that you have identified as numbers 2 and 3 each receive a score of 10.
- The four letters above that you have identified as numbers 4, 5, 6, and 7 each receive a score of 8.
- The six letters above that you have identified as numbers 8, 9, 10, 11, 12, and 13 each receive a score of 6.
- The four letters above that you have identified as numbers 14, 15, 16, and 17 each receive a score of 4.
- The two letters above that you have identified as number 18 and 19 each receive a score of 2.
- The letter above that you have identified as number 20 receives a score of 0.

Add up your scores for the following groups

A.	B.	C.	D.	E.
F.	G.	H.	I.	J.
K.	L.	M.	N.	O.
P.	Q.	R.	S.	T.

Totals

(Nolan & Badiali, 1990)

The total of column AFKP represents your reaction to **Individually Guided** professional development assumptions.

The total of column BGLQ represents your reaction to **Observation/ Assessment** professional development assumptions.

The total of column CHMR represents your reaction to **Development/ Improvement** professional development assumptions.

The total of column DINS represents your reaction to **Training** professional development assumptions.

The total of column EJOT represents your reaction to **Inquiry** professional development assumptions.

REFLECTION

Compare your results on this ranking activity on professional development with a peer. Discuss the implications for your ranking and your partner's ranking for your professional development.

Professional Development Models

There are numerous approaches to professional development as described in some detail by Dennis Sparks and Susan Louckes-Horsley (1989). They describe staff development as professional growth that is consistent with the mission and goals of a school or community of learners. They address the question, "What do educators need to become more effective in their work?" Since you now understand that the work of a teacher leader includes such a wide number of tasks, it only makes sense that professional growth opportunities occur in many ways as well. Too often, professional development has been defined narrowly as "training."

The exercise that you have just completed examines your preferences for the ideas that underlie Sparks and Louckes-Horsley's five approaches or models of staff development. Your high score indicates which model or models would result in productive professional growth activities for you. At the end of this section, I introduce a sixth model for professional development for you to consider.

Individually Guided Professional Development

Teachers learn so many things out of a natural sense of curiosity or as a by-product of solving problems in school. When this process is formalized, it can be a legitimate form of professional growth and should be acknowledged as such by everyone in the school community. "Formalized" means that there are several distinct phases: (1) the identification of a need or interest; (2) the development of a plan to meet that need or interest; (3) specific learning activities; and (4) assessment of the learning has met the need or interest. The following statements from the survey indicate your preference for this model.

- A. Teachers are capable of self-initiated learning.
- F. Teachers are the best judges of their own learning needs.
- K. Teachers learn most effectively when they initiate and plan their own learning activities.
- P. Teachers are most motivated to learn when they select their own learning goals.

Observation/Assessment for Professional Development

It is so useful to have another pair of eyes watching what occurs in the classroom. Having an observer collect data on an area of interest identified by the teacher can lead to discoveries about what enhances student learning. This form of staff development should not be confused with evaluation. The observation/assessment process in this case has professional growth as its purpose, whereas the process of evaluation seeks to certify whether or not a teacher is competent. Cognitive coaching (Costa & Garmston, 1992) is a good example of this model. The phases of coaching are (1) a planning conference with the teacher to identify an area of focus for the observation; (2) observing a class and collecting data; and (3) conducting a reflective conference to analyze and make sense of the data. This model can be very helpful when a teacher is implementing a new approach with students. The following statements from the survey indicate your preference for this model.

B. Providing opportunities for analyzing their classroom performance is an important avenue for promoting teacher growth.

G. Teacher self- analysis and reflection can be enhanced by the observation of others.

L. Classroom observation and assessment benefit both the observer and the observed.

Q. Once teachers begin to see positive results from changing their classroom behavior, they will be motivated to improve even more.

Development/Improvement Process for Professional Development

It is true that problems abound in schools. Therefore, a large part of teaching is problem solving. This model of professional development has more to do with school-wide problems rather than classroom problems. Curriculum problems, staff development problems, and problems that impact the entire school fall into this category. When teachers band together to solve these problems or to address issues that concern the entire school community, they use and develop skills important to their professional growth. Phases of this activity include (1) identifying a problem or need; (2) deliberating on various ways to address the problem or need; (3) coming to consensus on a plan to address the problem or need; (4) implementing the plan; and (5) determining whether or not the plan has been successful. The following statements from the survey indicate your preference for this model.

C. Teachers learn most effectively when they have the need to know or a problem to solve.

H. Teachers have the best understanding of the improvements needed in curriculum since they are the closest to it on a daily basis.

M. Teachers grow professionally through their involvement in curriculum development and school improvement projects.

R. Experience in school improvement projects provides teachers with guidance for recognizing problems and developing relevant solutions.

Training for Professional Development

Training has been the most prevalent model of staff development in the history of education. Some even refer to your education as "teacher training," a term that is wholly inappropriate. Dogs are trained. Teachers are educated! "Training" is a much narrower, technical word and idea than "educating." Training connotes changing behavior, routinizing practice, and technicizing activities (Eisner, 1994). This is not to say that all programs designed to teach us new approaches to classroom learning are no good. Rather, training too often takes a narrow and mechanical view of learning and of teachers' work. Under certain conditions, training can be quite valuable, particularly if it is delivered by a peer who has special expertise in teaching. Training has better chances of impacting learning if there is a follow-up component inside the classroom. Observation/assessment acts as a good companion to training, insuring more transfer to practice. The following statements from the survey indicate your preference for the training model.

D. Research based techniques and behaviors are worthy of replication in the classroom.

I. Teachers can learn new behaviors that were not previously in their repertoire of teaching behaviors.

N. Workshops conducted by experts are an excellent way to improve teacher performance.

S. Experts can be very effective in showing groups of teachers how to adapt research-based teaching methods to the teacher's own classroom.

Inquiry for Professional Development

Inquiry is an indispensable practice if you are to grow as a professional, as I have tried to establish throughout this book. Having devoted an entire chapter to this model, you know how important it is for teachers to generate their own knowledge through action research. I hope you will inquire about any and all aspects of teaching and schooling, alone or with partners, during your teaching career. The phases of activity are (1) identifying a problem or issue; (2) deciding on a question or questions to be answered; (3) conducting a systematic investigation, collecting data; (4) using your findings to enact an intervention; and (5) sharing the results with peers in some kind of public forum. The following statements from the survey indicate your preference for this model.

E. Teachers are individuals who are inclined to formulate valid questions about their own teaching practice.

J. A most effective avenue for staff development is cooperative study by groups of teachers themselves of problems that arise from their daily teaching practices.

O. Teachers are inclined to search for objective data to answer important questions about their own teaching practice.

T. Teachers develop new understandings and change their behavior as they work in groups to study questions that are directly connected to their daily teaching practice.

Professional development depends so much on the context in which you find yourself. Your school setting will be unique. Questions relevant and important in your own school will be irrelevant in another. Things that are critical for teachers to know and do in one school might be very different from what teachers need to know in the school just across town. Teachers' interests and experience levels differ. What can be said with confidence about staff development is that it must be ongoing and that there are certain school conditions that support and encourage it:

1. There must be norms of collegiality and responsible experimentation.
2. There must be administrative support and involvement.
3. There should be some relationship between teachers' professional growth and student learning.
4. There must be ample resources, rewards, and time devoted to professional development.

If you are determined to be a great teacher, continuing your own learning is the key. It will be easier in some settings than it will be in others. But part of your commitment to the field requires that you continue to grow and learn yourself. Your students deserve no less.

Mentoring: A Sixth Model for Professional Development

I want to add to the five models outlined above by describing a sixth model of professional development that may be the most powerful of all. Some of you have seen this model in action throughout partner schools during your field experiences where there is a sense of community and a shared sense of responsibility for student learning. In partner schools, sometimes called "professional development schools," veteran classroom teachers agree to mentor preservice teachers. Mentoring is a powerful and comprehensive way for veteran teachers to learn and grow professionally. If they create a relationship with their intern or student teacher that is open and inviting, a mentor can learn every bit as much about teaching as the intern can. Why? How?

When they feel "safe" enough to do it, students of teaching ask the best questions about teaching and learning: "Why do you pass out papers in the beginning of the class and not at the end? What do you do with a student who gets stuck at the same place in a problem every time? How much individual attention can parents have a right to expect for their child in this school? Who is in charge of the curriculum? Why did you give one student so much time to answer your question when you gave the other student virtually no time at all? How do you keep your own values out of the class discussion? Why do you do that? Should we do that?"

The number of questions is endless. A good mentor has asked herself these questions before, but having a student of teaching raise them again requires a mentor to revisit the answers. Questions require deeper, more continuous reflection on practice. Small questions that take only a moment can provoke new understanding. Large questions that take an entire semester and require collaborative inquiry lead to new discoveries. The mentor role expands a veteran teacher's skill and knowledge in the same way having to teach anything requires deep understanding of the subject.

There will be a time in the not too distant future when you will be asked to mentor a beginning teacher. It isn't easy to be an inspiring role model, but I encourage you to try it on for size if the opportunity presents itself, and it no doubt will. You will be better off for having done it as a teacher leader yourself. You will be passing along a healthy conception of the profession of teaching.

A Final Case Study

I want to conclude the book with a case study. Please attend to it and discuss it with peers and your instructor.

Case Study: The Professional Development Committee

Marcia Gonzalez was surprised at first at how difficult it was to teach. There were so many distractions, classroom interruptions, behavior problems, and administrative requests. During her student teaching assignment, she was part of a team that took care of these matters together. Now, virtually isolated in her own classroom, she felt unprepared to deal with the press of everyday problems by herself. She realized more and more how important it was to have what her university supervisor used to call a "safety net," that is, having really good colleagues around to help her. What she also realized after her first month in the classroom was that the best way to improve her school was to foster closer relationships among the staff so that they could act more as a team. When the opportunity came to serve on the school's Professional Development Committee, Marcia volunteered. Some teachers were surprised at this. They thought getting involved in this committee was audacious and would perhaps be too much responsibility for someone just starting a career in teaching. They thought decisions about in-service were better left to the veteran teachers and the principal.

The person least surprised, however, was Marcia's principal, Tony Smith. This was Tony's second year at the school and he knew when he hired Marcia that she would bring fresh ideas to the staff. During her interview she impressed him with her understanding of teamwork and collaboration. He thought that Marcia might influence the way others on the staff viewed the school. Sure enough, he was right.

During the first meeting of the Professional Development Committee, as teachers began to talk about the three in-service dates for next year, Marcia asked a series of good questions.

Jorge: I know this teacher from Smithtown who said they had a great motivational speaker during the last in-service. This guy was a former football coach and he really cared about kids. He knew how to set a fire under them and he did the same for the teachers.

Tyrone: I know the guy you mean. He is good. He's been on the circuit for a few years. Our teachers would like him.

Marcia: What is the actual purpose of the three days we have coming up for professional development this year?

Tony: In the past, in-service days were used to present programs to teachers. This committee constructed a list of choices for them to pick and then lined up programs.

Jorge: We always got teacher input. If we didn't structure it by giving them choices, they really didn't seem to know what to tell us.

Tyrone: Yeah. They were always interested in learning CPR. Some wanted to know more about their retirement programs. We had a film once on caring for children, but most people thought it was sappy.

Phyllis: They always like to hear motivational speakers, though, especially those who have a sense of humor.

Tony: My view of professional development is a little different. I hope this committee can come up with a plan for the long run that will focus on student learning. I'd like to see us zero in on test scores.

Marcia: I'd love for my students to do well on district tests, too. Would most of the teachers here be interested in programs like that?

Jorge: I doubt it. We used to have all in-service days controlled by administration and they would always pick something like test scores to work on. We used to have a lot of teachers absent during in-service. Then we got this committee. Attendance has been better since we've been picking the topics.

Marcia: How are the teachers involved in choosing topics for their own professional development?

Phyllis: We ask around. We call other schools.

Tony: I think Marcia has something else in mind. Am I right Marcia?

Marcia: Can we give them a questionnaire, or could we each take four or five teachers in the school and ask them about this?

Tyrone: Ask them what?

Marcia: Well, ask them what they need to grow professionally. Or ask them what kind of program they would like to experience that could help them get more from their students. I for one would like to know how to get more out of the time my students spend doing group work.

Tony: I suppose we could do a kind of needs assessment. I think consulting the teachers is fine, but I am also concerned about student performance. I want them to be a little focused in what they say they are interested in.

Phyllis: I heard about this consulting company who has a program on brain-based learning. They are supposed to be good.

Marcia: I guess I am interested in hearing from the staff. I would be surprised if everyone would be interested in the same thing. Perhaps we need to see.

Tony: Remember now, we only have three days next year.

Marcia: Do we always plan one year at a time?

Tony: I'm new here. Are you suggesting we need to plan long-range?

Jorge: We have always planned for one year. Next year, a new committee can plan.

Tony: I think there is some advantage to planning long-term, particularly if I understand what Marcia is suggesting. Marcia, do you mean that different teachers might want different professional development experiences?

Marcia: I guess what I'm thinking about professional development is that "one size fits all" approaches can be a waste of time for many of the staff, especially if they are just training exercises or filling time. I do have a copy of a survey that could begin a conversation among the staff. It helps teachers to preference what they think they need in order to grow. Our committee could start by asking them to take the survey. It's self-scoring, but we could collate the scores and see if we have a majority in one or two areas.

Jorge: This committee is turning out to be more work than I thought. Does anybody like the idea of the motivational speaker?

Phyllis: I think we should see the survey. It might be good to get more input about this. The staff will take in-service more seriously if we can find programs they all are interested in.

Tony: Our time is almost up. I think we are off to a good start. The way I understand it, we are going to think about professional development long-term and we are going to give a survey to teachers to help us determine what kinds of programs they would benefit from. I'm not setting aside my concern about test scores, but I am willing to work along with you to see where the staff is on this. Thanks for coming. We'll meet again next Friday.

REFLECTION

What role did Marcia play in this meeting? What will be her greatest challenges in meetings to come? How can she overcome those challenges?

Teachers like Marcia are on their way to making a difference in schools, altering the status quo. She has a good grasp of what it means to teach well in the classroom. She recognizes the challenges and the difficulties that teachers face day to day. She invents lessons that engage her students, constructing a community of learners including herself, and she wants to improve. She seeks to broaden her community by reaching out to colleagues in a diplomatic way. She understands the necessity for inquiry. She knows how to interact deliberately. She is very conscious of the impact of her actions and realizes that some might take her intentions and ideas the wrong way. Yet she perseveres, and leads. Marcia knows how vitally important working together with colleagues is to transforming a school. She knows how to employ principles of change. Marcia is committed to becoming a teacher leader. I wish her, and you, well in the quest.

Reflection: *What's Left?*

As my time as a preservice teacher comes to an end, I find myself excited to get out into the world of work. I get frustrated when I am out of schools or not around children for extended periods of time. As I have been wrapping up this semester, I know that I can never be truly ready to begin teaching. Teaching is definitely a profession that is about learning by doing. We have been talking a lot about teacher leadership, and what that is. I think I am getting a clearer picture of the skills and tools of being a teacher leader.

The first part of being a teacher leader is having a critical eye when looking at the world. Paulo Freire talks about reading the word and reading the world, and that is crucial for a teacher leader. Teaching is under attack lately, but we will all have students who have been under attack in the US since its inception. It is important to look critically at what is going on today, as well as to make historical connections.

Second, I think teacher leaders have to be a part of the community they teach in. I have lived in three states and have found so many accepting and welcoming people in them. Many of these people are often overlooked because of the bodies they inhabit or the neighborhoods they come from. Teacher leaders can only make the best decisions in school if they are connected to what is happening outside of school. Every community has great assets.

Finally, I believe a teacher leader has to be all about openness and listening. We do inhabit a privileged position, and it is our job to be great listeners. As I graduate from the university and enter teaching and ask "What's left?"—the answer is <u>everything</u>.

—Rob Cron, preservice teacher

References

Adler, M. (1982). *The Paideia proposal: an educational manifesto*. New York: Macmillan.

American Institutes for Research. (1999). *An educator's guide to schoolwide reform*. Arlington, VA: Education Research Service.

Anastasi, A. (1976). *Psychological testing*, 4th ed. New York: Macmillan.

Anderson, G., Herr, K., & Nihlen, S. (1995). *Studying your own school: An educator's guide to qualitative practitioner research*. Thousand Oaks, CA: Sage.

Anderson, J. (1988). *The education of blacks in the south: 1860–1935*. Chapel Hill: University of North Carolina Press.

Apple, M. (1979). *Ideology and curriculum*. London: Routledge and Kegan Paul.

Armstrong, T. (1994). *Multiple intelligences in the classroom*. Alexandria, VA: Association for Supervision & Curriculum Development (ASCD).

Banks, J. (1994, May). Transforming the mainstream curriculum. *Educational Leadership*, pp. 4–8.

Bayles, F. (1999, March 5). School equality, N.H. tradition come in conflict. *USA Today*.

Beamish, R. (2011). Back to school for the billionaires. *Newsweek*, May 9, pp. 38–43.

Beane, J. (1998). *Integrated curriculum: Designing the core of democratic education*. New York: Teachers College Press.

Benne, D., & Sheats, P. (1948). Functional roles of group members. *Journal of Social Issues*, 4(2), pp. 41–49.

Bensman, D. (1986). *Quality education in the inner city: The story of Central Park East Schools*. New York: The Center for Collaborative Education.

Bode, P. (2013). Multicultural education, by the Gale Group. Retrieved from http://www.education.com/reference/article/multicultural-education/#C

Boyan, N., & Copeland, W. (1978). *Instructional supervision training program.* Columbus: Merrill.

Bracey, G. (1997). On comparing the incomparable: A response to Baker and Stedman. *Educational Researcher, 26*(3), pp. 19–26.

Bracey, G. (2009). *Education hell: Rhetoric v. reality.* Alexandria, VA: Educational Research Service.

Brandt, R. (1999). *Rethinking leadership: A collection of articles by Tom Sergiovanni.* Arlington Heights: Skylight Press.

Brookfield. S. (1995). *Becoming a critically reflective teacher.* San Francisco: Jossey-Bass.

Cochran-Smith, M., & Lytle, S. (1993). *Inside/outside: Teacher research and knowledge.* New York: Teachers College Press Columbia University.

Codell, E. R. (1999). *Educating Esme: Diary of a teacher's first year.* Chapel Hill, NC: Algonquin Books.

Combs, A. (1959). Personality theory and its implications for curriculum development. In Frazier, *Learning about learning: Papers and reports from the third ASCD Research Institute* (pp. 5–20). Washington: ASCD.

Connelly, M., & Clandinin, J. (1988). *Teachers as curriculum planners.* New York: Teachers College Press.

Costa, A., & Garmston, R. (1994). *Cognitive coaching.* Norwood, CA: Christopher Gordon.

Cremin, L. (1977). *Traditions of American education.* New York: Basic Books.

Dewey, J. (1959). *Dewey on education: Selections with an introduction and notes by Martin S. Dworkin.* New York: Teachers College Press Columbia University.

Dillon, S. (2011). Foundations join to offer online courses for schools. *New York Times,* April 28.

The Education Watch 1998: The Education Trust State and National Data Book, Vol. II. (1998). Washington, DC: The Education Trust.

Eisner, E. (1994, 2001). *The educational imagination: On the design and evaluation of school programs.* New York: Macmillan.

Elashoff, J. D., & Snow, R.E. (1971). *Pygmalion reconsidered.* Worthington, OH: Charles A. Jones.

Engel, A. (2009). *Seeds of tomorrow: Solutions for improving our children's education.* Boulder, CO: Paradigm Publishers.

Fashola, O., & Slavin, R. (1998, January). Schoolwide reform models: What works? *Phi Delta Kappan,* pp. 370–379.

Fullan, M. (1991). *The new meaning of educational change.* New York, NY: Teachers College Press Columbia University.

Gewertz, C. (2000, April 26). A hard lesson for Kansas City's troubled schools. *Education Week.*

Giroux, H., & McLaren, P. (1994). Between borders: Pedagogy and the politics of cultural studies. New York: Routledge.

Gitlin, A., & Bullough, R. (1995). *Becoming a student of teaching: Methodologies for studying self and school contexts.* New York: Garland Press.

Glatthorn, A. (1987). Cooperative professional development: Peer-centered options for teacher growth. *Educational Leadership, 45*(3), pp. 31–35.

Glickman, C. (1993). *Renewing America's Schools.* San Francisco: Jossey-Bass.

Glickman, C., Gordon, S., & Ross-Gordon, J. (1998). *Supervision of instruction: A developmental approach,* 4th ed. Boston: Allyn & Bacon.

Good, T., & Brophy, J. (1973). *Looking in classrooms.* New York: Harper & Row.

Goodlad, J. (1979). *Curriculum inquiry.* New York: McGraw-Hill.

Goodlad, J. (1992). *Teachers for our nation's schools.* San Francisco: Jossey-Bass.

Goodlad, J. (1994). *Educational renewal.* San Francisco: Jossey-Bass.

Haberman, M. (1995). *Star teachers of children in poverty.* West Lafayette, IN: Phi Delta Pi.

Henry, E., Huntley, J., McKamey, C., & Harper, L. (1995). *To be a teacher: Voices from the classroom.* Thousand Oaks: Corwin.

Hershey, W., & Wagner, M. (2000, May 12). Court: School funding still a mess. *Dayton Daily News,* p. 1, 6.

The Holmes Group. (1990). *Tomorrow's schools: Principles design of professional development schools.* East Lansing, MI: The Holmes Group.

Hovda, R., & Kyle, D. (1984). A strategy for helping teachers integrate research into teaching. *Middle School Journal, 15*(3), pp. 21–23.

Huyvaert, S. (1995). *Reports from the classroom: Cases for reflection.* Boston: Allyn & Bacon.

Ingvarson, L. (1987). Models of inservice education and their implications for professional developmental policy. Paper presented at the conference on "Inservice education: Trends of the past, themes for the future." Melbourne, Australia.

Jackson, P. (1968). *Life in classrooms.* New York: Holt, Rinehart and Winston, Inc.

Jacobs, J. (Ed.). (1997). *A school teacher in old Alaska: The story of Hannah Breece.* Amherst, NY: Prometheus Books.

Jones, B. (2013). Update. Seattle MAP test "window" extended, teachers still threatened, students opt out. Retrieved from http://brianpjones.tumblr.com

Kaestle, C. (1983). *Pillars of the republic: Common schools and American Society, 1780–1860.* New York: Hill & Wang.

Keizer, G. (2011). Getting schooled: The re-education of an American teacher. *Harper's, 323*(1936), pp. 33–40.

Kohlberg, L. (1981). *Essays on moral development, Vol. 1: The philosophy of moral development.* San Francisco: Harper & Row.

Kohlberg, L. (1984). *Essays on moral development, Vol. 2: The psychology of moral development.* San Francisco: Harper & Row.

Kohn, A. (1994). *No contest: The case against competition.* Boston: Houghton Mifflin.

Kozol, J. (1992). *Savage inequalities.* New York: Crown Publishers.

Lindsey, T., Robins, K., & Terrell, R. (1999). *Cultural proficiency: A manual for school leadership.* Thousand Oaks: Corwin Press.

Lipsky, D., & Gartner, A. (1997). *Inclusion and school reform: Transforming America's classrooms.* Baltimore: Brookes.

Lortie, D. (1975). *Schoolteacher: A sociological study.* Chicago: University of Chicago Press.

Loewen, J. (2007). *Lies my teacher told me: Everything your American history textbook got wrong.* New York: Simon & Schuster.

Lucas, C. J. (2006). *American higher education: A history,* 2nd ed. New York: Palgrave Macmillan.

Lucas, T. (2000). Demystifying the learner. In Senge et al. (Eds.), *Schools that learn* (pp. 124–127). New York: Doubleday.

Mager, R. F. (1962). *Preparing instructional objectives.* Palo Alto, Calif.: Fearon.

Matczynski, T., Rogus, J., Lasley, T., & Joseph, E. (2000). Culturally relevant instruction: Using traditional and progressive strategies in urban schools. *The Educational Forum,* 64(4), pp. 350–353.

Matthews, D. (2012, September 10). Everything you need to know about the Chicago teachers' strike, in one post. Retrieved from Dylan Matthews' blog at http://www.washingtonpost.com/blogs/wonkblog /wp/2012/09/10/everything-you-need-to-know-about-the-chicago-teachers-strike-in-one-post

McCarthy, M., Cambron-McCabe, N., & Thomas. (1998). *Public school law: Teachers' and students' rights,* 4th ed. Boston: Allyn & Bacon.

McCarthy, M., Cambron-McCabe, N., & Eckes, S. (2013). *Public School Law: Teachers' and Students' Rights,* 7th ed. Boston: Allyn & Bacon.

McCutcheon, G. (1995). *Developing the curriculum: Solo and group deliberation.* New York: Longman Press.

McCutcheon, G. (1995). Curriculum theory and practice for the 1990s. In Ornstein & Behar (Eds.) *Contemporary issues in curriculum* (pp. 3–9). Boston: Allyn & Bacon.

McNeil, L. (2000). *Contradictions of school reform: Educational costs of standardized testing.* New York: Routledge.

Meier, D. (1995). *The power of their ideas: Lessons for America from a small school in Harlem.* Boston: Beacon Press.

Moyers, B. (1996). *Children in America's schools.* Television documentary on school funding. South Carolina: South Carolina ETV.

Newman, J. (1998). *America's teachers: An introduction to education,* 3rd ed. New York: Longman.

Newman, J. (2005). *America's teachers,* 5th ed. Boston: Allyn & Bacon.

Newmann, F., & Wehlage, G. (1995). *Successful school restructuring: A report to the public and educators by the Center on Organization and Restructuring of Schools.* Madison, WI: Center on Organization and Restructuring of Schools.

Newton, A. (1994). *Mentoring: A resource and training guide for educators.* Andover, MA: Regional Laboratory for Educational Improvement, Educational Resources Information Center.

Noddings, N. (1999). Renewing democracy in schools. *Phi Delta Kappan, 80*(8), pp. 579–583.

Nolan, J., & Badiali, B. (1990). [Instrument for gauging perspectives on professional development]. Previously unpublished instrument.

O'Hair, M. J., McLaughlin, H. J., & Reitzug, U. C. (2000). *Foundations of democratic education.* Fort Worth, TX: Harcourt, Inc.

Orenstein, P. (1995). *Schoolgirls: Young women, self-esteem, and the confidence gap.* New York: Anchor Books/Doubleday.

Ornstein, A., & Behar-Horenstein, L. (Eds.). (1999). *Contemporary issues in curriculum,* 2nd ed. Boston: Allyn & Bacon.

Ornstein, A., & Hunkins, F. (1993). *Curriculum foundations, principles, and issues,* 2nd ed. Boston: Allyn & Bacon.

Palmer, P. (1998). *The courage to teach: Exploring the inner landscape of a teacher's life.* San Francisco: Jossey-Bass.

Palonsky, S. (1985). *900 shows a year: A look at teaching from the teacher's side of the desk.* New York: McGraw Hill.

Peck, M. (1987). *The different drum: Community making and peace.* New York: Simon and Schuster.

Perelman, L. (1989, November). Closing education's technology gap. Briefing Paper No. 111. Indianapolis: Hudson Institute.

Peterson, K. (2012). Teachers are right to resist Race to the Top evaluations. Retrieved from http://www.oregonlive.com/opinion/index.ssf
/2012/11/portland_teachers_are_right_to.html

Pinar, W. (1989). A reconceptualization of teacher education. *Journal of Teacher Education*, Jan–Feb, p. 11.

Pinar, W. (2012). *What is curriculum theory?*, 2nd ed. New York: Routledge.

Pinar, W., et al. (2002). *Understanding curriculum: An introduction to the study of historical and contemporary curriculum discourses*. New York: Peter Lang.

Pipher, M. (1994). *Reviving Ophelia*. New York: Grosset/Putnam.

Poetter, T. (1994). Making a difference: Miss Conner and Bunker Hill School. *Teaching Education*, 6(1), pp. 149–152.

Poetter, T. (2006). *The education of Sam Sanders*. Lanham, MD: Hamilton Books.

Poetter, T. (2012). *Teaching again: A professor's tale of returning to a 9th grade classroom*. Charlotte, NC: Information Age Publishing.

Poetter, T., & Badiali, B. (2000). Look who's talking: Learning from student teachers. In Senge, Cambron-McCabe, Lucas, Smith, Dutton, & Kleiner (Eds.), *Schools that learn* (pp. 422–424). New York: Doubleday.

Poetter, T., & Badiali, B. (2001). *Teacher Leader*. Larchmont, NY: Eye on Education.

Poetter, T., & Knight-Abowitz, K. (2001). Possibilities and problems of school choice. *Kappa Delta Pi Record*, 37(2), pp. 58–62.

Poetter, T., Badiali, B., & Hammond, DJ. (2000). Growing teacher inquiry: Collaboration in a partner school. *Peabody Journal of Education*, 75(3), pp. 161–175.

Poetter, T., Pierson, J., Caivano, C., Stanley, S., Hughes, S., & Anderson, H. D. (1997). *Voices of inquiry in teacher education*. Mahwah, NJ: Lawrence Erlbaum.

Posner, G. (1995). *Analyzing the curriculum*, 2nd ed. New York: McGraw Hill.

Posner, G. (2004). *Analyzing the curriculum*, 3rd ed. New York: McGraw-Hill.

Posner, G., & Rudnitsky, A. (1986). *Course design: A guide to curriculum development for teachers*, 3rd ed. New York: Longman.

Postman, N. (1995). *The end of education: Redefining the value of school.* New York: Vintage Books.

Ravitch, D. (2013). Good news! Students in Portland, Oregon, are speaking out. Retrieved from Diane Ravitch's blog at www.dianeravitch.net /2013/01/30/good-news-students-in-portland-oregon-are-speaking-out/

Rosenthal, R., & Jacobson, L. (1968). *Pygmalion in the classroom.* New York: Holt, Rinehart and Winston.

Rotuno-Johnson, R. (2010). Democracy and special education inclusion. *Education in a Democracy: A Journal of the NNER, 2,* pp. 169–182.

Rousamaniere, K. (2000). From memory to curriculum. *Teaching Education,* 11(1), pp. 87–98.

Schlechty, P. (1990). *Schools for the 21st century: Leadership imperatives for educational reform.* San Francisco: Jossey-Bass.

Schniedewind, N., & Sapon-Shevin, M. (2012). *Educational courage: Resisting the ambush of public education.* Boston: Beacon Press.

Schon, D. (1983). *The reflective practitioner: How professionals think in action.* New York: Basic Books.

Sergiovanni, T. (1994). *Building community in schools.* San Francisco: Jossey-Bass.

Sergiovanni, T. (1996). *Leadership for the schoolhouse.* San Francisco: Jossey-Bass.

Sergiovanni, T., & Starratt, R. (1998). *Supervision: A redefinition.* Boston: McGraw-Hill.

Simon, H. (1976). *Administrative behavior: A study of decision-making processes in administrative organization,* 3rd ed. New York: Free Press.

Sirotnik, K. (1995). Curriculum: Overview and framework. In O'Hair & O'Dell (Eds.), *Educating teachers for leadership and change* (p. 235–242). Thousand Oaks, CA: Corwin.

Sizer, T. (1996). *Horace's hope: What works for the American high school.* New York: Houghton Mifflin.

Slavin, R. (1995). *Cooperative learning: Theory, research, and practice*, 2nd ed. Boston: Allyn & Bacon.

Slavin, R. (1997). *Educational psychology: Theory and practice*, 5th ed. Boston: Allyn & Bacon.

Sleeter, C. E., & Grant, C. (1988). *Making choices for multicultural education: Five approaches to race, class, and gender.* Columbus, OH: Merrill.

Sleeter, C. E., & Grant, C. (2006). *Making choices for multicultural education: Five approaches to race, class, and gender*, 5th ed. Hoboken, NJ: Wiley.

Smith, K., & Berg, D. (1987). *Paradoxes of group life.* San Francisco: Jossey-Bass.

Sparks, D., & Loucks-Horsley, S. (1989). Five models of staff development for teachers. *Journal of Staff Development, 10*(4), pp. 40–57.

Stedman, L. (1997). International achievement differences: An assessment of a new perspective. *Educational Researcher, 26*(4), pp. 4–15.

Stuart, J. (1950). *The thread that runs so true: A mountain school teacher tells his story.* New York: Touchstone.

Tannen, D. (1994). *Talking from 9 to 5: How women's and men's conversational styles affect who gets heard, who gets credit, and what gets done at work.* New York: W. Morrow.

Tanner, D., & Tanner, L. (1975). *Curriculum development: Theory into practice.* New York: Macmillan.

Thomas, S., Cambron-McCabe, N., & McCarthy, M. (2008). *Public school law: Teachers' and students' rights*, 6th ed. Boston: Allyn & Bacon.

Tienken, C. H. & Orlich, D. (2013). *The school reform landscape: Fraud, myth, and lies.* Lanham, Maryland: Rowman and Littlefield.

Turning Points 2000: Educating adolescents in the 21st century. (2000). New York: Teachers College Press.

Tyack, D. (1974). *The one best system: A history of American urban education.* Boston: Harvard University Press.

Unruh, G., & Unruh, A. (1984). *Curriculum development: Problems, processes, and progress.* Berkeley, CA: McCutchan Publishing.

Watts, H. (1985). When teachers are researchers, teaching improves. *Journal of Staff Development, 6*(2), pp. 118–127.

Weiner, L. (2012). *The future of our schools: Teachers unions and social justice.* Chicago: Haymarket Books.

Zemelman, S., Daniels, H., and Hyde, A. (1998). *Best practice: New standards for teaching and learning in America's schools,* 2nd ed. Portsmouth, NH: Heinemann.

Zimpher, N. (2000, March). Keynote address, University of South Carolina National Professional Development Schools Conference. Columbia, SC.